Spir Justice

Beatrice & Present Company Publishers
P.O. Box 9247
Scottsdale, AZ 85252-9247

© 2004 by Beatrice & Present Company

All rights reserved. No part of this publication may be reproduced, stored in a retrieval system, or transmitted in any form or by any means, electronic, mechanical, photocopying, recording, or otherwise, without prior written permission of the publisher.

ISBN 0-9755793-0-4

Acknowledgement

Many thanks to family and friends who have been what I've needed, when I've needed it. They have been my unpaid editors, motivators, prayer counselors and so much more. I have been blessed by their presence in my life. Jerome Carlton White, Theresa "Bonnie" Kerns, Novi and Don Colbert, Fred Campbell, Sylvia Abbott-McMorris, Richard Freeze, Marcia Atkins, Patsy Logue, Mary Blount, Maria Baxter-Nuamah, Elvena Mouzon Jarvis, Jeweldine Hancock, Janice and Keren Orr, Olive Swearengin, Mildred Mason, Daisy Joe, Geraldine Rooks and Calestine Williams.

A very special thank you to Mary K. Dougherty for her obedience, advice and assistance in getting this book published.

A warm and bright thank you to my dentist, Dr. Matthew Mitchell of Scottsdale, Arizona, for keeping a lady's smile pretty.

Dedication

This book is dedicated to the life and memories of Elijah, Sr., Edna Mae, and Agnes Elizabeth "Suzie" White, Lannie Harris and William "Bill" Tenner.

Foreword

Often, the journey of life takes us to places and through situations that we think would kill us. While we're going through the situation in that place we don't have a clue about why we are there, or why we have been brought to where we are. We discover while going through the situation that we don't have any control over it and more often than not, the situation is controlling us. We do things that we never thought that we would do.

While in the midst of the situation, we tell ourselves that if we knew the reason for what we are going through we would be accepting of it. The truth of the matter is that we believe that knowing gives us a sense of control. We deceive ourselves into believing that knowledge is power or control, sometimes that is true. How about the times when we have believed, as a result of knowledge, that we have fully accepted a situation only to have that belief shattered by new facts. What's more devastating is when the new facts compel us to take some sort of action. We then take the action that we have deemed necessary, based on the new facts, which aren't just facts, but undeniable truths. We take the very necessary action and find ourselves in situations more incredible than before the new facts, or undeniable truths appeared on the scene.

What part then does love play in all of this?

Spirit In The Dark: Justice of The Buzzard is a book that I believe will answer some questions and provoke the asking of many others about the incredible and about the length, depth, and height of selfless love and its unseen lover. Readers, even those who may not believe in or have a relationship with God, will understand that the only explanation for the unbelievable is Divine manipulation. Life is not always fair, and this book will also reveal that God is never fair, but, He is always just.

Spirit In The Dark: Justice of The Buzzard is representative of many life living situations. Real life is the life that is lived. Real life begins before the recorded date of birth and is experienced after the descent from eternity into time through the birth canal, and after the doctor's or midwife's smack on the buttocks. Or is it?

Spirit In The Dark: Justice of The Buzzard is a story of fairness, a story of justice, a story of great love and great hatred. It is a story that brings eternity and time face to face, right here on earth. This story shows that in spite of the fact that evil lives in darkness, the truth is that God is the landlord of darkness.

To Angela
From your cousin,
Beatrice

BEATRICE & PRESENT COMPANY

PRESENTS

SPIRIT IN THE DARK:
JUSTICE OF THE BUZZARD

1

    The procession of cars made its way down Highway 17; one straight line of less than fifteen cars. The hearse carrying the body of the old woman slowly led the caravan of mourners and the curious to the final resting place for the remains of Gertrude Elizabeth Spann, age seventy-eight. The youngest of five children, she had mourned the passing of her mother when she was a child of eight or nine years old. She had also mourned the passing of a much-loved nephew, a husband, her father, three brothers and a sister.
    Gertrude and her younger brother, Herman, had virtually been left alone after the death of their mother. There were three older children who were their half brothers and sister, children of their mother's previous marriage who went to live with relatives of their father when their mother had married again. But they had all kept in touch with each other during the years, even visiting and spending time with each other although they lived in different states.
    The lone limousine directly behind the hearse carried all of Gertrude's children, except Toni, the eldest daughter. Toni followed in her rental car several cars behind the limousine, preferring to be alone during this time. Being alone had seemed to be a lifetime assignment for Toni. Everyone had said from the time that she was a baby that Toni was not only a loner, but a beyonder, whatever that meant. Often she had been accused of being uppity, a hankty heifer, of thinking that she was better than others and an assortment of other less than kind or endearing names. But Toni had taken it all in stride even when it had come from her mother and siblings. Toni had determined that she would not dignify others asininity by either denying their accusations or explaining her actions.
    Toni smoked her cigarette and listened to the CD of songs that her mother once loved and claimed to have danced to when she was a young woman. As Ivory Joe Hunter belted out his song Toni softly sang along. She knew almost every word of the song by heart.
    The cars now had entered a different county and policemen on motorcycles were now leading the caravan. The policemen stopped traffic and directed cars through traffic lights. Toni saw the respect shown by the people as they obeyed the policemen. Strange, she thought, this was perhaps the only respect ever shown to her mother by so many white people. They had never shown as much respect to her in life; especially after all of the homes of whites she had cleaned in her lifetime. Strange thing about death, Toni thought, it is perhaps the one time folks are respected the most, regardless of the type of life that person had lived. Well, she thought, her mother would never have to clean another house again.
    As the caravan made its way down the old country road, Toni could see the old church steeple up ahead. The cemetery was directly across the street from the small Baptist Church. It looked like some fixing up had been done since she was last here. The church had a quaintness about it, Toni remembered, from the first time she had seen it.
    She had never been inside of the church; it looked like it could hold a maximum of three hundred or so people. The churchyard was so clean and the grass so green. It seemed to be the earthly witness of what heaven must be like. Suddenly, Toni had an urge to go inside of the church. The red brick building and steps seemed to have been

polished with the sun. The white mortar between each brick looked like someone had permanently frozen snowflakes and used them as the mortar between each brick. The stained glass windows in the front and on the side of the church went straight up until it got near the top of the roof of the church. At the top of each stained glass window the shape of a crown could be seen. The architect had meticulously formed each window with a small peak on the left and the right, then bent the curves so they flowed into the one larger peak in the center at the top forming the crown. Surely, she thought, this scene more than qualified as a Hallmark card.

Toni shook her head; a small but beautiful piece of heaven on earth was just across the street from a cemetery. The remains of so many lives lay in dirt covered boxes under the earth, never to be enjoyed, celebrated or tolerated by human beings, again. On the other side of the street, a sweet retreat for spiritual life on earth. A place, Toni thought, where the living dead could go and have their souls comforted and their lives resurrected. To Toni, the church was the compass for the lost to find their way back home to God. At that moment, it seemed as though the church was etched in her heart. The thought of this little country Baptist Church would stir her spirit and start a revival.

Toni watched the church for what seemed an eternity. With her eyes, she took in everything and analyzed it as quickly as she saw it. The church, though small in size, looked like a cathedral of peace. A place that had the power to take away every earthly problem, if one could just get in the yard. Walking through the doors, she thought, could cleanse the heart and soul of the worse sinner and fill it again with peace and joy.

As she watched, a man walked out of the front door of the church putting a jacket on as he walked down the red brick steps. Her attention was turned from the man when the cars came to a complete stop. After a short while, the cars were moving again.

The cars again began to move and several entered the cemetery behind the hearse. Others chose to park along the outside of the cemetery's fence on the edge of the street. The old country road appeared to have been swept and raked, there was no litter. Either the litter laws were strictly enforced, or the people were very prideful, Toni thought.

Toni parked her car inside of the cemetery a short distance from the other cars and stood next to it, not hurrying to sit in the graveside seats for the family. As her mother's Pastor spoke, she watched from the distance. Several people had laid a single flower on the casket. Then Toni noticed a brown-skinned lady who looked very familiar. Her mind began to race as she tried to remember who the woman was. Without a doubt, Toni knew the woman, but her memory failed to release a name or hint of a time and place from when she had known the woman. The brown-skinned woman laid a small bouquet of red and yellow roses on the casket and blew a kiss at it. Toni thought that this was real class, but still could not remember who the woman was. As the woman walked away from the casket Toni said "God bless you, sister." After her mother's Pastor had spoken, the man from the church across the street said a few words as well, but she never moved closer to hear what either man had said.

The graveside service was over in a very short time and everyone began to leave the cemetery. Toni held her ground and watched as her brothers and sisters got back into the limousine. Then she slowly began to walk toward the grave. Several people who were now leaving the cemetery reached out to touch her as she walked to the seats in front of the grave.

Toni had not paid attention to much else as she stood near her car. As she got closer to the seats in front of the grave, Toni shifted her purse from her hand to under her arm so that she could unbutton her jacket. As she sat looking at the casket and the bouquet, she noticed a shadow and realized that someone was standing near. She turned slowly and saw that it was the man from the church across the street.

"Didn't mean to disturb you young lady. You're related to the deceased, aren't you?" the man asked.

"Oh you didn't disturb me at all. And, yes sir, I'm her daughter, Toni."

She extended her hand to the man, but never got up from her seat.

"It's certainly a pleasure to finally meet you. I'm Rev. David Anderson, the pastor of the church right across there. Are you the one who is the lawyer in New York?" The Preacher asked.

"Yes, sir, I'm a lawyer, but I live in Connecticut." Toni responded.

"I knew it was up north there someplace. I knew your mother, she had talked a lot about you. So I don't have a crystal ball or anything like that." The Preacher smiled.

"No, I just thought that you had word of knowledge from the Holy Ghost."

"Oh what you know about the Holy Ghost?" The Preacher jokingly asked.

"Not as much as I need to know, but He's still teaching me. Sometimes I'm not a very good student, but I'm getting better."

"Your mama she used to come here often and she would stand there at your daddy grave. She come out here one day, many, many years ago in the pouring rain. Something was troubling her heart and mind. I come cross the street here with a parasol to try and at least keep some of the rain off of her. I was finally able to get her to come back over to the church with me until the rain stopped. I called my Missus and she brought a little something to eat here for both your mama and me. I was able to minister to your mama then. It was right after your brother had gotten sentenced to the penitentiary for killing her boyfriend who had shot her."

"That's was almost twenty-five years ago, Rev. Anderson."

"Yes it was. I was a much younger man at that time. Plenty time has passed since then daughter. But like I was saying, she would come and pull the grass from around your daddy and her nephew grave, then she would come over to the church to see if I or the Missus was there. She even come to church here. She sometimes would just call to talk to me rather than call her Pastor; she was kind of shame faced, you know. Couldn't much blame her, cause people remember your past better than you do. Folks' past is a dead thing that judgmental people just won't let stay buried. They always want to try and resurrect the dead thing and ain't never successful. The judgmental don't realize that by keeping other folks' past alive they bringing a harsher judgment on themselves from God. The Missus called your mama often when she was down sick. We even made the trip there to Joyce's house to see her several times. But, she at peace now, Toni. I'm glad she made peace with God before she left here, too. Well, I'll leave you here for now, it's almost one o'clock and I got to take the Missus to the Winn Dixie. God bless you child, you did a lot for your mama and your family. She told me that you had a call on your life, too, and I can see it."

"Thank you Rev. Anderson, and you and Mrs. Anderson be blessed indeed."

"Oh, thank you so much. I see you know about Jabez, too?" he said as he walked away.

Toni turned around and watched as the Preacher left the cemetery and walked back across the street. All of the cars were gone now and the only people left in the cemetery were Toni and the two young men who were filling the gravesite.

Toni sat in the chair facing the grave and lit a cigarette. One of the men saw her smoking and asked whether she smoked menthol or non-menthol. When she said non-menthol he asked if he could have a cigarette.

4

"I thank you mam, I would rather beg than steal. It's real bad to have a habit and not be able to support it. But, smoking helps me to keep my head straight. I took this little hustle today so I could make a few dollars to keep me going."

The man stood away from the grave as though he was trying to make sure that no ashes went into it.

"My name's Roland Aiken, mam, what's yours." The man asked.

"Toni Spann, and it's a pleasure to meet you, sir."

"This your mother, mam?"

"Yes."

"Please accept my condolences. I don't know how it feels to lose a mama. I still live with mine." He said. "My daddy dropped dead when I was too young to even remember."

"Thank you so much, Roland." She replied. The young man did not appear to be a fool or anything remotely akin to a fool. He seemed real sincere.

"Why you stayed after everybody else left the cemetery, mam? People usually scared to come in a cemetery even if it is daylight and it is their mother."

"Well, a long time ago, Roland, I learned that a cemetery was not just a place to bury the dead, but it was also a place where some of the greatest writers are buried with their stories unwritten. The person with the cure for cancer might have been buried here without ever finding his or her way to the laboratory to do their thing. The cemetery, Roland, is my reminder that I was not born to live forever and should not leave this world until I have done all that God ordained me to do. Everything that God put in my heart to do, no matter how far fetch it might seem to somebody else, I've got to do it, or die trying. A cemetery, Roland, is a reminder that when this body is done so are all the dreams that I carry in my heart and should not carry them to the grave. A graveyard is a place for dead bodies, not for unrealized dreams, dreams keep us alive so long as we're still working on them. Like Dr. King, the dreamer might die, but the dream lives on."

When Toni looked around after her statement she realized that both men had stopped working and were staring at her. They had clung to every word she had spoken as though they had been caught in an invisible web.

"Oh my God, I feel that in my spirit." Roland said. "The Lord trying to tell me something."

"I felt that all in my spirit, Ms. Spann." The young man standing next to Roland said. "I've got goose bumps on me. I can't let my dreams die before I do. Can I too, please get a cigarette from you Ms. Spann?" the young man asked.

"You ain't from around here are you, Ms. Spann." Roland asked.

"Oh please call me Toni. No, I moved away from here almost thirty years ago. I live in Connecticut."

The young man laid his shovel to the side of the grave and smoked the cigarette.

"I've always wanted to leave South Carolina and go somewhere else to live. You know, to try and get a decent job. Then come back here and build me a nice house on my land. What kind of work you do in Connecticut, Toni." The other young man asked.

"I'm a lawyer."

"Now see there. That's what I'm talking about, getting some education, a degree from a college so that you can make real money. I always wanted to go to college, but I never had the money. I can see me now in one of the high schools teaching math, then becoming Assistant Principal, then Principal." Roland said.

"Was you raised here in South Carolina, Toni?" Roland asked.

"Yes, I was."

5

"Sometimes Toni it seems like there's a cloud or something that's over our life. You know it's almost like having shackles on your feet, body, hands, everything. Seems like no matter what we do, or how hard we try, it's almost like being in a grave and we can't get out. Everyday it's just like having dirt thrown on you until you get to a point where it feels like you're being buried and you ain't dead yet, but you feel like you're dead. I might not be explaining it right, but that's just how I feel."

"Oh I know the feeling real well, Roland, trust me. When I left South Carolina it was like I was running for my life. It was during a time when common sense would have said stay until things get better in your family. But there was a feeling deep down inside of me that kept saying if I didn't go now, I would never get out of here. It was like my life was ahead of me and if I didn't follow it I would die where I was. It felt, just like you said, being in a coffin and I could sense the coffin top shutting down with me inside. I know exactly what you're talking about, brother."

"Yeah, yeah, that's just the way me and my friend here feel. We sit down for hours sometime Toni and talk about that feeling. But you know what, we always end up talking about our dreams too. It don't matter how bad things might have been for us that day or that week, Toni somehow right in the middle of our conversation about the trouble, we just get to talking about our dreams. I tell you the God in heaven truth, Toni, if I had the money and knew somebody somewhere else I would be out of here in twenty minutes. I would finish what I'm doing here and wouldn't bother to change clothes. I would just go, truthfully." Roland said.

"Sounds like what you fellows are hoping for is a breakthrough." Toni said.

"Yeah, a breakthrough. It's like being in a circle that won't break. If you can just get a crack in it you can get out or something could get in."

Roland had stopped his work and stood looking around the cemetery. The sorrow in his eyes and on his face seemed to tell of years of disappointments and hours of dreaming of a better life. But underneath the story of disappointment and sorrow, Toni saw a glimmer of hope flickering like the wick of a kerosene lamp when it's almost empty. She felt sorry for the young men, she, too had been where they now were. Roland looked like he wanted to cry; tears had welled in his eyes. He stared up at the pine trees, then shook his head as though in bewilderment.

"How old are you, Roland?"

"Me, I'm twenty-four, be twenty five in January." He responded.

"Do you have any commitments that would keep you from going to college now?"

"No mam, my girlfriend she quit me about five or six month ago. She moved to Boston with a friend of hers. She works for the Telephone Company up there. I live with my mama not too far from here. I catch these little jobs to keep a little change in my pocket and to help my mama out as much as I can."

"If you really want to go to college, Roland, I can have you in college in January. But you'll have to go to Minnesota. I have a very dear friend, who is just like a sister to me. She's a teacher and department head at a college there. If you promise me that you will graduate and can get to Minnesota, I will get you into college by January and you can teach math or whatever you desire."

"Don't kid me Miss Lady, please don't kid me. The Lord is my witness and with His help lady, if you can get me into college, I don't care where I have to go, I'll go." Roland said excitedly.

The young man who had been smoking the cigarette seemed to come alive, again, when Toni said that she could get Roland into college by January.

"Miss, look here, I graduated from high school too, I ain't never been in no kind of trouble and I was almost an A student, can you get me into college along with Roland? Oh by the way, my name Horace, Horace Petry. I'll get to Minnesota, just tell me when and I'll be there."

"Yes, I can get you and Roland into college, if you really want to go. It's cold in Minnesota, you can freeze your tutu off there, if you're not careful, but you guys can make it. Just get yourselves plenty of warm clothes and start buying them now so when January rolls around you're ready."

"Toni, what we got to do to get into college?" Roland asked.

The possibility of going to college seemed to generate an uncontainable excitement in the cemetery. Toni pulled out her cell phone and called her friend, Marsha, in Minnesota. After telling Marsha what she was trying to do for the young men and getting Marsha's word that she could get them in, Toni gave the phone to Roland and Horace so that they could speak to her friend and give her their addresses to send their application packets. The two men gave all of their information to Marsha and began praising God in the cemetery. When the telephone conversation was over the two men were in tears because they were bound for college. The flicker of hope had burst into a raging fire of limitless possibilities. Toni smiled as her heart was warmed watching the near quiet transformation of two lives.

"Complete the applications that Marsha will be sending you all and do it very quickly. Start saving your money so that you can buy your plane tickets to Minnesota, that is, if you plan to fly there. Of course, you can always choose a different mode of transportation. Save as much of any money you earn so you can buy food or any of your personal stuff. If you have any questions about anything at all, just give Marsha a call and she'll help you to find the answer. In the meantime, start considering yourselves university men, or college boys. This is November, you guys have less than two months to get yourselves together. Hey, I want an invitation to that graduation, too."

"Toni, look how God works. I came out here today to make a few dollars and the Lord done open a door wide for me to be a teacher. Praise the Lord. Pastor said that the Lord would put people in your path that you would find favor with. Now just who would have thought that our life could take a change in the graveyard? I just bless the Lord right now and I bless you too, Toni. Toni, I'll never ever forget you, I mean that." Roland said.

"Roland, even if you forget me, please, don't ever forget the God I serve, the same One that Abraham, Isaac, and Jacob served." Toni said.

"I had laid in my bed the other night, Miss Toni, just imagining myself as a man who worked for a big computer company. I seen myself hopping on an airplane and flying to California to check out a big job and solve a problem that other people couldn't. I seen myself driving a nice car out of my garage at a nice brick house. You know that white brick, not the red brick. Lord look at us now, Roland we going to Minnesota and get us an education, a college degree, in the name of Jesus. All we need to do is find us a church up there and keep God's covering on us while we in school. Who knows, we might like Minnesota enough and stay after we finish school. But I tell you right now, Toni, I'm gonna get my Masters degree before I leave there. Yes, mam, you can bet the farm on that." Horace said. "I always sit down and just write my name, Horace Petry, BA, MBA. I just love the way that sound, Miss Toni."

"Dr. Horace Petry. Now that has a sound that I love." Toni said.

"Toni, I'm gonna put that bouquet at the head of the grave, " Roland said, "it's too pretty to bury." Toni nodded her head in agreement.

Toni gave each of the men twenty dollars so they could buy their own brand of cigarettes. They were so grateful and began to sing an old hymn as they finished filling the grave. The men had beautiful voices and Toni joined in the singing.

"Oh you got a good voice, Toni." Horace said.

The young men began finished the grave with a renewed energy and began making their life's plan at the same time. They continued to rejoice at their prospects of going to college.

<u>2</u>

Toni saw a blue car pull up along the side of the fence of the cemetery. The brown-skinned woman who had laid the bouquet of roses on the casket had returned. Toni watched as she made her way to the graveside. The closer the woman got to Toni the more familiar she looked, but Toni was still unable to remember her. She stood up at the chair to receive the woman and learn who this familiar face belonged to.

"Toni, it looks like you getting some company." Horace said.
"Tonitia Spann, that's you isn't it?" The brown-skinned woman asked.
"Yes, mam, it is. Please forgive me if I don't remember you." Toni responded.
"Titi, this me, baby, Helen Baker, I'm the one who named you baby?"
"Oh Miss Helen, darling how you doing? Please forgive me." Toni said.

No one had called Toni by that nickname in almost thirty years. Helen Baker had given her the nickname when she had named Toni at birth. Helen had thought that the chocolate baby was the most beautiful little girl she had seen and wanted her to have a name that showed off her beauty. Tonitia Renee was the name Helen determined to be most suitable for her best friend, Trudy's first daughter. The two women hugged and cried as Horace and Roland watched in joy.

"Toni, we're through here. Miss Marsha said to get her phone number from you. Toni, Roland and me, we can't tell you how much we appreciate what you doing for us. This means a lot to us. You come out here today to bury your mama and you ended up giving hope and new life to two country boys in Branchville, South Carolina. God bless you. " Horace said.

"God bless you guys, too. I'm going to be checking those grades too. I hope I find a couple of little brothers name on the Dean's Honor Roll, too, that could be a hundred dollar bonus for somebody." Toni replied.

As Helen walked over to the fence to tell the driver that he could leave, Toni took out her business cards and wrote down Marsha's telephone number on the back and gave each one of the young men a card. Toni wrote her home and cell phone numbers on the cards just in case the young men wanted to reach her. She also took the young men's telephone numbers and addresses so that she could be in touch with them as they prepared for college. Horace and Roland put the shovels on their shoulders and walked across the street to the church and around the back.

Toni and Helen sat in the chairs facing the grave. Horace and Roland had taken care to smooth the grave then make a small mound. The bouquet of roses was placed in a hole made in the dirt at the head of the grave, making it look like it was sitting in a vase.

"What that you doing for them boys, baby?" Helen asked.
"I'm helping them get into college in January. My best friend, Marsha, is with the University up there and she does recruiting as well. I've helped a number of other kids go to college with her help. I called Marsha up and she said that she could get them in undergraduate school in January, if they can get to Minnesota. She's sending the application packets to them today." Toni responded.

"Oh baby, that is so wonderful. God blesses you for helping people. Them boys look like they was floating out of this here cemetery. You thought you was coming here to bury your mama and God had another little something He wanted you to take care of for Him. I want you to come by the house and get your graduation present I bought a long time ago. You hear me child?"

"I will, and I thank you." Toni said.

"But that's a good thing you doing for them boys. They just need somebody to give them a little help. Sometimes peoples just need a little help to bring out the best in them. You hadn't forgot where you came from baby, thank the Lord. Somehow I feel in my spirit them boys is gonna make it. I feel a joy rising up on the inside of me for them. God'll bless you too, Titi. That's my baby girl. Just look at you, got some hips on you too. You always had them long pretty legs just like Trudy. But you gotta spend a day with your old godmother now."

"I will certainly do that. But tell me this, Miss Helen how did you know that I was still here in the cemetery?"

"Well something inside me said go back to the cemetery and talk to your godchild. It was like I knowed you was still here Titi. I told old Melvin to just don't ask me no question, just turn around and bring me back here. I told him if he didn't want to turn around to just stop the car and I would walk back. He got to where he could turn around in the road and brung me right back here. It wasn't nothing but the Lord, sweetie. And you stop calling me Miss Helen, I'm your godmother."

"Godmother, I'm sorry, but I am so glad to see you. I thank you for the flowers you brought for mama."

"Honey, Trudy was a queen so she suppose to get nothing less than roses. Even though a wedge was driven between us, I never stopped loving Trudy. We go too far back for that. How many peoples can you say you know for more than sixty years, child?"

"I don't know, godmother, I guess not many."

"Me and Trudy used to work on the farm just up the road a piece from here as young girls, just after her youngest brother joined the Navy. Wasn't nobody but Trudy and her daddy then, but he was living in the next county over there most of the time with his woman when he wasn't working."

Toni and her godmother sat facing the grave in silence. Tears streamed down their faces as they just watched the grave. Neither woman spoke for what seemed to be an eternity. The warm November sun shined warmly upon them as the gentle breeze ruffled the tops of the pine trees. Every now and then a rabbit could be seen running through the underbrush. Still the old woman and the younger woman sat in silence and watched.

"You think she watching us Titi?"

"I think so. The Bible says something about us running the race and there being so great a cloud of witnesses. Who are the witnesses, if they aren't those who made their peace with God and went ahead of us? They're the ones cheering us on, godmother. If we really listen with our inner ear, we can even hear them cheering us on, or urging us to do the right thing, trying to guide us around obstacles. " Toni responded.

"You know I never thought of that scripture like that before, but I believes it baby. We all come here to earth from heaven. Some of us forget that heaven is our real home. Many of us don't make it back home either. The devil tricks us and we get led away and some of us never find our way back so we can return to the Father. I wonder how many times God's heart been broken cause one of us didn't make it back home?"

"I know mama made it back home. Joyce said that she prayed all night long. Three days before she passed, godmother, Joyce said mama told her thank you for all that she had done. Then she told Joyce to tell me the same thing. The night before she passed,

Joyce said she wanted to put on this silk pajamas set that I had bought her a few years ago. She even put on her satin bedroom slippers that I had sent her when I went to China. She just laid in the bed Joyce said dressed in her silk and satin."

"Oh she was preparing, honey. Trudy wanted to look good when she meet Jesus. I wonder sometime if the end is really like they show it on Touched By An Angel?"

"I don't know godmother. But it could be, I just don't believe that God allows his people to hurt so bad, like you see in some of those terrible car accidents. I think before impact, God sends an angel who escorts our spirit back to eternity."

"I hope so Toni, but whatever way He decides to do it is fine with me, I just want to be sure that God is the one that send the angel for me, and I'm going back home to glory. Amen. Now come on let's go and get us a bite to eat."

"Well, where do you want to go. Everybody has left the church by now." Toni said.

"Oh child, we ain't going to no church. I got me a pot in the freezer. I seasoned up my whiting fish before I left home so I can fry 'em when I get back. We going to my house."

"What kind of pot you got up in that freezer, godmother?"

"Gal, I got me some butter beans and okra. I seasoned it down with them smoked ham hock and neckbones. You know that seasoning done gone all through that pot."

"Get up off that chair Helen Baker and let's tap that pot. I hope you got a piece of cornbread with that."

"I ate all of the cornbread but we can fix some more."

"I've got to change clothes. I'll take you home, go back to the hotel and change, then I'll come back to your house. How's that?" Toni asked.

"Now Titi, that sound good, but don't fool me, now. For true you coming back?"

"Yes, mam. I just want to put on my sweats and tennis shoes, then I'll be back to your house."

"Okay, sugar, don't break godmother heart."

The two women walked arm in arm to the car. Toni opened the passenger door and let Helen get in. Toni and Helen waved at Horace and Roland who were still sitting on the front steps of the church. Toni saw the Pastor pull up in front of the church and the two young men talking to him. As Toni started to walk around to the driver's side of the car, the Pastor began yelling across the street to her. Toni waved to let him know that she had heard him and pulled across the street to see what he wanted.

"Oh Sister Spann, the fellows just gave me the praise report. I'm so full of joy for them; God came through, again. Let's just thank the Lord and have a word of prayer right now before you drive another mile."

The Pastor, Toni, the two young men and Helen stood in a circle holding hands as the Pastor prayed and thanked God for what was about to happen.

"Now, I tell you what, Sister Spann, we here at the church gonna start getting Roland and Horace ready to go to college. If we got to sell some chicken dinners and fish sandwiches, we gonna send these fellows off to school with a blessing on them and a bit of it in their pockets."

"I'll tell you what Pastor, I'll pay for one round trip ticket if you can get the other one. That way they'll even have a ticket to come home for Christmas." Toni said smiling.

"Oh shoot, you ain't said nothing but a word, daughter. We got them covered for transportation." The Pastor said and he and Toni high fived each other.

Toni gave the Pastor her card with her phone numbers on it so that he could also keep her informed about the dates the fellows would be leaving for school. Horace and

Roland's complexion seemed to have taken on a golden glow. Their joy was showing over their entire being.

As they slowly drove down the old country road Toni remarked that she was surprised that even in such modern times that this part of the country had managed to maintain a rural innocence. It had all of the modern features of the big cities, such as indoor plumbing, modern homes and well cared for lawns. But somehow there was that little country flair that set it apart from every other place.

"You think you might come back here to live one day, Titi?"

"I don't know godmother. Connecticut got some country in it, too."

"Well, I guess where you born at on earth ain't where you got to die at. Look at all of them folks who left here to fight in the war and they died in bloody fields overseas. My Bobby went off to the Marine Corp and he died in Viet Nam. Some folks bodies never come back to they hometown to be buried, they have what they call memorial services for them. The best thing though is that you be saved so you can go back to your real home."

The two women drove in silence until Toni saw the little market and pulled in.

"Godmother, do you like Jiffy cornbread mix?"

"Girl, hush your mouth or whisper. I been doctoring up Jiffy for years, that's why I don't have any at the house cooked. Shoot, I figure like this, why mix up all of that stuff when you can get the same or better result with Jiffy. I always liked my cornbread a little sweet anyway."

"Well let's go on up in here and get us some Jiffy for our butter beans and okras. I can smell that whiting frying already."

"I hope we hurry and get this show on the road, honey cause my backbone was playing patty cake with my stomach, now they seem to just be hugging each other, tight."

The two women laughed as they made their way around the little market. They picked up everything they needed, paid for it, and headed out of the door. As they got to the car, Helen saw a couple she knew and waved to them.

"How you doing Sister Baker?" the man asked.

"I do just fine, Brother Wash. How you and Ruth doing?"

"I'm getting around, Sister. If I can find something else for Art and Burt to ride on, I might be able to run." The woman said.

"Who Art and Burt, your grandsons?" Helen asked.

"No girl, Arthritis and Bursitis. They with me and on me so much, I decided to give them nicknames." Ruth said.

Everybody burst into laughter at Ruth's remark.

"Ruth you too jokey, girl. Maybe you should just give Art and Burt a roll of quarters and show them where the bus stop is." Helen said.

"Well sister Helen is this one of your daughters?" Brother Wash asked.

"Sure tis, brother, this here is my goddaughter, Tonitia Renee Spann, she a lawyer in Connecticut. This here is Trudy Spann oldest daughter. She here to bury her mama which we did a little while ago and she gonna spend some time with her old godmother before she head back up that road."

"Sure you right. I forgot that Trudy's funeral was today. Tonitia, please accept me and my wife's sympathy for your loss. We all been knowing each other for at least a good fifty some odd years." Brother Wash said.

"Well thank you both." Toni said.

"We got to go on to the house. I left my fish seasoned in the refrigerator this morning. Me and Toni just about starved out by now. Y'all take care now."

Toni pointed the car onto the highway and the two women rode in momentary silence. Then Helen spoke up.

"Child that old Wash wasn't nothing but an old poontang pooch. He was too low down and sleazy to be a hound. He thought that he was gonna get Trudy but that's when your daddy stepped on the scene, honey. Big Aaron was something then, child. He and Trudy took a look at each other and that was all she wrote. Wash didn't stand a Popsicle's chance on a summer's day in hell then."

"God mother, you're crazy."

"Crazy like a fox, baby. The only thing that changed about that old Bo Cat, Wash, is the color of his hair and his belt size. Don't you think for one minute that fool been all nice, Ruth had to put a whipping on his tail a time or two. I remembers it too."

Toni laughed as she inserted the CD into the player. Helen was taken aback when she heard the music coming out of the speakers.

"Titi, where you got that music from baby? Oh honey that sound sweet. Me and Trudy used to sit this one out when we lived in New York. We wouldn't dance with any of the fellows off this here song. I sure would like to have that record. Pump it up a little tad, as them young kids would say, let me feel that."

"I ordered that from the television one night. You know how they advertise all of that stuff, so I ordered it because I like the Platters. It even got Ivory Joe Hunter on it. If you got a stereo I'll leave it with you while I go to the hotel and change clothes, you can do your thing in private."

"Oh girl, mama is in the now time. My little fancy stereo set sound like one of them big ones. My stereo can even duplicate. I got me a few blank tapes so when you get back you can make a copy of that for me. Shoot, I'm gonna have my private party after you leave. I'm gonna call Inez and tell her that I got a tape of our kind of music." Helen said.

"Now godmother, tell me when was this you and mama lived in New York, and was acting like Paulette and me?"

"Oh Titi, that was so long ago, before either one of us got married or had any chilrens. Another friend girl of ours, Viola, who used to work in the fields with us, got fed up and she went on up there to New York and got one them sleep-in jobs with the white folks in Long Island. After about a year or so Viola, she come down here to see about her mama and them. That girl was looking good baby. She tell me and Trudy that she could get us a job too. Then she tell us all about Harlem and how all the sleep-in girls would take the train to Harlem and dance at that Savoy Manor. Titi, me and your mama got so excited. Honey, the next thing you know, me and Trudy in New York City trying to put the lights out and hang some new ones."

"Godmother, I bet the two of you were a riot. I can just see you and mama getting off a train making your way down the streets of Harlem with your red fox stockings on with the seam up the back."

"Hush your mouth child or whisper! We was something else then honey. As y'all would say, now, we was fine baby cakes. Titi we had nice shapes and knowed how to put a few rags together. We worked right down the street from each other in Hempstead, Long Island and made good money in them days. The white folks wasn't so bad, either. Most of the colored girls at that time came from the south. We all was poor and trying to make it. A lot of them girls still in New York till this here day, if they ain't dead."

"How about Viola, the lady that turned you and mama on to the sleep-in jobs?"

"Oh Viola, she died back in eighty-nine or ninety. She married a fellow who was a teacher in Queens. She had two kids by the time she married him. None of the two kids was his, though. But he was good to her. You should remember Viola though. Trudy went to New York and stayed right there in Brooklyn on Livonia Avenue with Viola when you and Aaron, Jr. was in elementary school. You remember when she left Big Aaron?"

"Mama left daddy?"

"Oh sugar, I thought you remembered that cause Trudy was gone for about eight or nine months."

Toni had completely forgotten that her mother had left her father. As she pulled in front of Helen's house the memories began rushing forward like an open faucet.

"Oh my goodness! Godmother, you're right, mama did leave daddy. I had swept that clean out of my mind until you said it just now. How could I have ever pushed that out of my mind?"

"Easy. Sometimes when things hurt us so bad Titi, the Lord let us push it aside until when we can deal with it. Sometimes pushing things aside save our lives. But you and Paulette was both in the third grade then. I remember that cause you had lost a tooth and it was picture taking time. Big Aaron sent you over to me and Willie, my dead husband, for me to do your hair that morning. You was crying so much for your mama that I had to hold you in my arms like a baby and rock you. Willie, he would hold you some so I could feed the other chilrens. You was pretty heartbroken over the whole thing Titi. I think that's where you got that thing about being alone. Yeah, I watched you as you was growing up, no matter how close you got to people you had to put down some fences about how close they could get to you."

"Godmother, I remember it all now. Daddy took me to school that day. The ribbon you had put in my hair fell off and daddy tried to put it back on. Daddy started crying, too because he couldn't get the ribbon just like you had it. Daddy kept saying that he was sorry and asked me to forgive him. He ended up taking the lunch that he had fixed for me and Aaron, Jr. and giving us money to buy hot lunch that day. Godmother please tell me why mama left daddy."

Toni cut the engine off and rolled down the window. She asked her godmother whether it was okay for her to smoke a cigarette, lit it and held it out of the car window.

"Well, sweetheart, Big Aaron made a great mistake. Trudy caught him in the act with this woman and that darn near destroyed her mind. She say she didn't want nothing to do with Big Aaron. Trudy came back here to get her chilrens, she was gonna take all four of y'all back to New York with her. See it was you, Aaron, Jr., Margaret and Wilson, then."

"Godmother who was the woman mama caught daddy with?"

"The woman that lived right across the street from y'all. Trudy could have killed both her and Big Aaron that evening. Trudy caught them in the act. Neither one of them could have lied about what was going on. Everybody knowed about it too, sugar."

"Godmother, mama had to look at that woman everyday while we were growing up. Everyday that woman would come out of her door and go down that street and come back in the evening. Mama had to see her and not say anything. Then here I was with my silly self admiring how that woman dressed and thinking that she was really something else."

"Hell, she was something else. She had bought that house across from y'all and she couldn't up and leave it, either. But you didn't know what was going on baby, so you wasn't silly. Trudy come right cross here and she was so hurt by Big Aaron. Trudy couldn't even talk to Big Aaron. Your mama prayed and she prayed, but her heart was so broken, Big Aaron had destroyed her trust. Then about two weeks after that Trudy say she was going to the A&P and asked me watch y'all till she get back. That was about four thirty, cause y'all hadn't been too long get home from school. I looked at the clock and it was after seven o'clock. I knowed it didn't take that long to go to the store, even walking. It was way pass dark when Big Aaron come home and there ain't no dinner cooked and he come cross here and ask me if I had seen Trudy. I told Big Aaron what I knowed, then I told him that I believe Trudy was gone for good."

"Godmother you know what, that thing stayed with mama for most of her life. Everybody she loved had either died or deceived her. Tell me how daddy reacted to that."

"Well, your daddy took Margaret and Wilson in his arms, and told you and Aaron Junior to walk close to him. I could see the tears in his eyes. I had feed all of y'all so he didn't have to cook for y'all that night. He kept his head down after that. You could see the shame that laid on Big Aaron like a quilt or something. He was a broken man. We never talked about what he did that night, course he knew that Trudy had told me everything. Yeah, that's why I could never turn my back on Trudy. We was just like sisters, Titi. But when your mama come back here to get y'all Big Aaron he was sorry and he was hurting. I love Big Aaron like a brother, but if anybody should have been hurting, it should have been him. After Trudy had been gone for a month or so, I talked to Big Aaron about that whole thing. Neither one of us knowed where Trudy was at that time. But all them years Trudy and Viola had stayed in touch and Viola sent her the money to come to New York. Big Aaron knowed he was wrong too, he say he don't know what got into him, but he didn't think Trudy would find out. It was ugly baby. Somehow Trudy stayed so she could take care of y'all, but it was never the same between them. Then my Willie got killed the next year and Big Aaron and Trudy was right there for me and my chilrens. I couldn't even take care of my own chilrens for a while. Trudy and Big Aaron had to do it for me, remember?"

"Yes, mam. Godmother God is still good, though."

"Yes He is, baby. Now go on and change them clothes and get back here to me. Oh and give me this thing so I can listen to it while you gone."

3

Toni decided to go to Joyce's house first, which was in the new subdivision about a mile and half from where Helen lived. As she turned down the street she could see a number of cars in the driveway and along the street in front of Joyce's house. Toni did not like crowds and knew that she would not stay very long but thought it was a decent thing to at least go in for a minute and say hello to the people.

Toni took the jacket off to her suit and left it in the car on the seat. She grabbed her purse and locked it under her arm and rang the doorbell as she walked into the house. She spoke as she walked past the people seated and standing in the house and went into the family room. Joyce was sitting on the bar stool talking with a few people who looked familiar to Toni.

"Girl, I don't care how much weight you lose, you cannot get rid those hips like Aunt Trudy." Toni's cousin Tammy said.

"Girl those aren't hips, that's my slip that's rolled up like that." Toni replied.

"Toni you need to stop lying, that's pure hips honey. You had them hips since you were a little girl. How you doing sweetie?" Tammy said.

"Girl I'm doing. How about yourself?" Toni asked.

"Well, I didn't think that I could make or even live after the divorce, but God was merciful, girl. I sleep at night, I don't cry anymore and I can see me with somebody else, but it's got to be somebody that God picks this time. How you doing, dating again?"

"No Tammy, after my divorce, I decided to just wait on the Lord like you're doing. I don't date and I don't fornicate, would like to again before I leave this world, but if I don't, I'll just thank God for the times that I did."

"I know that's right. I'm in the same boat, girl. Twenty-three years I put into one relationship and it was devastating to say the least when he said he wanted out. I didn't know what to do. Homeboy didn't wait around either, no sooner had he said he wanted to be free, he was packed up and gone. But I made it girl. I got enough strength and I filed the papers. After I had filed, he supposedly came to his senses. But the woman he was with came to her senses because she realized that half of homeboy's pension was mine."

"Tammy I finally realized that I was the anesthesia for mine. He was out there getting his heart broken by other women then he would go through his dumped lover thing and all the time I was just being his anesthesia to help him get over his many breakups. Girl, I got these hips in gear, dropped the weight of him and some of that so-called satisfied weight and turned my home into a single girl's chalet and laid before the Lord so He could heal me."

"Have you seen him since the divorce?" Tammy asked.

"Tammy, I was out at the golf course, taking lessons, of course. I stopped by a client's house on my way home and there he was down the street a little bit from this client. Girl the hips were working that day, too. I heard him calling me, but I didn't even act like I heard him. Before the client could come to the door, there he was standing on the sidewalk calling me. I turned around and he asked how I was doing? Tammy, Tammy, I couldn't pass the opportunity up. I turned around and looked at him said, 'can't you see, I'm fine, just fine, how about yourself?' Girl he couldn't say a word right then. When he finally spoke, he just said that he was doing good and that he

16

was visiting a friend. I told him that I was visiting a client and that I would see him later. Girl don't you know that weasel asked me what was my phone number he wanted to call me. I looked at him and told him that I wasn't taking applications this year for friends, husbands or pen pals and waved goodbye."

The cousins high fived each other.

"Toni, it seems never to fail, the grass always looks greener on the other side until them jokers get over there. They leap across that fence honey and find out that what they were looking at wasn't nothing but artificial turf. But when they try to get back on the other side where they came from they find out that the little picket fence has been replaced by a twelve foot concrete wall."

"I saw that fool another time after that, too. I had just bought my Lexus, honey."

"Hold up Miss Thang, you got the Lexus?"

"Sure did, honey. Bought me an LS 420 to match me."

"Now that's what you do sister, look good, smell good, and be good if they let you."

"Tammy, I almost sprained my ankle trying to make sure the joker saw me in my Lexus. He was with one of his girlfriends. I was walking with one of my colleagues who just happened to be a fine ass brother. Homeboy said, that's a nice ride you got Toni."

"What his girlfriend say?"

"Nothing, she just looked at me."

"What color your Lexus is, honey?"

"Black with the gold package on it and girl, I even did the bad wheels."

"I know you did. I put the same things on my Cadillac, honey."

"Girl, you always said that you would get your Cadillac. What kind you got?"

"The Eldorado, is there any other?"

"Wait a minute, I saw a white El Dog parked out there, is that you?"

"Yes mam."

The cousins high fived each other and laughed like schoolgirls.

"Tammy how are the kids?"

"Girl the twins graduated from college this past June and they got commissioned into the Marine Corps. My daughter is in college in Maryland, don't look like she'll be back here no time soon. So I'm turning my house into a single girl's chalet like you. You should come on back down here girl."

"Yeah, right. Look I promised godmother that I would be right back after I changed my clothes and I hadn't even gotten to the hotel yet. I'll be around for a few more days though, let's get together." Toni said.

"Girl where you been at?" Henry asked.

"I stayed behind at the cemetery and godmother came back and sat with me for a long time. Why?"

"I didn't see you at the church or anything and I got a little worried. I thought maybe you tried to make crab bait out of yourself." Henry said.

"Boy now I know you done lost your mind. I am not suicidal, I am homicidal. I was over to godmother's house. I'm going to the hotel to change clothes and go back to her house cause she frying some fish to go with some butter beans and okra."

"Girl your godmama know she can cook. I seen her about in May or April over at the Winn Dixie and I gave her ride home. She said something was wrong with her car. So I took a look at it to see if it was something I could fix. I had to get a few parts and tune it up for her but I got the old girl rolling again. Miss Helen stopped me from working and fed me. According to her, I needed to eat and have strength to finish fixing her car, cause she had plans of driving. But Toni, Miss Helen had some turnip greens and collards mixed together with some smoked neckbones and hamhocks. She had fried some chicken and had some candied sweet potatoes and hot biscuits, real biscuit, not that stuff in the can. Me and Miss Helen sat down in that kitchen and took the brakes off of our forks. Girl I almost hurt myself over there, then I asked her where was the dessert. Miss Helen said if I didn't get out there and fix her car she was gonna whip me with an extension cord. I told Miss Helen to just put the rest of them biscuits in a baggie cause they was going home with me. But she made me a whole pan of biscuit to take home. Me and Shantae tore up that pan of biscuits, the kids didn't get any of them. Tell her I'm bringing the pan back for a refill."

"Yeah godmother always could cook." Toni replied.

"I always liked Miss Helen, though. I still got a nice handkerchief she gave to me twenty-five years ago."

Henry looked Toni straight in the eyes as he said what he did about the handkerchief. It was strange, and Toni felt that there was more to that statement than she was being told by Henry.

"I'll probably see you tomorrow, Henry. Tell Joyce I'm still at the hotel, if I'm not in my room tell her to call godmother's house."

"Okay, drive careful girl, you know you ain't lived here in ninety-nine years." Henry said.

"Where you going missy?" Joyce asked.

"I'm going to the hotel and change clothes then I'm going back to godmother's house. She's cooking some fish for us now." Toni responded.

"Shoot, girl I should go to godmother's house with you. Last time I ate over there she had fried fish, spaghetti and cole slaw. I went to sleep right in that recliner in her den. Tell her I said thank you and I said hello. But you'll be at the hotel later on, though?" Joyce asked.

"Yes, call me there or at godmother's house. Where is Margaret?" Toni asked.

"She out there in the back yard talking to some people." Joyce responded.

"Well anyway, I'll talk to you later. Hey Tammy, I'll see you later, okay." Toni said as she left.

4

As Toni drove to the hotel her mind was flooded with the memories of when her mother had left her father and had left her, as well. How could she, for all of these years, have forgotten that time? It was as though she had taken that period of time out of her memory. Not once had that memory surfaced, or anyone had mentioned it until her godmother said it today. Toni began to realize that that period in her life had been traumatizing, so traumatizing that even as a child she had put it far out of her mind.

As she pulled into the parking lot of the hotel, Toni thought to herself that a lot of things had changed in the old town, it wasn't as rural as it was when she was a little girl. But she had thought that it was the best place to live. The hotel was something that she could never have imagined as a child. But there it stood, a very nice hotel, not quite a bread and breakfast but it didn't have the feel of the larger chain hotels, either. The rooms were quite homey and the small restaurant attached to it made it a very nice place to come and just get away, she thought. Many of her former classmates who had left had returned and built or bought homes in the area. But there were a few things that had not changed she thought.

Joyce was divorced, she was divorced, and Tammy and all of her sisters were divorced. Margaret had divorced her second husband. There was hardly anybody in the family who was still married. Henry had married the love of his life and Jeremiah was still single. Aaron Junior had retired from the Navy and was working as a Social Worker with a Juvenile program. He and his family lived near Uncle Clifford. Wilson and Alma shocked everybody when they revealed that they were going to get married. Before she got out of the car, Toni asked the Lord to help her reconcile with the town as well as reconcile in her mind and spirit those things that she did not understand.

Toni changed clothes and was back in the car headed to her godmother's house in no time. As she turned down the street where Helen lived it was already starting to get dark. Toni could hear her stomach growling and knew that she was ready for a big meal. As she parked and got out of the car she could see the figure of another person through the open blinds and curtains in Helen's dining room. She walked up the steps admiring the fall flowers along the yard and narrow walkway. She walked up the steps onto the porch and knocked on the door as she walked on into the house.

"Oh Titi, I'm glad you back. I want you to meet Darlene Pritchard. You remember Leroy, Amos and Franklin Pritchard? This is their mother. Darlene, this here my godbaby, Toni Spann, she a lawyer up there in Connecticut. We just buried her mama today."

"How you doing Mrs. Pritchard?" Toni said.

"I'm doing fine, just fine, baby. I'm sorry to hear about your mama. How long you gonna be here with us?" Mrs. Pritchard asked.

"I don't know, I'm playing it by ear." Toni responded.

"Look at you, sweetie, that's a cute little outfit you got on. I'm glad you put on something with long sleeves cause it can still get chilly here in November." Helen said.

"Helen, let me walk on back round this corner before it get too dark. Toni, you take care of yourself, baby and have a safe trip back home. Don't be long before you come back and visit us. My Franklin and his wife built a house in one of the new subdivision and they'll be moving back here before Christmas. His wife already said that she gonna cook Christmas dinner in that new house." Mrs. Pritchard said.

"Oh yeah, where are they moving from?" Toni asked.

"They live in New Jersey now. Franklin is a supervisor with the post office and his wife is a Practical Nurse. She say she want to get situated here so she can work and go to school to get her R.N. degree. She a hard working girl, though, she'll make it." Mrs. Pritchard responded.

"Yes, mam, I believe that she will. Having the mind to do is half the battle."

"But Toni, I'm proud of you girl, a lawyer. I don't think none of you chilrens from here but you, of course, is a lawyer. Mabel Anderson boy who moved here last year is a doctor." Mrs. Pritchard said.

"Which one of her sons?" Toni asked.

"Helen what that boy name? He about two or three years older than Toni and your girl Paulette?"

"Chile, I can't think of the boy real name. He the one they call Bear, used to play football there at Bonds-Wilson." Helen replied.

"Oh, I know which one you talking about. I didn't know that. I knew he had played professional football for a good while, but I didn't know he was a doctor. That is fantastic." Toni replied.

"Yeah, he a single man, too. He got three kids but they all grown with they own families. I think they stay wherever they mama is, but they come and visit him though. Now if you moved back here we would have us a black doctor and a black lawyer from the same neighborhood." Mrs. Pritchard said.

"You starting trouble, Mrs. Pritchard. I don't know when or even if I'll leave Connecticut. I'm fairly comfortable where I am and the only place that I've really thought about living is perhaps retiring to Scottsdale, Arizona so that I can golf as much as I'd like. But it's always good to know that you're always wanted somewhere else." Toni responded.

"Now you can't stop a person from trying, can you? Y'all go on and get your supper, I'll see you before you leave, honey. Good night Helen."

"Okay girl, be careful going down them steps, now." Helen replied.

Toni and her godmother sat down for dinner. It had been such a long time since Toni had sat at a table of food prepared with such love. It had been a long time since she had sat down to break bread with another person. Her dining had been alone. She had cooked the food and ate as she watched television or reviewed a case. Seldom would she go out with friends or colleagues for a meal. She worked when she worked and the time after work she had kept to herself. But tonight she sat with her godmother and knew that if no one else on the planet that night loved her, Helen Baker did and that was good enough.

"Godmother, you can make a person hurt himself with this good cooking. Henry said that he was going to return that pan you had baked him some biscuits in. He said that he was bringing it back for a refill, seems you didn't give him no dessert."

"Girl let Henry go on way from here. Titi, I swarney, that Henry can eat, girl. Bless his heart, though, he don't put on weight like some other folks do. Henry brought me home that day, girl, and got my car fixed. Baby, I was back on the road that night. I was so glad to have that car fixed and it didn't cost me all that money folks claimed it would. I guess I do owe Henry another pan of bread and a peach cobbler."

"Oh, now I ain't gonna tell him about that peach cobbler cause Henry would sleep right here until it's ready. "

The two women ate and laughed at their own jokes. The golden brown whiting fish lay on the platter like pieces of gold. The cornbread looked like it was prepared for two queens. Toni and her godmother said grace and put their forks to work.

"Godmother, why didn't you get married again after your husband died? You stayed single all of these years. I know there was somebody who wanted to make you his wife."

"Titi, I asked the Lord to give me just one good man, one who would marry me, and treat me good. I had that. I didn't ask the Lord for but one. But I did have a little boyfriend or two since that time."

"You must be kidding, I don't remember you ever having a boyfriend godmother."

"I always tried to keep my little business to myself, so I just let them court me right here in my house. I stop even seeing men folks after that Isiah Henderson. Lord have mercy on his soul."

"Wait a minute, you used to go with Isiah Henderson, too?"

"Yeah, I ain't too proud of it, but I did. That was fore Trudy started dealing with him. I tried to warn Trudy that Isiah wasn't nothing but trouble, but she got mad with me and accused me of trying to get him back after he supposedly quit me. I loved Trudy too much to argue with her, so I just let her tell me off and left it at that. I just told Trudy that she would see for herself and look at what happened. Poor Henry had to spend time in that there penitentiary behind that mess."

"Godmother, mama got mad at you about that man? I told mama, the first time I found out that she was messing with him, that he was too young for her. There was something about him that just didn't sit well in my spirit. Even that night when the police found his body right back there and asked me to identify him, even in death there was something evil about him."

"You don't even know the half, Titi. That man had fixed your mama and she was crazy over him. He was all sweet and stuff when I first started letting him come around here to see me. But one night he come here about three or four in the morning, that was just before my Walter went into the service. I had already loss my Bobby. Honey that Negro was as drunk as a cooder cat and wanted me to let him go in my bedroom and have his way with me. I told Isiah he had to go cause I wasn't that kind of woman. Before I knowed anything that Negro had knocked me in the eye and throwed me on the floor to fight me. That's when Walter jumped on him. Isiah pulled a pistol on my child and cussed him like he was a dog. The Lord was with us that morning."

"Did you tell mama about that?"

"I tried, honey, but Trudy sweared out that I was just lying on Isiah and a whole bunch of mess. I was too shame to say anything to anybody after that. I had to change my phone number cause he kept calling here talking about how sorry he was. I told him that I didn't want him to even speak to me anymore. That fool told me that nobody quit Isiah Henderson, that he did the quitting."

"Oh so he was one of them kind of Negroes?"

"That ain't the half, girl. I went to the Masonic Hall for an oyster roast and fish fry one Friday night with another friend girl of mine. We was sitting at this table when I seen Isiah, I told my friend girl let's go cause I don't want no trouble, that's when I seen Trudy coming in. Isiah was just showing off, hugging and feeling up on Trudy just to let me know he was with her. So, me and my friend, we sit there for a little while. Trudy she come over to the table and sit with us. We was just cutting the fool and listening to the music when Isiah come back and tells Trudy to get up from the table with me cause I wasn't no good. First, Trudy looked at him like he was a fool, cause me

21

and Trudy been like family for almost all of our life. Then Trudy just tell me that she'll talk to me later. I was hoping that Trudy would start to see what she was dealing with."

"So mama just did what he told her to do?"

"Well Titi, there was other people who had come out that night trying to enjoy they self. So I thought that Trudy was just going along so that Isiah wouldn't start no mess up in there. But that Sunday after church, I went round there to talk to Trudy. But baby that was a different Trudy. I just told Trudy that she would see for herself. I didn't know that it would end up with Henry going to the penitentiary for killing that Negro. Heck, I didn't think that the Negro would be crazy enough to shoot Trudy, either."

"So, did mama ever thank you, godmother?"

"For a few months there, Trudy she just avoided me, she would not even look across the back fence there. I knew that damn Isiah had his hooks in her so deep she didn't know whether she was going or coming. It was just too much for me to look at. Trudy had really flipped out by then, but she had a little help. That Isiah Henderson and his family wasn't nothing but root workers and devil worshippers from their hearts. Them folks made me do something that I ain't never done before. I had to get before the Lord and stay right there until He released me from that."

"I tried to forget that night and over the years it's not come to mind as often as it once did. I did a lot of praying and asking God to forgive Henry for taking the life of another person."

For a moment the two women sat quietly eating their dinner. Toni had spent a lot of money on attorney's fees trying to keep Henry out of prison. She had had to get a second job to try and keep up with the bills that she was getting from the lawyer. No one had helped at all and she had worked herself almost sick to try and keep up.

"Isiah wasn't no good to nobody. I remember one time he asked me to ride with him to visit his mama and them. They from way up the road there from out the country, almost to North Carolina. I remember the feeling that come over me as soon as we drove up in front of his mama's house. Girl it felt cold and something seemed to be right close up on me, I couldn't see it, just felt it. There was something evil about that house, too. I couldn't eat or drink anything there. It was like something made my stomach upset and I asked where was the store so I could get me an Alka Seltzer or something like that. I believe that it was the Lord that allowed me to have an upset stomach so that I could have an excuse not to eat or drink anything. Sweetheart, I threw up all in his mama yard."

"I have had that feeling a few times. Sometimes it feels like something is trying to move on and into you and it'll cover one side of your body sometimes." Toni said.

Looking across the table with the most serious eyes, Helen stared right at Toni.

"Titi, these was evil people, I tell you. Not long after that night at the Masonic Hall, I walked in the front door and got about right there when Isiah come walking out my kitchen."

"Say what? How he got in your house."

"I don't know to this here day, but I know he'll never come again, not even as a spirit. Titi, that Negro scared the living dodo out of me. I backed up out that door screaming and hollering like a wild fool. The girl cross the street there called the police. I took out a warrant for his arrest. The police could see he had left out the backdoor."

Eyes wide and mouth open, Toni laid her fork down on the plate and shook her head in disbelief.

"How in the world did he get in this house, godmother?"

22

"I still don't know, Titi. But that was a week or so, less than two weeks before he shot Trudy. The police say they was looking for him, but my oldest boy he come here and brung me a pistol for my own protection. I intended to use it if I even seed that fool near my gate."

"He was a bold one, huh? He just didn't believe that anybody would stand up to him. He must have thought all that roots and witchcraft would scare death, too."

"Now before that night, Titi, I used to try and go to sleep at night and something would come like a man and lay right on top of me and try to have sex with me. I couldn't even sleep at night."

Toni had finished her meal and was now just listening to her godmother reliving the horrors of Isiah Henderson. Watching and getting angry that a person could torment another with witchcraft, Toni was glad that Isiah was dead.

"What did you do?"

"I told my cousin who live there in Barnwell about what was happening and she come here and took me to see this here Pastor named Rev. Hunter, in Georgia. Them peoples in that church prayed down fire from heaven for me sugar and prayed for my house and family. I got baptized again while I was there and I ain't never had no more troubles like that."

"Praise the Lord, there was a man of God, a real man of God, not somebody playing with God and practicing voodoo. This here preacher had the power and the know-how to deal with that kind of mess."

"Praise God for that."

"But that Satday night I was sitting right there on the front porch with no lights on when I seen this here car pull up on the other side of the street with no lights on. I could see them better than they could see me from where I was sitting. I was waiting for that same cousin of mine to come here. She was gonna spend the weekend with me and go to church with me that Sunday. See that Monday was a holiday and none of us was working. So I seed that it was Isiah, I started to get up and grab that pistol, but something just told me to wait and watch him. I seed him put something down in his pants and pull his shirt down. He cut there between my house and the one next door. So I got up from the porch and looked out the bathroom window and seed him going over there to y'alls house. I said to myself 'what he doing going over there, the police looking for him for shooting Trudy.' It wasn't long before I hear the gunshots. I ducked down and crawled out the bathroom and went back to lock the front door. Then I hear the footsteps and somebody running but the footsteps and the running stop. I went in the back bedroom and I could hear somebody breathing real hard, they never moved. I then seed Isiah running back toward this way, trying to get to his car, that's when I hear the shots and seen him fall down right out there where you seen him, too. Then I seen that it was Henry who had been outside there waiting for him right under that bathroom window."

Toni had been following the story until Helen said that she had seen Henry shoot Isiah. Toni knew something was wrong with this story because she had pulled Henry into the house and he never left until the police arrested him for the murder. Toni thought, maybe her godmother was fabricating some parts of this story. Old people don't always remember things as clearly after twenty-five years. But Helen continued.

"Isiah was trying to make it back to his car and get out of here but he never made it. Henry let him have it before he could getaway, and then Henry and Jeremiah walked out there to the street and went around the corner. Henry was still carrying Jeremiah in his arms when he shot Isiah."

Henry carrying Jeremiah? Toni thought. Helen had not seen Henry. Henry had not killed Isiah. Toni knew who was carrying Jeremiah that night because Jeremiah was in her brother-in-law's arms when they came into the house before the police arrived. Alma had called the police after she had pulled Henry into the house. Toni remembered that she and her girlfriend, Alma, had been sitting in the kitchen when they first heard the shots fired. Alma had not moved from the spot where she had been sitting. The nearness of the gunfire had caused Alma to freeze in her seat.

"Godmother, you said you saw Henry when he shot Isiah?"

With her head hung low, Helen nodded her head up and down to answer yes.

"I knew somebody was outside that bathroom window, cause I could hear 'em breathing hard and I had heard the footsteps before that. But the footsteps had stopped just before I heard the heavy breathing. Then I seen Isiah running back this here way and the gunshots. Isiah had a pistol in his hand, but Henry surprised him when he got right long up in here. Then I seen Henry walking toward the street, toward Macon, to go back around the corner, I guess and wait for the polices to come."

"Did you see Henry's face, godmother?"

Toni did not want to let Helen know that the person she had seen was not Henry, but Lloyd. But needed to know just how much of the person she had seen that fateful night.

"No, I didn't look him straight in the face. I just knowed it was him because he was carrying Jeremiah in his arms. He just shot Isiah and didn't look back, just kept walking toward Macon Street with Jeremiah in his arms. You know, protecting his little brother."

Toni, for the first time in twenty-five years, realized that she had spent money for something that Henry had not done. No wonder Lloyd wanted Margaret to marry him so quickly. He had shot and killed Isiah that Saturday night and on Monday he and Margaret decided that they would get married at Rev. Pryor's house. Smart thinking, Toni thought. Lloyd must have believed that being married to Margaret would prevent him from testifying against Henry at trial. Or, Lloyd might have thought that if someone ever figured out that he was the one that had killed Isiah, he could use the excuse that it was his mother-in-law, and have someone to bring him cigarettes to the prison.

Toni sat with her legs stretched out in the kitchen floor. She could not believe that Lloyd had kept this secret for so many years while Henry spent nearly two years in the penitentiary. No wonder he was so helpful when Henry got out of prison in helping him find a job, then helping to redo the little house Henry had bought and expanded. He was trying to make up for what he had done. If Henry knew that Lloyd was the one that had shot and killed Isiah, he would probably shoot and kill Lloyd and spend time for a murder that he had actually committed.

No one had paid any attention to what Jeremiah had said about his ears. Jeremiah was only about seven at that time. Jeremiah had said a number of times that the bullets had flown past his head and that his ears were ringing. The bullets had not flown past his heads; they had more than likely come from behind his head from Lloyd's pistol.

"Toni, I had to repent to the Lord for the way I felt. I was so glad that Isiah was shot and was hoping that he was dead out there. I went out the back door and walked over to where his body was. I called his name three or four times but he didn't answer. I walked closer to his body and the pistol was still in his hand with his fingers still in the little piece there like he was gonna pull the trigger. His eyes and mouth was wide open, like he was trying to say something. He had a wild and surprised look on his face, too, child. He was sweating like I don't know what. But he was sure enough dead. Then I thought about what was gonna happen to Henry, now."

"He still had his shoes on, too. But you know what, godmother? Isiah didn't even have on a pair of socks and there were no laces in his shoes. I remember his eyes being open and staring straight up into the sky. I wonder if he had enough time to repent, or whether he knew that he could repent even then?"

"Only God knows for sure, baby. But Isiah had probably been evil all his life. His mama taught them how to be evil. She was the one that folks would come to put evil spirits on other peoples. I hear tell that people would come from North Carolina and Georgia to see that old woman. She didn't do nothing but root work for people. People in New York knowed about her and would make the trip to get her to do dirty old evil things for them. She ain't never had no job, other than the root work she did."

"Now that's a shame for people to involve their children in that old evil stuff." Toni said, but her mind was so far away from where she was sitting.

"My cousin she got here right about the same time the police got here. I told her what had happened and she started praying for y'all. Oh child, Hester put down a piece of praying up in here that night. Hester even went out there where Isiah body was, after the coroner took him away, and she prayed the evil away from it. Hester, she knowed how evil Isiah and his peoples was. I had hated Isiah so much, Titi, that Hester had to pray for me to release that hatred before it hurt me."

Looking into the ceiling but not really seeing anything, Toni just responded, "yeah, unforgiveness don't hurt the person who you holding it against, it hurts you."

"Hester had just left here to drive back to Barnwell when my phone ring. I thought it might have been Hester to say she had car trouble, but that was a brand new Pontiac that she had just bought. This here woman's voice asked how was I doing and I didn't recognize the voice, but there was a cold chill that come across me. The hair on my body stood up, just from hearing that voice. I never did say how I was doing, I just ask who it was. Girl, it was Isiah's sister, telling me that her mama wanted to talk to me. First, I don't know how they got my telephone number because I had it changed to unlisted when Isiah got to bothering me."

"Come on, godmother, you mean to tell me those people got your unlisted telephone number and called you?"

"Titi, they sure did. I ask the old lady how she got my number and she tells me something about the operator dialed it for her. You know she was nothing but a lying wonder. But anyway, she had the nerve to ask me if I would take a package to y'alls house for her. She just says that all I had to do was just sit the package someplace where nobody would notice it for a while. Before I knowed anything, I had told that old woman to go to hell."

"No, you didn't?"

"Oh yes I did, honey. I said it to her before I knowed it. I told that devil's disciple that I was not her bag lady for carrying roots and that she should be on her knees thanking God for allowing her to live this long rather than trying to hurt people that her son had already hurt. I told her not to ever call me again."

"Good for you, good for you. Mama didn't have that much sense. She could've gotten me and uncle Clifford killed. Don't you know that she invited them people in that house?"

"That's what I know, honey. I knowed then that Isiah had put something on Trudy and she was not in her right mind. I seen Isiah car down there in front of y'alls house a day or so after the old woman called me. I could not believe my eyes. I knowed it was

Isiah's car cause it set there in front of my house from that Satday night until late that Sunday evening when the police wrecker come and pull it away from here."

Toni's mind was spinning as she tried to hear everything that her godmother was saying. She had heard something tonight that she herself could scarcely believe. Lloyd had actually been the person in the dark who had ambushed Isiah Henderson and killed him, but Henry had been the one that everybody believed had killed him and spent time for it. She could not wait for the moment that she faced Lloyd, now a respected elder in his church and in the town. Toni thought that this liar and murderer should be exposed for exactly who he was and for what he had done.

"That man sure did a lot to create enemies, didn't he?" Toni asked, not expecting an answer, but just to let Helen know that she was still a part of the conversation. "But to mama he was a perfect a gentleman, even though he tried to kill her. I wonder how many times he had hit her and she just played it off?" Toni asked, not really expecting an answer.

"Ain't no telling, baby." Helen said as she got up from the table and started putting the food away. "I know when he come up in here that morning and knocked me down in that floor and pulled that pistol on my son, he was a fool and didn't think nothing bout no woman, except what they could do for him."

Shaking her head in a bit of shame and much sorrow, Helen stopped and looked out of the kitchen window as though trying to see something. Helen looked at Toni then back at the widow, pointing her finger.

"But he got his just desserts right out there that Satday night. Isiah thought that he was going over there to scare or hurt Henry, but the Lord had other plans." Helen leaned against the wall as she stared out into the night. "Yes sirree, homeboy figured he would do his usual but he didn't figure God into none of what he was doing. I guess he figured he had God scared of him, too."

Toni sat with her elbows resting on her knees and staring down at the kitchen floor. "You know what godmother?"

Turning to look at her godchild, Helen seemed to return to the present. "No, what's that, sweetie?" she responded.

Sitting up straight in the chair and crossing her legs, Toni looked her godmother in the eyes and said, "godmother, that night Isiah died was not the end of anything, but just the beginning, something about that night still has to be settled."

Helen sat down again at the kitchen table and sipped her soda. "Titi, I got the strangest feeling in me." Pointing to her chest, Helen placed the glass on the table and with a frown on her face began to shake her head. "Titi, you know something I don't baby? Is the Lord telling you something?"

Toni could not look at her godmother; she just stared straight ahead.

"I don't know what's going on godmother. But something about that night ain't right and it hasn't been right since that night." Helen looked at Toni with curiosity dancing in her eyes like miniature ballerinas on a frozen lake. "Too many strange things happened then and even after that man was killed." Toni said, never lifting her eyes from the floor.

Toni and Helen put away the remainder of the food and washed the dishes in almost virtual silence. Helen wondered as she dried the dishes that Toni had washed whether she should tell Toni about something else. Helen could see that Toni was in deep thought and perhaps their earlier conversation had triggered something. She resolved that she would not say anything else, unless, of course, Toni asked her.

Toni's mind was still on the truth that she had just discovered, Lloyd having been the one who had killed Isiah. Lloyd had done a tour in Viet Nam and killing certainly was not foreign to him. He had been trained to kill his enemies, or at least trained to kill those whom America had said were its enemies. Was it so hard for Lloyd to see Isiah Henderson as his enemy? No, it wasn't Toni rationalized. After all, Isiah had fired on them first and he had done it under cover of darkness. Isiah had not had any training in real covert warfare. He had just made himself a target that's all. But Henry had been made to pay for the training as well as the crime of Lloyd. Henry was the person that everybody saw as being a murderer. No matter how much everybody hated or disliked Isiah Henderson, Henry was still seen as being his killer.

Silence had become a dominant third person in the kitchen with Toni and Helen. Although the third person was not saying anything it still disturbed Toni. Throwing the dishtowel over her shoulder, Toni leaned against the sink and began to ask Helen a question. "Godmother, let me ask you this."

Knowing that she would answer any question that Toni asked, Helen put the pan in the drawer and turned to her goddaughter. "Go on sugar, what is it?" Helen replied.

"Do you think that Isiah's people tried to work roots on any of us?"

Helen knew now that she would certainly have to tell Toni all that she knew and all that she had done.

"Titi, I believe that them folks tried and I believe that they did."

Sitting down, now so that she could tell Toni something else, Helen folded the dishtowel that she was using to dry the dishes and neatly placed it on the table beside her.

"Sit down here, I needs to tell you this here before I leave this world."

Helen's eyes filled with tears as she pulled her dress down over her knees.

"Don't nobody know anything about this here except me and Paulette, and the man we both went to see. Now, you know about it, too. I prayed to God that this thing would never ever come back to haunt me."

Toni was puzzled, now. She didn't know that her question would cause Helen to cry or to tell something that she too, was trying to forget.

"Godmother, I didn't mean for my curiosity to make you cry."

"No, no Titi, it's not what you asked me, it's what I didn't ask the Lord before I did what I did."

Helen composed herself and told Toni to give her one of the cigarettes from her purse. As Toni got her purse, Helen pulled out the coffee can and asked Toni whether she wanted her to brew enough of the decaf for her a cup. While the coffee brewed Helen went to the bathroom and changed into her snap-up housedress.

"Titi, bring that coffee pot and plug it in right here in this den. Just carefully pick the whole thing up, like I usually do and bring it right here," pointing to the little snack table near the wall. Helen then got the coffee mugs and the sugar and creamer containers and brought them into the room. Toni laid her purse and the cigarettes on the seat of the recliner and went back to the kitchen to let the water out of the sink.

5

Helen took a cigarette from the pack and lit it, sitting an ashtray before herself and one in front of Toni. The two women made their coffee and sat down for what Helen was about to say.

"Baby I told you that the old woman called me after Isiah died, didn't I?" Helen asked to be sure that Toni was following what she was about to say.

"Yes, mam, cause your telephone number was unlisted at that time." Toni was curious why Helen would again tell her about the telephone call.

"Well when I seen Isiah car down there in front of y'alls house that day and his people going in, I knew they was not there for good. Something come over me and I couldn't shake that feeling for love nor money, uh, huh, it just wouldn't go away." Helen shook her head as she blew the smoke from the cigarette toward the ceiling.

"Paulette, she called me from New York that same night just as I was getting ready to go down on my knees and make my prayers."

Looking up as though she was seeing something in the other room, Helen squinted her eyes and looked again at Toni.

"Paulette talked a little bit, what she was really doing Titi, was beating about the bush. I had told Paulette that very night after them folks had called me and told her what they had asked me to do. Unbeknownst to me, Paulette had talked to somebody about that situation and they told her that all of us was in danger. Finally Paulette told me what she had called me for."

Toni's eyes were beginning to widen as she listened to Helen.

"Now you say Paulette had spoken to somebody who said that all of us were in danger, who was they talking about?"

Helen crushed the cigarette in the ashtray and lifted her hand in a motion suggesting herself and Toni.

"Me, you, Henry, Trudy and all of y'all. These people really wanted to hurt us because of that Isiah." Taking a sip of her coffee and putting the cup down, again, Helen looked at Toni. " Baby, I learned that them folks wanted to do us serious harm. Paulette had this here man in New York to call me up, cause I couldn't believe what I was hearing."

Taking another cigarette from the pack, Helen lit it, sat up straight in the chair and glared at Toni. As she exhaled the smoke from the cigarette, Toni for a moment was frightened.

"Titi, this here man began to tell me about some things that I knew he couldn't have known. That man told me about something that me and Trudy did back in New York before we was twenty-one years old and I know we ain't never told it to nobody else. Then he started to describe the old lady and he told me that she had already done something evil in your mama house. He said that the old lady didn't come here to claim the body, but he told me who she had sent and that she had put something on each one of them chilrens of hers that was supposed to stay in the house when they leave out. He say that she was doing something with my name cause I wouldn't do what she wanted me to do. So he give me this Bible verse, Isaiah 54 and verse 17, to say everyday. He told me what they had planned to do to Henry, and Toni it was nothing pretty."

Toni felt her anger kindled as she listened to Helen. She had always believed that Isiah's people had done something evil from that day they showed up at the front door of their house. That very same night Toni had experienced something that she knew was so evil and had always believed that there was a battle between good and evil that took place in the living room of their house after Isiah's people left.

"Godmother, just as sure as I am sitting here, those people did something in that house. I know they did. But look at how the Lord defeated that, too. Henry never set foot in that house from the night he was arrested until after he got out of prison. So whatever was meant for him never touched him."

Helen was now looking at Toni as though she was looking through her.

"Praise God, you so right. He stayed there Big Aaron's brother, your uncle. But, Titi that was the same night the man talked to me on the phone and told me them peoples had started working their roots and evil. He told me that their intent was for all of y'all to be found dead in there. I almost had a heart attack. But he told me not to worry, because God had put an angel of light to stop the spirit in the dark."

"You know the thing that gets me is that these people defended all the evil Isiah did. They didn't care about the hurt that he had brought to other people. They didn't even care that he had shot mama. All they wanted to do was avenge what happened to him."

Toni lit a cigarette and stared off into space. She was angry because her thoughts over the years were almost confirmed. There had been something supernatural, on the evil side, working against her family. Helen frowned and shook her head because she too, knew that there had been more going on than met the eyes of the average person.

"But Titi, Paulette told me that she wanted me to come to New York right away to stop anything them folks was doing."

"Is that right? Did you go?"

Helen was reliving that period of time, again. It had been a particularly difficult time for her as well as for Toni and her family, but neither had known what was happening to the other.

"I ain't had no choice, baby, Paulette, she tell me to come to New York quick, she was gonna make all the reservation for me to fly." Looking at Toni in a sheepish sort of way, Helen laughed as she told Toni of her fears. "Baby, I ain't never been one for riding higher than I can step, but bless John I got on that airplane that following Satday morning. I just tell everybody that I was going to New York to take care of my daughter. You know what I mean, just to keep them out my business."

Toni smiled as she watched Helen and couldn't restrain the laughter that was moving up in her.

"Godmother, you mean to tell me that that was the first time you had ever flown?"

Helen did not appear to be amused by Toni's laughter.

"Hell, they always had that old gray dog going every place else I needed to go, or Trailway. You think that funny, huh?" Soon Helen was laughing at herself.

"I'm just tickled about how matter-of-factly you said that you didn't ride no higher than you could step. I'm one those people who believe that if all its got is four wheels and have to stop at red lights, its too slow for me."

Toni and Helen fell over in their chairs in laughter at their different philosophies and preferred modes of transportation.

"Now you know I had to be serious to choose that darn airplane over my two old standby's, Gray Hound and Trailway."

Still laughing, Toni looked at Helen and asked, "did you enjoy the flight, godmother?" Another round of laughter broke out in the room. Helen had to stand up and cough so that she could answer Toni's question.

"Let's just put it like this, I had a good piece of change in my pocketbook, they had a pretty good supply of Smirky and we didn't cheat one another. By the time the plane landed in New York I think I could've flown right beside it without a parachute."
Laughter filled the room. Helen walked over to Toni and they high fived each other.

"But Titi, I tell you I was a little shaky about what I was about to do. I didn't want to be involved with no voodoo, hoodoo, or anything else with the devil cause it ain't nothing but a bunch doodoo when you get right down to it."

Helen was leaning forward in her seat talking to Toni. Her voice had taken on a more serious tone than it had had earlier.

"I went with Paulette to Brooklyn. First we come pass this here church and went to the house next door to it. The man and his family lived on the first floor and the basement. The two floors above that was where his office was."

"Oh yes, a brownstone," Toni said.

"Yes, you right, that's exactly what it was. The man told me and Paulette to go back up the stairs and he would be up there to open the door. I couldn't see him at first when he answered the bell downstairs."

Helen looked around the room as though she was looking for something. Toni looked as well to make sure she followed everything Helen was either saying or showing her.

"See that piece of paper there, the brown piece," Helen said pointing to a magazine.

"Yes, I see it." Toni responded.

"See that brown on it, this here was a dark skin man but he had eyes about that color. At first it was kind of scary, child."

The telephone rang and interrupted Toni and Helen's conversation. It was Helen's daughter, Paulette.

"Girl, you gonna live a long time, me and Titi sitting right here talking about you. You wanna talk to her? Wait a minute."

Helen called Toni to the phone. After exchanging telephone numbers and setting up dates when they would get together, Toni gave the telephone back to Helen.

"Now where was I girl. Oh yeah, Paulette say call her the minute you get back to Connecticut cause she need to get out of the city, she gonna come and spend the weekend with you."

"Oh that's fantastic, we gonna have ourselves a good old time, too." Toni replied.

Helen smiled because the two most precious females in her life were going to be getting together.

"Oh yeah, the man. He had an accent, but honey he was a very proper speaking man. He sounded like them people from England, but that's not where he was from, though. The first thing this here man told me is that he is water and fire baptized and filled with the Holy Ghost. He said that the church next door was where he Pastored, but he used his God given gifts for the body of Christ. He say that if I had not been a tongue talking Christian he would not have consented to meet with me."

Helen began clapping her hands and praising the Lord. Toni began to praise the Lord with her godmother. Helen was soon able to finish her story. Drying her eyes, Helen looked at Toni and said, "God is good, you hear me? God is good."

Toni nodded her head in agreement with Helen. Helen began to tell Toni the remainder of the story about her trip to New York. Toni listened intently to every word that Helen said.

The preacher prayed with Helen and Paulette and anointed them both with oil. Helen wrote down the names of each of Trudy's children, including Toni. She told the minister that Toni was her goddaughter. The preacher prayed over each name and also prayed for Trudy. The minister told Helen and Paulette that Trudy was stubborn and strong-willed and that she was not yet ready to hear what anybody had to say. The minister knew that Trudy had turned away from God after having walked with Him for a while. Trudy, he said, was angry with God and had blamed Him for everything that had happened to her since her mother died. Trudy had walked away in her heart before she stopped going to church and started drinking. Aaron's death just allowed her the freedom that she had longed for before he died.

Toni listened and she could see what the preacher was talking about. For many years Toni had believed that her mother's dramatic turn was the result of something that she had longed for, not some sudden reaction.

Isiah's mother, the minister said, was wicked. She had sold her soul and that of her children to the devil a long time ago. Toni's eyes were the size of saucers as she listened to what Helen was saying to her. Silently Toni began to thank God for protecting them.

Helen went on to tell Toni that Isiah's mother had planned to drive Helen insane as well because she refused to do what she had been asked to do. The minister took out a handkerchief and blessed it. He prayed over the handkerchief and put it in a plastic bag. The preacher gave the plastic bag to Helen and told her to get to the jailhouse as soon as possible and give it to Henry with the instructions to keep the handkerchief on his body at all times. The handkerchief could be in his pocket or around his neck or tied to his wrist, so long as it was on his body. Now Toni understood why she had the feeling that there was more to the statement that Henry had made to her. Henry still had the handkerchief after all of these years.

Helen told Toni that the minister had given her prayers to pray specifically for Henry.

"But Titi, the preacher said something that just didn't sit well with me, at least I didn't understand what he said. He say something about everybody gotta be prepared to understand what happened in the dark that night."

Toni smiled to herself because she knew that the preacher was right. It had taken twenty-five years for her to see the truth but now she knew that she and Lloyd were not the only two human beings that knew the real truth. Helen shook her head and continued.

"The minister said that God would have to prepare everybody to understand what He was going to show them."

Helen went to the bathroom before she finished telling Toni what the minister had said.

"So as soon as I got back here from New York, I called the jailhouse to find out how I could get in to see somebody. That's when I found out that Henry wasn't even in jail. I was in a fix then, 'cause I never seed him over there at the house. Then I seen your cousin, Tammy, and she told me that Henry was living cross the bridge with your uncle. I got in touch with Henry and gave him that handkerchief."

Helen shook her head and clapped her hands.

"The last thing the minister said to us was that if they did try Henry anybody involved had better do the right thing. He said if they did not, regardless of who they was, they would suffer by the evil in their own hearts."

Toni remembered the people who had sat on the jury during Henry's trial. She remembered Mr. Hosea Shephard, who lived on Macon Street and had been a friend of her fathers, as well as Mr. Lindsey Buchanan a mason in her father's lodge. There was

Yvonne Bowman, who had gone to school with Toni. Mrs. Sally Ruth Gordon was a member of the same church that Trudy had been a member of before she had quit going and being an active member. Yvonne had been seeing Lloyd for a few years before he began dating Toni's sister, Margaret. Toni believed that Yvonne held a grudge because Lloyd had not married her. Everyone had expected the two of them to get married soon after Lloyd returned from Viet Nam, but he had stopped seeing her.

Helen interrupted Toni's thoughts. "You remember what happened that day when the judge sentenced Henry?"

Toni hung her head because that had been one of the saddest days of her life. She had shed more tears that day than when her mother died.

"Godmother, I will never forget that day. I believe that was the day that my heart was broken so badly that there are still pieces of it missing."

"Yeah, baby, there's things that can do that to you. But I remember what Paulette's preacher said when I saw that dark shadow on top of the courthouse and looked up seen that buzzard just flapping its wings. Then that breeze that started blowing and circling them folks of Isiah's as they tried to come down them steps and get to they car. They was driving that old car of his. Honey that old mama of his started to scream like she had seen the Lord Himself shaking His fist right in her old evil face."

Helen poured more coffee into her cup and reached for the spoon to stir in some cream and sugar. Toni lit another cigarette and blew the smoke toward the ceiling.

"That old mean behind solicitor come strutting out that door about the same time hisself. He saw what was going on and he turned whiter than a brand new sheet. That wind wrapped that suit coat around him like it was a blanket. I tell you all I could do was stand cross that street and think that them folks had done some damn evil stuff."

Reaching for the cigarettes, Helen pointed her finger at Toni and said, "baby, I tell you right now, it was a whole bunch of drawers that needed to be changed in a hurry that day, mine included."

"That was something else that day." Toni said as she sipped her coffee. "You know what else, godmother?"

Helen looked up. "Uh, uh, baby what is it?"

"Yvonne Bowman never got married and she never had any children before she committed suicide." Helen's eyes widened.

"Hush your mouth, child. I thought somebody say that she overdosed on some prescription medicine that the doctor had written for her."

Toni stood up to go to the bathroom, but before she left the room she responded to Helen's statement.

"Yeah, a doctor wrote the prescription for the pills but girlfriend left a note for her mama and them to read. She said she couldn't live in this world no more if this was all that life had to offer, she didn't need anymore of life. Now that's what I heard."

Helen, who had stretched out on the sofa raised herself up. She began to speak loud enough so that Toni could hear her in the bathroom.

"Well Paulette pastor ain't never lied about what them folks was gonna cause for they self. Hosea he had a reaction to something that he ate and they say that his tongue swoll up and choked him to death. Then Lindsey drowned trying to save his grandson. Both of them end up dying. Sally Ruth just lost her mind and they had to put her in that crazy house where she died at about three or four years ago."

Toni returned to the room and sat on the floor this time. She lit another cigarette and looked Helen in the eye.

"So whatever happened to Isiah's old evil people, godmother?"

Helen looked around the room as though she were looking for somebody. With her head tilted to one side like a hound listening for the sound of a rabbit in the bush, she quietly said to Toni, "they all dead except for that baby daughter who was at Trudy's funeral today."

Toni almost choked on the cigarette smoke when she heard that.

"You say one of those people was at the funeral today? I don't remember seeing her. Not that I would know who I was looking at anyway."

"Well she sure enough reached out to try and touch you as you passed by. She was sitting there in the back of the church with a cane on the left hand side as you go out the door."

Toni had remembered someone reaching out to touch her but she had been just a little too far ahead to see who it was. But she had remembered the woman as she walked up to the casket.

"What you suppose she was doing there, for real, godmother?"

"Only God knows for sure, Titi, but she sure ain't no trouble to nobody but herself. The girl so sick it ain't funny. She look like God done turn his back on her, the devil done rejected her, and death has refused to touch her. She can't even walk to the highway by herself and fall in the path of a truck so she can get taken her out of her misery. She got some of everything wrong with her and she got to pay people to take her where she want to go cause she can't see out of but one eye."

Toni laughed to herself, thinking how could Helen know all of that.

"Godmother how do you know all of that?"

Helen adjusted the pillow under her head and cleared her throat, "cause I asked her. She recognized me before I recognized her. I had only seen her once or twice when I was seeing Isiah, but she remembered me and stopped me outside the church."

Toni was excited and wanted to know what else Helen had found out.

"Well how is the rest of the family? Did she say or all of a sudden you had a desire to mind your own business?" Helen and Toni burst into laughter at Toni's remark.

"No, I asked her about them. The old lady, she said died less than a year after Isiah."

"Hush your mouth, see there!" Toni said, excitedly.

"The older brother what come into y'alls house with them, he got hit by a bolt of lightening, she said, as he was coming in the house from work about a year or so after the mama died. Then the older sister she got burned up in her car on her way to North Carolina. She ran off the road, hit some trees and the car flipped over and burned."

"Yep, she was probably on her way to try and put voodoo on somebody there." Toni said.

"You probably right Judge Spann, and they all died, including the grandson who was twenty three and got cancer and died so quick, she said. She said that when they found out he had cancer, the boy died within four or five months. She the only one living now, but all of them died within a five year period. That's probably what the old woman wanted to happen to all of us, but those demons turned on them. Those demons they sent out to hurt other people couldn't cross the blood of Jesus. That buzzard carried death back to them who sent it. Glory be to God, He not only got a heart to love us, Titi, He got a hand to fight for us."

Titi got up and went to the kitchen to get water so that she could brew a little more decaf for her and Helen. As she stood at the sink filling the container she began to cry. Her tears were a combination of joy and sadness. On the one hand she was thankful that Helen had cared enough about her and her family to pray for them and seek godly help.

On the other hand, she was sad because her mother, now dead, had not realized that her selfishness and stubbornness had almost destroyed the family.

Toni turned the water off and walked back into the room where Helen lay stretched out on the sofa. Pouring the water into the pot, she looked over at Helen. "Godmother, do you think mama ever really knew what those people were doing?"

Without moving or opening her eyes, Helen replied. "I don't think she did right away, Titi."

"Did mama ever say anything to you later on about Isiah?"

"Oh yeah, after Henry went to the penitentiary. Trudy, she come round here one day and she ask me if I could talk to her for a minute. She ask me to forgive her and she said how sorry she was that she hadn't listened to me. She said that she just didn't feel right and didn't know what to do. She thought that you was mad at her, too."

"I was very angry with mama, but I kept praying for her. Mama just had this idea that everybody was trying to run her life. I was mad because the things that she was doing kept causing so many problems for us. But mama was stubborn and she would cuss us of every foul word she could muster up. I can't even count the number of times or the ways that she told me to kiss her backside."

Helen laid still, believing that it was better to just listen to her goddaughter without commenting for now.

"Godmother, did you notice that very few people were at mama's funeral?"

"Yes I did, but most of them people Trudy used to party with they dead honey, been dead for years, except for a couple who ended up in the nursing home. They can't even do nothing for they self these days. If more of them was alive I believe they would have been there. Trudy and me ain't no spring chickens honey. We closer to eighty than we was ever before." Helen got up to go to the bathroom, leaving Toni sitting on the floor. "I'm gonna warm me up a piece of that cornbread, baby, I feel just little bit lunchy."

"I think I'm gonna warm me up a piece of that fish."

"Honey hush," Helen said, "I did have that fish on my mind, but I wanted to act like I had some manners, but now that you mentioned it I guess there ain't no need in letting you eat by yourself, I'll join you. Thank God for microwaves." The two laughed about Helen's sudden decision to eat again and proceeded to the kitchen for seconds.

Helen tried to get Toni to stay the night at her house rather than drive to the hotel, but Toni was insistent that she wanted to be alone and rest. Helen knew that there was something on Toni's mind that she had not said anything about but she didn't want to pry. Perhaps, Helen thought, the past week had taken its toll on Toni, with her mother's death and the funeral, no matter how you rationalize it grief was grief. Even the worst child in the world felt the hurt and abandonment when his mother died, Helen reasoned.

"Titi, you gonna come by here tomorrow, though?"

"Oh yes, I'll come by don't worry, remember, you got my music up in your house. We have to record a tape for you before I leave."

Helen smiled as Toni began to put the cigarettes back into her purse. She was proud of her goddaughter and in that instant she was overwhelmed with a feeling of love for the younger woman. She didn't know whether it was because Toni's own mother was now dead, and she had an opportunity to be a mother to her, or she was looking at the little ebony princess she used carry on her hip because she had felt that she was too cute to walk. Either way, Helen thought, the princess had grown into a fine woman and although she had not been there every step of the way she was here now for her goddaughter. She walked over and hugged her real tight.

"Tonitia Renee Spann, don't you ever forget this here old woman love you as if she carried you in her womb and birthed you." The tears streamed down her face. "I loved you from the first moment I laid eyes on you," wiping her tears and her goddaughter's, "when I seen that you was a girl, it took me two days to come up with a name that I believed was suitable. I wanted you to have the prettiest name and everything and you such a beautiful woman, God bless you always." Helen kissed her goddaughter right on the lips as she had done when she was a little girl.

"Thanks godmother for everything and I really love you, too. I would love you even if you didn't love me."

Toni walked down the steps and out of the gate to her car. The words "I love you," still rang in her ear and heart. As she started the engine of the car more tears began to fall from her eyes. I love you was something that she had seldom heard. She couldn't recall a time even hearing it from her parents. Sure there were the few times that they had said it as part of some point they may have been trying to make. But it was never an individual "I love you," with a hug or with any degree of sincerity, nothing that would cause her to feel the words like she had just heard. It was always "I love y'all kids…" But, Toni thought, if parents themselves had never been told that they were loved and had never been shown love, how could they sincerely tell it to others?

With her mother now dead, Toni knew that she could only believe that she really loved her and that her inability to say it or show it was based on her never having been shown or taught how to. But she would not hold it against her mother. Her mother's own life had been filled with pain and grief, so filled that as an adult she tried to get the attention and affection that she had longed for from childhood by any means necessary.

<u>6</u>

As Toni put the key in the room door her mind was instantly focused on Lloyd. How Henry had suffered during the years because of what Lloyd had done. Until today she had believed that Henry had actually shot and killed Isiah, but the truth was that Lloyd had ambushed him behind Helen's house. She wondered how she would tell this to Henry without arousing enough anger in him to confront and possibly hurt Lloyd? For sure, Toni thought, she had to confront Lloyd and let him know that his secret was not secret anymore.

The hot shower did not help to calm Toni's passion about confronting Lloyd. But what if Lloyd denied that he had shot Isiah behind Helen's house that night, then what? She thought. She'd talk to Jeremiah again about what he heard and saw that night. For twenty-five years they had all ignored what Jeremiah had said about the bullets flying past his head and how his ears were ringing. But she had to figure out a way to ask Jeremiah without arousing suspicion in him about that horrible night.

Toni laid in the middle of the bed in the dark praying that her brain would stop and turn itself off so she could get some sleep. It had been a long day and a long week. She had already commanded her mind to be joyful because God had given her the assurance that her mother had made it back home to Him.

Joyce said that their mother had prayed nearly all night the night before she died. For the first time, Joyce said, she had heard their mother speaking in tongues. It was as if she were "petitioning God and heaven," Joyce said. Toni had heard her speak in tongues when she was younger and her mother was an active member of the church, the praying band and the Missionary Board. So, she was not going to spoil her mother's going home celebration with whooping, hollering and crying. Truly, Toni was grateful and full of joy that her mother had gone to heaven and she would meet her there.

Sleep would not come, although she was tired. So Toni just laid in the dark and looked up, not really seeing anything, but staring upward in the dark anyway. She couldn't help but think how she had shut a whole period of time out of her mind and life like her mother leaving her father. But when Helen had said it today she remembered the entire incident as though it had been yesterday. Then the telephone rang, Toni didn't even know what time it was.

"Hello." Toni said, trying to sound as though she had been asleep.

"Girl you don't know how to check your messages?" Joyce asked.

Toni laughed because she had totally forgotten about checking messages or anything.

"Girl, I forgot. What time of night is it?"

Joyce laughed at the question. "What you mean what time of night it is, you sound like you got some place to go, or somebody to meet. It's twelve forty-five, are you late or early?"

Toni laughed because Joyce had been the one with the sense of humor and who had taken things in stride.

"Neither one, unless Denzel left me a message. What you still doing up?"

"Now see, I didn't call you for you to dip all in my Kool-Aid. But since you asked, I'm waiting for my little honey to come by here."

"Girl who you seeing that he can't come to your house before midnight?"

"Now you see why I don't mind other people business or let them in on mine, cause you have to explain things to them, let it suffice to say that he's my undercover man."

The sisters burst into laughter at Joyce's statement.

"But tell me this and I won't ask another question," Toni said, still laughing at what Joyce had said, "do you always use covers?"

Joyce laughed before she answered. "Sometimes, but just for decoration."

The sisters chattered away about different things. Joyce was divorced with two children that she was getting ready to go to college, arranged by Toni. Joyce had managed to buy a rather nice home on her own and after years of taking a couple of college courses at a time, she had managed to get her teaching degree and was enjoying her fairly new job as a Social Studies teacher at the new Middle School.

Joyce was proud of what she had done, graduated from college before her children graduated from high school. Toni was proud that her younger sister had taken her advice and completed her education. Toni had given her a computer as a graduation present. There had been times when Toni had to pay the tuition for Joyce but she saw it as money well spent, an investment in greatness she called it. Now Joyce would often send Toni a check for a hundred dollars with a thank you note enclosed. Joyce had made Toni promise that the money they sent each other would be "stupid money," money to spend on stupid stuff. Joyce knew that she would now always be able to take care of herself.

"Where is Margaret?" Toni asked Joyce, thinking that Margaret was perhaps watching television.

"Miss Thang went some place with Lloyd." Toni had to pause before she said anything to Joyce.

"She went some place with Lloyd? What they trying to do, make a comeback in each other's lives?" Toni almost demanded to know.

"I guess so, girl. They got two grown kids together. Lloyd ain't never really got serious with nobody, except God, after he and Margaret broke up. Hey, it'll probably be good for both of them to try it again. She could and has done worse"

This was not the kind of talk that Toni wanted to hear because as far as she was concerned, Lloyd was a liar and a murderer and she planned to expose him.

"So you think she went to his house to spend the night or something like that?"

"Girl I don't expect Margaret back here tonight, matter-of-fact, I hope she stay gone all night." Toni was furious.

"Isn't that your doorbell, Joyce?"

"Yes mam it is, let him sweat for a few minutes so he'll be glad to see me when I get there."

"Shoot, you wait too long and the undercover man just might take cover somewhere else."

"Hold on a minute, okay?" Joyce asked Toni.

While Toni was waiting for Joyce to return to the telephone she could hear Joyce telling the person to look in the refrigerator and make a plate from all of what was there. Toni wanted to get out of the bed and go to Lloyd's house and drag Margaret out of there.

"Hey, you still there?" Joyce asked.

"Where am I going, you said for me to hold on."

"Oh girl, you getting a little huffy in your old age, maybe I should find you an undercover man in Connecticut."

Toni laughed at Joyce and came back quickly.

"If you find me anything at all make sure he's under and above cover trained."

Joyce started laughing uncontrollably.

"Oh, you sound like you got a little freak in you that you want somebody to draw out sister."

"Girl, you had better go see about your company. Was he at the funeral?" Toni asked.

"No, he was at the wake last night, though, but he just kept his cool so nobody knew who he was. I didn't want to have to explain anything, you know what I mean?" Joyce asked Toni.

"Yes."

"Toni, I feel like this, we did all that we could for mama when she was alive and even when she got down sick and everything. You couldn't be here but Lord knows you sent money so I could keep her as nice as possible. Nobody else helped me Toni, but you. So, I just don't have it in me to drag about feeling sad or putting on mourning clothes and that kind of junk. Just like you said before, mama went to heaven and I thank God for His mercy. Toni, I ain't going through all that mess. Mama lived a long life, she did some of everything that she was old enough, bad enough, and bold enough to do, then we took care of her at the end. Mama did a lot of celebrating, or what look like celebrating in her days, so I'm gonna celebrate her living."

Toni knew in her heart that Joyce was right and she had nothing to be ashamed of, or anything to be regretful of.

"Joyce, we did the best that we could. How many people can say that they gave their parents more than their parents gave them and we ain't talking about just material stuff either. But I want you to do this one thing for me Joyce, everyday, you hear me," Toni said emphatically, "everyday, please, hug your kids and tell them that you love them. I don't care what they may have done, please, do this for me, promise me, Joyce, that you will do this. Let them feel love each and every time you say it, it's important to me and to them."

Joyce started to cry. "Toni I promise I will do it. I can't remember mama and daddy doing that with us. I needed that Toni."

"That's why it's important to me that you do it with your kids, Joyce. It's not enough to keep them fed and dressed and give them a place to stay, they have to hear you say, that in spite of all the other things you've done, you love them and hug them so they can feel it."

"Toni, I will, matter-of-fact let me go to their rooms right now and give each one of them a hug. I'll even give them one from you."

"Thanks Joyce, good night."

"I love you Toni," Joyce said.

"I love you more, Joyce."

Toni was all teary again, but she meant what she had said to Joyce. Toni could scarcely remember a sincere I love you, even from her ex-husband. She was grateful that Helen loved her enough to hug her and kiss her like she was still that little smarty pants girl of years before.

Tony had never turned the lights on even as she talked to Joyce. The darkness allowed her to see what she would not dare to look at in the light. She fluffed up the pillows and tried to put Lloyd and Margaret out of her mind. But her mind seemed more like a video tape on continuous rewind. Toni was drawn backward to look again over her life and that of her family's.

7

It was a Saturday morning in October. Toni had just moved into a brand new apartment building. The building was safe, had a security man at the entrance to check those coming in and out, and she could well afford it on her salary and send money to help her family when needed. The telephone rang about six thirty that morning waking Toni from a much needed and sound sleep.

"Toni, this here your Aunt Clara, baby, wake up, your mama been shot."

Toni could not believe what she was hearing, her mother was not a teenager.

"I'm awake Miss Clara, did somebody break into mama's house? Is mama alive?" Toni began asking.

"No baby, Isiah he just went crazy and shot Trudy in her back."

"What do you mean he just went crazy? Where was mama when this happened?" Toni asked. Clara seemed a bit a hesitant to answer the question. "Miss Clara, did you hear me, where did this happen at and where is mama now?"

Between sobs, Clara tried to answer Toni's questions. Toni knew that Clara had been drinking and her mother more than likely had been too, because they were party partners.

"We had gone out to have a little bit of fun and had ourself a drink or two. Just as we was getting in Trudy's car, Isiah he come up from behind and started a nutsy ass argument. Trudy walked away from him then he shot her in the back. Somebody called the ambulance cause we was right outside the club and they heard the shots. Toni I don't know what got into Isiah, he just crazy as hell, I told Trudy he was crazy."

"Miss Clara, how was mama doing when the ambulance took her away?"

" She was alive and bleeding pretty bad, cause like I told you, Isiah shot her in the back."

Toni hung up the telephone and sat on the side of the bed. She was shaking uncontrollably. Anger overtook her causing her to sweat and cry. How she had prayed since her father's death that her mother would give up the drinking, partying and the assortment of men. Like a wild teenager who had gone boy crazy, so had her mother after her father's death. Toni had believed that the only way her mother would stop the things she was doing was if death overtook her. In her heart, Toni did not want her mother to die as a result of her lifestyle. Toni wept this morning because unlike the other old party mamas, hers had been shot in the back.

Toni called her younger brothers and sisters to see how they were doing and to let them know that she was on her way to South Carolina to take care of them. Her brothers and sisters were pretty quiet, none could really talk about what they had heard. Joyce had said that she wished that her mother would just stop trying to be eighteen or nineteen years old and act like she had grown children. Joyce asked how was she supposed to answer the questions of the kids at school because she knew they would hear about her mother having been shot. Wilson already was being teased badly by the other fellows at work about how his mother drank and partied.

Toni hung up the telephone and sat on the floor beside her bed. Never in a million years would she have imagined her life being cast into situations like those she had seen and experienced since her father's passing five years ago. It was almost impossible to figure out what had triggered this behavior in her mother. If it had been grief because of her father's death, surely, Toni thought, her mother should have recovered by now. But as the months and years had passed her mother's behavior had grown worse. Toni could not see an end to all that her mother was doing or perhaps would do. Her mother had made it almost as clear as glass, that this was her life and nobody was going to tell her how to live it. The arguments between her mother and her grandfather were like mini wars. He had not been able to talk to his daughter about her behavior and how it was impacting her children. Her mother was completely and insanely out of control, she now lived for the thrill.

Toni called her grandfather; he was nearly eighty years old. She did not know what, if anything, her grandfather could do, but she called him anyway. She picked at a small bump on her knee as the telephone rang.

"Yes," the voice on the other end said.

"Granddaddy, this is Toni, how are you?"

The old man cleared his throat; "I do pretty good, baby girl. How you doing?"

"Granddaddy mama done gone out there and got herself shot."

There was a very pregnant pause. Finally, the old man spoke.

"What she did now and who was it?" he asked.

"That guy Isiah she been seeing, he shot her in the back, Miss Clara said."

"Oh so she and Clara was out whoring when this here thing happen? She and Clara both should have been home with their chilrens. See that's what happens when you want to live the fast life. Baby girl, there ain't nothing I can do for my daughter, she just something, I can't figure out what, but it ain't nothing I can talk to. It's like she got a signed contract with hell and she won't listen to nobody but them other drunks she dealing with. I told her before that Isiah was entirely too young for her and that boy and his peoples deal in all that roots and stuff, but she cussed me out like I was a dog."

Toni began to cry because even her mother's father seemed to have given up on her.

"Granddaddy, you know it seems like from the day we buried daddy mama's just been acting like a crazy person. She started all that drinking and just seeing different men."

Her grandfather interrupted her, "seeing different men, hell, she having them like one of them women who sells themselves, only difference is Trudy ain't getting paid."

Toni was hurt because her mother's behavior was so blatant that even her father knew of her many indiscretions.

"No, Tonitia, Trudy had that in her all the time. Big Aaron was the one person that was keeping her from it. I know my daughter, your daddy was the person who had kept her from her own self."

Toni tried to ask her granddaddy if he would meet her at her mother's house. She needed his support.

"No, baby girl, your mama she told me not to ever darken her door again, and I intend to respect her wishes. Trudy has been mad with me since her mama died."

The old man went on to tell Toni that he had been a young man at that time and had married Trudy's mother who was a widow with three children.

Toni's grandfather had worked on the railroad and traveled wherever the railroad work had taken him. He was gone for as many as three months at a time from his home in South Carolina. There was not much work for black men in those days, the old man explained to Toni, except the pulp wood and the mill, which did not pay enough to keep a family. The railroad paid a little salary and the men could save most of their money, he said, because they lived in camps, which resembled or could well have been the places where slaves had once been housed.

The old man admitted that he was not always faithful and at the time that Trudy's mother died they had had two children. He was gone most of the time because he and the other "colored men" on his crew did not have the same privileges as the white men and the crew leaders were cruel to the "colored men."

"You might as well know this now, Tonitia, you got some peoples out there in the world who will do anything to gain the advantage over other people. So you be careful, baby girl. I do believe that somebody done put roots on Trudy and controlling her mind. I know, cause somebody did it to me. I was seeing this one woman on the side and somehow she got her claws up in me good. That bow-legged gal put a hex on me like you wouldn't believe."

Toni couldn't believe that her grandfather was one who had fallen to witchcraft, but she listened silently as he spoke.

The old man told Toni how he had been drawn to the woman and when he didn't want to see her he could not help himself. He told Toni how his wife had begun to be ill and no one, not even the doctors at the big hospital that treated colored people, could figure out why she was pining away. He was taking almost all of his money to the other woman and nothing she wanted that he would not try to get for her. He said that eventually everybody in his town knew that he was having an affair with the woman. But everybody also knew that his wife was sick and had taken to the bed. He said that there had been a few times when his wife had had to send their son to the woman's house to get him to come home.

"Oh child, that bow-legged woman had me messed up and bound up like a little slave."

When Trudy's mother was so sick that she could not eat and had to be changed like a baby, her grandfather started to come home a little more often. He still went to the other woman's house because she was fixing his meals. He told Toni that after his wife had passed and he buried her, not ever knowing what she had died of, he had given Trudy some money and told her that he would be back in a little while. But the other woman would not allow him to go home for days.

Herman lied about his age and joined the Army shortly after their mother had passed.

The old man said that for a while he did not know that Trudy had been living in the house alone because Herman was gone. A cousin of his realized that Trudy was living alone when she received money from Herman asking that it be given to Trudy. Trudy hated him, he said, and she had a right to hate him.

"I was so messed up, child by that woman and them roots she had put on me, I couldn't help myself." The old man said. "I was in a little place somewhere there in Georgia working with a crew of fellows. We all decided to go into town this here Friday night and do us a little good timing at one of the juke joints there for coloreds. I just wanted to have myself a little drink of whiskey. I used to dance with the all the gals everywhere before I got myself mixed up with that woman. After that, I just didn't have a desire for nothing. I used to love to dance and talk trash with the women folks, but I just didn't have it in me no more. I wasn't even thinking about my dead wife, that's how messed up that woman had me." The old man continued to talk to Toni.

The old man told Toni that for several weeks he would go into town with the other men and he would sit and have a drink by himself. Then one night he was coaxed by one of the other fellows to go up the road from the juke joint to a teahouse and do some gambling. He said that the house belonged to a lady named Alice. As he walked through the door, Alice stopped him and told him that he couldn't come in. He was surprised because he had never been denied entrance anywhere. He asked Alice why he couldn't come in and Alice told him there was a black hand on him and he would jinx her house and everybody in it. He didn't know exactly what she was talking about, but he pleaded with Alice to tell him. It was then that he realized that his wife's death was not natural and the other woman had put a voodoo curse on him. Alice told him that she could take him to somebody to help him the next day and he agreed. He said that he slept outside on Alice's back porch that night so that he could make the trip to another town with Alice that Saturday.

"Baby girl, I never believed that people could do all that evil stuff, but I'm here to tell you as living proof, they out there and they can do all kinds of mess. This here woman Alice, bless her heart, was gifted by the Lord. But she hadn't found her way to the church. Alice could see things like that and she took me to a preacher man. This here preacher he begin to tell me some of everything that had happened to me from the time I was a young man to the time I met that bow-legged heifer until I got on with that crew in Georgia."

"Granddaddy, did you ever tell mama about all of this?"

The old man sucked his teeth and cleared his throat. "No, I ain't never had the courage to just force her to listen. When I would try to tell Trudy anything about that time she just start an argument and say she didn't want to hear anything from me. So I finally stop trying."

The man that Alice had taken Toni's grandfather did something mysterious to him and prayed. He then took her grandfather down to a creek where the water was running and made him bath. Her grandfather was told to send the woman a letter telling her that he knew what she had done to him and to his wife and that he would never see her again.

"Did you ever see the woman again, granddaddy?"

"Yep, but she couldn't come near me or even look me in the eye. I seen her with one old fellow that I knowed. I got bold enough to call the fellow by his name and tell him that I had something to tell him about his woman. I told him what that old bow-legged gal had done to me and that fellow took off running."

The old man laughed until he began coughing. "Baby, that old gal was so mad with me she didn't know whether to spit or piss. But I told her if she tried any of that voodoo mess I would have her hands and feet cut off from her body so she couldn't walk or be able to wash her ass or feed herself. I told her that I would tell everybody in South Carolina about her and that mess she did to other people."

"Ooh, granddaddy, what did she say?" Toni asked.

"She told me that I wasn't never no good anyhow. I told her I was still a whole lot better than she was cause I ain't never killed nobody to get what I wanted. I walked away and ain't seen her until about six or seven years ago, right before she died. She died before Big Aaron. But concerning your mama, somebody I believe done something to her, too. But your mama hatred and stubbornness opened the door. She'll live Tonitia, but don't fret yourself over her, she gonna do exactly what she wanna until I'm dead and gone. She'll wake up one day and see all the stuff torn up and down because of her and she'll try to change."

"Granddaddy, what am I supposed to do now? The kids want to quit school and they're ashamed of mama." Toni was frustrated and desperate.

"Tonitia, ain't nothing we can do, except pray. I belongs to the Methodist church here by my house and I keeps y'alls name and everything on the weekly prayer list, you chilrens gonna be alright, the Lord on y'alls side. Don't get yourself all swallowed up in Trudy's mess."

Toni again sat with her head down on the floor. She did not know what else to do. She felt a sense of hatred begin to rise up within her. Her mother had made a mess of her life and was making a mess of Toni's and her brothers and sisters lives as well.

Toni tried to pray, but all that she could get out was the Our Father prayer and the Twenty-third Psalm. She did not know how she would pull her brothers and sisters lives together after this. She prayed that this would be the one thing that would cause her mother to take a look at her life and see how it was effecting her children. Trudy had all but forsaken her children for whatever thrill she could get from a man.

Aaron Junior had left home and no one knew where he was. He had been so ashamed, he had said, of his mother that he could not bear to live in the same town with her. The shame he had felt when another fellow said that his mother was the town's slut and drunk was too much. He could not fight another person or the fellow that said it, because it was true and he couldn't beat up everybody that spoke even the ugly truth about his mother.

The other children seemed to be stuck and had nowhere to go. Toni cried that day because she had known a time when not a profane word crossed her mother's lips. She cried because the woman who had once prayed down fire from heaven couldn't tell you where her Bible was now. She cried even harder because a bullet had pierced her mother's back and she lay in a hospital when she should have been home preparing breakfast for her baby boy. The tears flowed like open streams because Toni knew that she would go to South Carolina as she had so many times before in crisis and her mother would spew the ugliest profanity at her that she had ever heard and nothing would change.

Toni called the airlines to see whether she could get a flight out to South Carolina that day. After making the necessary arrangements to fly that evening, Toni called her friend Kim and asked her to drive her to the airport. They had met at church shortly after Toni had moved to Connecticut to attend college and had become very good friends after learning that they both were from South Carolina. The two of them had started college together and had spent the last two years working on their degrees going to classes year round. Both young women looked forward to graduating in another year or so. Toni explained to Kim what had happened and why she was going to South Carolina.

"Look, let me get dressed, Toni, I'll be over there in a few minutes, okay." Kim said before hanging up.

Toni sat on the floor feeling sorry for herself until the buzzer rang letting her know that someone was in the lobby. She got up from the floor and walked to the kitchen and answered the buzzer.

"It's me, Kim, buzz me in."

Without effort or thought, Toni pushed the buzzer until she thought that Kim had entered the door from the outside lobby. She waited by the kitchen door until her doorbell rang and opened the door.

Kim began to cry as she walked into the apartment. "Toni, this too shall pass, and you got to believe that. Maybe this will wake your mama up."

With tears streaming down her face, Toni shook her head; "I don't think so Kim. I just have to find myself a little peace somewhere on this earth until this does pass."

Kim felt helpless, unable to do anything that would help her friend find that little bit of peace she so needed now. Tragedy had been something that Kim had lived with for many years. Her mother, too had been a drinking and partying woman in South Carolina. She had told Toni how she had watched as her mother's lifestyle had brought her own life to an end one Friday night. The shooting of Toni's mother began to bring back memories of Kim's mother's death. Kim walked into the kitchen and began to brew some coffee for her and Toni. As she poured the coffee into the filter she began to give Toni more details about that sad and awful Friday night.

"Toni I tried as best as I could to stop that fool from beating and kicking my mama. My mama was so drunk that night it seemed like she couldn't fight back or even run. As I look back, I think I did more fighting back than my mama and she was the one who was getting her ass kicked. Girl I hit that man with everything that I could lay my hands on, but he seemed to be possessed by the devil himself, not a demon. His purpose seemed to be to kill my mama and that he accomplished his mission."

When Kim was only fifteen she watched as one of her mother's boyfriend beat her into a coma. Kim had tried to pull the man off of her mother who was too drunk it seemed, to defend herself.

"Toni that Negro kicked my mama like she was a football or a piece of trash. This guy had slept with mama many times and he beat her like she was a foreign stranger. Girl, he had spent the night at our house with my mama just two nights before that. But he beat her unmercifully." Kim said as she wiped the tears away and lit a cigarette.

The boyfriend had kicked her mother in the head several times and stomped her body as though she was a piece of trash. Kim saw the blood running from her mother's nose, then her mother tried to cover up herself to ward off the blows. Kim said that she had run across the street to one of their neighbors and asked the woman to call the police because the man was beating her mother badly. The woman told her "child get on away from here and let your mama handle her own business."

"Toni, there were four women sitting on that porch, one of them was the first cousin of the man. Those evil heifers were enjoying the fact that my mama was getting her ass kicked. Toni, women are their own worst enemy. We do more harm to ourselves and each other sometimes than any man could ever do."

Kim said that she ran back to her house and grabbed the broom to keep the man away from her mother. She was pulling at the man and screaming for someone to call the police, but none of the women moved from their positions on the porch. Blood was all over the living room floor and the furniture. Her mother had stopped moving. When the boyfriend would kick her, she didn't try to cover herself anymore. The boyfriend finally stopped beating Kim's mother and tried to pick her up by pulling one of her arms, but there was no reaction. He began yelling at her and calling her names telling her to get up and clean herself up. Kim said that her mother's eyes were open but the stare was blank. She kneeled down and called to her mother, but she didn't move. Kim knew that something was wrong and she ran nearly a mile to a service station and asked the man there to call an ambulance.

"Toni, those jealous bitches did not move off their behinds until they saw me dash out of the front door and down the street screaming."

When Kim got back to her house, the women were on her porch telling her not to go inside. The boyfriend had left by the time she returned. Kim said that she knew her mother would not have died if just one of the women had just called the police, or allowed he to use the phone to make the call herself.

"It wasn't that they didn't have a telephone, Toni, two of those heifers did. But they were glad as hell to see my mama get the snoot kicked out of her. No, it wasn't right that mama was dealing with another woman's husband. But she didn't deserve to die like she did. Nobody deserves to die like that. My mama had never done anything to those women."

Kim's mother never regained consciousness and died three days later in the County Hospital. Her brain had been so swollen from the beating that the doctors said, if her mother had lived she would have been institutionalized for the rest of her life with severe brain damage. Kim said that when she saw her mother in the hospital, that she barely recognized her. The boyfriend had beaten, stomped and kicked her mother so badly that even the doctors and nurses were asking how many people had attacked her. Her mother's arm had been broken, pelvis crushed and so many other internal injuries. Kim said, that at the boyfriend's trial, she learned for the first time that her mother had also been pregnant. Her loss had been two-fold, her mother and a baby brother or sister.

"You know what was so sad about all of that, Toni?"

"No, what?"

"The Solicitor asked whether he knew my mama was pregnant and he said that he did. But get this, he said that the baby wasn't his, that my mama was trying to stick him with a baby."

"You have got to be kidding."

"No, I wish that I was. Even though he had no way of knowing the baby wasn't his, he thought nothing about beating it out of my mama. He really let the devil use him."

Toni's mind had left the room having been taken captive by her thoughts. She could see Kim's mother that night as she realized that the intent of her lover was to kill her. The initial shock perhaps had paralyzed her and she could not fight back. But somewhere within her a spark of survival flared up and she tried to cover up to ward off the blows. Too little, too late. Maybe her eyes saw that which only the spirit could reveal, death. Maybe, just maybe, she slipped into the coma unable to surrender earthly ties as a mother, or to give herself more time to think of her children, the past, perhaps, even her future. She probably stopped fighting for her life after looking at it up to that point. Sad, Toni thought, Kim's mother had given up on life perhaps before that Friday night beating.

"You know Kim, betrayal is a spirit breaker and will kill you quicker than any beating or bullet. Once your spirit is broken, death looks like a friend."

"I think you're right, Toni. The old people never explained to us what they meant when they used to say 'don't put all your eggs in one basket.' If you trust your life or future to anybody other than God you've just signed your spiritual death certificate."

"Yeah, even people who don't die immediately they somehow ain't never the same."

Kim's eyes looked like they were staring into a place that was eternity's next door neighbor. Toni sat quietly for a moment, not knowing what to say to Kim, and too frightened for her mother to think. Finally, Kim wiped the tears from her eyes with the back of her hand and cleared her throat.

"They called those women at the trial to testify, too."

Kim looked straight ahead as though she were seeing that day in the courtroom, again.

"Did they tell the truth?"

"The woman who lived in the house across the street said that my mama's boyfriend pulled up in front of our house and his cousin, the fat one sitting on her porch, yelled across the street to tell him that he had just missed my mama. He then walked across the street to where his cousin was. She told him who my mama had left the house with and where the people she left with hung out at. She said that she had told him what kind of car my mama got into, who owned the car and the color of the car. Toni, that woman set my mama up and then she sat on her fat behind and watched my mama get kicked and stomped to death. She knew what she was doing and she knew what could happen to my mama, then she wouldn't call the police for me, nor let me use her phone to call them. Toni that woman will pay for what she did as well as what she didn't or wouldn't do."

"I don't believe any of them will leave this world without reaping what they've sown. The Lord said something in Proverbs about people whose feet are quick cause the shedding of other people's blood."

"I forgave all of them, Toni. It took me a while and even today I still have to ask the Lord to help me to truly forgive them."

Toni felt helpless now to comfort her friend.

Kim's aunt lived several miles away from her mother. Her aunt moved into the house where they had lived with their mother to take care of her and her brother, Neal, because their house was bigger. Her aunt had cleaned the house to remove the blood and any signs of the struggle.

Everyday after her mother was buried, Kim said that she sat on her porch and stared at the house across the street. In her mind, she saw the women sitting as they had the night her mother was beaten. She imagined that each of the women was standing before her. She studied their faces as she explained to them how it felt to do your best and still not be able to save a life; to beg for help, just a phone call and be denied. The women could not bring themselves to look directly at Kim, her brother, or their aunt. Until they moved to Connecticut the women never congregated on the porch across the street.

"Toni, I came to realize that a lot of women often envy the bold lifestyle of the party queen, but they hate the party queen for her boldness and they pray that she would meet with destruction and ruin. You know it's their justification for not being bold enough or given the opportunity to hang with the same people the party queen hang with. You know what I mean?"

"Yeah, I know what you mean. It's like the virgin whose still a virgin because ain't nobody ever ask her for none and she can't even give it away." Toni replied.

"Yeah, that's what I'm talking about. But she'll call another girl a whore cause the boys want to get next to her, not that the boys have, just cause they want to." Kim said, sadly.

Kim and her brother left South Carolina a little more than a year after the death of their mother when their aunt moved to Connecticut. The man that killed their mother was still in penitentiary and probably would die there. He was sentenced to life plus forty-five years. Kim never wanted to live in South Carolina, again.

"Guess what Toni, the man that killed my mama was a married man with a wife and four children. I heard his wife divorced him and she left South Carolina right after we did, and moved either to New Jersey or Philadelphia. That man's wife, Miss Mattie, was the only woman in South Carolina that offered any comfort or kindness to Neal and me. Toni, the lady sent food for me and my brother while my mama was still barely alive. I didn't know that she was his wife at the time. After my mama died, Miss Mattie sent her oldest daughter, Marie, who was about my age, with a nice white and pink dress for me to wear to my mama's funeral. I thank God for that lady's kindness, girl, because she was hurting, too."

"When did you find out that she was the man's wife?" Toni asked.

"My aunt told me that Miss Mattie had talked to her before my mama passed and told her that she didn't hold anything against us. She said Miss Mattie was praying for my mama cause they both had children. Then I saw Miss Mattie in the courthouse during the trial. At first, I thought that she was one of my mama's decent lady friends. The day that I had to testify against my mama's boyfriend, Miss Mattie hugged me in the hallway and told me to tell the truth and shame the devil. Then I heard my aunt say that she was too decent to have been married to that man. But I found all of that out after the trial."

"What did the guy do throughout the trial, Kim?"

"He sat there at the table with his head down. He never said a word. The judge asked whether he had anything he wanted to say before he sentenced him and he shook his head and said that he was sorry. He said that he didn't know what had happened."

"Was Neal at the trial, too."

"No, cause he wasn't home that night when it happened, he was spending the night at my aunt's house."

There was a period of silence. The two young women just stared into space and sipped their coffee.

"How you doing Tee?" Kim asked as she sat back on the sofa.

Toni's eyes were swollen and she still shook as though she had been locked in a block of ice naked.

"Kim, I don't know what's ahead. But, I've been thinking, the devil hates women. I need to quit school and bring all of my brothers and sisters who are still young here with me. Kim they're so ashamed of mama they want to quit school. Mama don't even care what her life is doing to her kids."

Kim bowed her head and cried with Toni, she felt her friend's pain and wanted to do more than cry with her or to drive her to the airport. But she was too familiar with the situation that Toni was going through. There was nothing shy of a miracle that would help Toni and Kim felt helpless.

"Toni, don't quit college, you'll be a better help to your brothers and sisters if you stayed in school. I'm your friend, girl, when you're too weak to lean on me, Toni, I declare I'll carry you. If you have to bring the kids back, we'll take care of them. I've been there girl and until your mama decides to change her lifestyle, you'll make yourself sick trying to force it on her and running up and down that road every time something happens. This is a case for God Toni, like Pastor said the other Sunday, 'only He who make em can fix em.' God is your mama's maker and not even He will force a change on her. Do what you have to do now and give it to God. My mama didn't live through her mess, your mother did, let's just hope that this is her wake up call. If not, I'm living proof that you can still survive."

After Kim left to run some errands, Toni washed her face and packed her suitcase. She called a co-worker to ask her to tell her supervisor that she had flown to South Carolina to see about her mother because she had been shot that morning.

Toni again became angry and her mind began to conjure up ways that she could kill Isiah Henderson and the last face he would see on the earth, would be hers. Toni's mind was obsessed with murder. More than anything she wanted Isiah dead. Nothing in the world would please her more than to see him dead.

The sadness and the self-pity that had earlier blanketed her entire being, had now been replaced by an over whelming desire to kill Isiah Henderson herself. Toni fanaticized how she would walk up to Isiah, speak to him in a quiet voice, turn to walk away pull out a pistol, turn back around and call Isiah's name so that he could turn as well and shoot him in the face. She did not want to pray today, Toni wanted revenge.

It was just after eleven o'clock and all that Toni had heard so far that day was bad news and sad stories. She remembered that she needed some cash and had about forty minutes or so to get to her bank and get it. Quickly she threw on a pair of slacks and a sweater and headed down to the garage to her car. As she drove to the bank she thought about how Kim's mother had died. She remembered Kim saying once before that her mother had only been thirty-three years old. Her birthday had been earlier that week and she went out that Friday night to celebrate. Instead of enjoying her thirty-third birthday, Kim's mother was beaten and kicked to death by a man who had made love to her two days before he stomped her brain to mush.

"How could he do it?" She heard herself ask.

Her own mother was forty-seven years old, an age when most women were not thinking of drinking and partying anymore, but settling down. Toni's mother had been a widow for about five years. Kim's mother had never married; she had had Kim and her brother for the same man, though. Then Kim's father left South Carolina to go north to find a better job. He was supposed to send for them after he got a job and an apartment, but he never returned, and even stopped writing or calling. Kim said that when he did return to South Carolina for a visit, he brought his new wife and their child.

Toni wondered if Kim's mother was trying to heal a broken heart she had suffered when the man she loved and had borne two children for decided that she was no longer good enough to be his wife as well as the mother of his children? Was her own mother's heart broken, Toni thought. How did Trudy now feel; the man she was so in love with and had given up her family for tried to kill her.

Toni became angrier as she stood in the line. How could her mother be out in the street at that hour of the night partying when her children were home, alone? Then she realized that she had not even called the hospital to find out how her mother was doing, she had been more concerned about her brothers and sisters. No, she had been concerned about her mother; that's why she had called her grandfather. But, like her grandfather had said, there was nothing that they could do for or about her mother, the decision to change her life was up to her mother. Until her mother decided that she wanted to change her way of living Toni knew that she had to find a way to have peace in her life and help her brothers and sisters live through this until they could stand on their own.

Toni stopped at the Seven-Eleven to buy cigarettes before returning home. The woman at the cash register smiled as she entered the door. Toni stood behind the person who was being served by the lady. Toni could see a fairly good-size scar on the right side of the lady's face just above her chin.

"How you doing today girlfriend?" the lady asked.

Toni, not wanting to lie shook her head as she responded. "I have been up since just after six o'clock this morning and all that I have heard so far is bad news and sad news about mamas. Other than that girlfriend, I think I'm okay."

A sympathetic sadness appeared in the lady's eyes as she looked at Toni.

"Let me encourage you sister, tough times don't last, but tough women do, and you look like a real tough lady. You'll make it and all them other women, too. What can I get for you?"

Toni told the lady what she wanted, paid it for it and left the store.

As she took the elevator to the twelfth floor where she lived, Toni prayed that her brothers and sisters would be okay until she got to South Carolina. She prayed that they would be okay even after she left, because she could not bring them all back with her. The children needed to be in a better and healthier environment. She became bitter at

48

her mother for not doing what she should be for her children. Why, she thought, did she have to take on her mother's responsibilities, they were not her children, but she loved her brothers and sisters.

"Why do people have children, if they're not going to do right by them?" She asked God. She sincerely waited for God to answer.

If her mother were dead, then she would have to take care of the children, but her mother was alive and wanted to good time and drink. Toni was angry with her mother. She could hear the telephone ringing as she got to her apartment door. Hurriedly, she unlocked the door and caught the telephone.

"Hello, hello." She hoped she hadn't missed the call.

"Toni? This is Margaret."

"Yeah, Margaret, how you and the other kids doing?"

"We're okay. We just talked to the hospital and they said that the bullet didn't hit any vital organs and mama should be able to come home in another day or two."

Toni sighed, and hoped that this would be a wake up call for her mother. "Where were you all, Margaret when mama got shot?"

"We were right here home where she should have been, too. Toni, this is too crazy, I just turned nineteen and I got plans for my life too. I can't sit here and raise mama children until she feel like she wanna be a mama, again and quit all of that partying, and messing with Tom, Dick and Harry. Toni, it's by the grace of God that mama hadn't brought somebody up in here and killed all of us while she sleeping her drunk off. I know daddy done turned over in his grave. If daddy's spirit could rise up, I know he would take his children out of here and burn this house down to the ground with mama up in here."

Toni could feel the anger in Margaret's voice. All of the kids were sick and tired of their mother's way of living. The way that their mother was living was not just effecting her; it had taken and continued to take a toll on everybody.

"Margaret, I don't know what to do. I have prayed for mama since she started living like hell. I've made arrangements to fly there in a few hours."

"Oh that's good, I sure would feel better with you here. That old Isiah Henderson called here not too long ago talking about he was gonna get Henry next."

Toni flew into a rage when she heard this. "Oh hell no! I'll kill that bastard myself, Margaret, just find me a pistol by the time I get there, and I swear, I'll blow his fucking brains out before daylight tomorrow morning. The police might not be able to find him, but I will and I declare I'll make sure he's dead before the sun rises again."

"Yep, he had the nerve to call here and threaten to kill Henry. God make em and mama pick em, she got hold to a fool this time, girl." Margaret seemed to be a little frightened.

"Where is Henry right now?"

"Oh he went over to Lloyd's house. I called Lloyd when that jackass called here and threatened Henry. Lloyd came over here and took all of the boys to his house."

"That was good thinking. Well you girls stay in the house and keep the doors locked, okay. Oh yeah, Margaret call the police and let them know that Isiah has started calling there threatening y'all, okay?"

"I'm on the case, girl, I called the police immediately and they sent a couple of cars over here. Lloyd was here when the police came. I think they are watching the house anyway trying to catch Isiah."

Toni was a little relieved when she hung up. She still had some packing to do before her flight.

Kim returned to Toni's apartment with a couple of sandwiches for them to eat.

"I figured you hadn't eaten anything, just like me." Kim said. "I stopped by the church and asked Pastor to pray for you and your family. Prayer works when nothing else does."

Toni picked up the bag and took out the sandwich and laid the pickle aside.

"I just got through talking to Margaret."

Kim wiped her mouth and looked at Toni. "So, how are they holding up?"

"Well Margaret said that Isiah called the house and told my brother, Henry, that he was next. Girl, I'll track that dog down and shoot him myself. He is bold, he shot my mama and the police have yet to pick him up for that. Now he's talking about getting my brother? I'll go to prison gladly for killing that bastard."

Kim sat at the table with her head down. Then she looked up, not really looking at anything in particular.

"Toni, please don't take that attitude with you. Just let the Lord and the police take care of that situation. Besides, if the ambulance was the one that took your mama to the hospital, the police was right there, too. Suppose your mama said that she didn't know who shot her, trying to spare his behind, then what?"

The statement sent shock waves through Toni's system. Suppose her mother had not identified who had shot her? The statement penetrated Toni's mind and spirit. For the first time she began to realize that maybe, just maybe her mother had not told the police who had shot her so that they could arrest Isiah. Usually the police would have a suspect in jail by now, if they knew who they were looking for.

"You know what, Kim, I think you're right."

"Right about what, Tee?"

"That my mama didn't tell the police who shot her. You know those policemen in South Carolina will have a joker in jail in no time when it's one of those Friday night shoot em up down there."

The friends sat and ate their sandwich in silence. Toni grew angrier now because she believed that her mother might be trying to protect a man who had tried to kill her. Toni wondered how she would respond now that the guy was threatening to shoot her son.

"Girl, you thinking too hard." Kim said to Toni. "Just thank the Lord that your mama still alive. As long as there is life, there is hope, don't forget that. I hated those people that watched my mama get beaten to death for a long time. I told you, I kept asking the Lord to help me forgive them. I just decided that I would never live in South Carolina, again in my life.

"Kim did your daddy come to the funeral or call to see about you and your brother when your mother died?" Toni asked.

"Did you call us?" Kim responded.

Kim looked at Toni with a smirk on her face. It was obvious that Toni had hit a sore spot.

"No, mam, I didn't know you then."

"Girl, me and my brother ain't heard a word from that man, yet. I know my aunt called his mama and asked her to let him know that his children's mother was dead."

"So, what did he do?"

"Toni my aunt said that he wanted to know what he was supposed to do with us, let my mama people raise us. He never gave Neal and me anything in our life, girl, not that I ever known of. I'm twenty-three years old and my daddy ain't never sent me a birthday card or anything."

Toni shook her head.

"How can people just forget their children and act like the children were never born?" Toni asked.

"Just like men screw women one night and stomp them to death the next night. It just don't mean anything to them."

"Girl, what this world coming to?" Toni asked.

"Now you really wanna hear something?" Kim said with a sparkle in her eyes. "When I was about twenty-one, this was just a few years ago. My aunt got a phone call from one of our cousins in South Carolina wanting to know whether it was okay to give my daddy my aunt's phone number. You see his daughter who was about eighteen died from an overdose of smack or heroin, or something, I know it was drugs. The way I understand it, he and his wife only had the one child and the girl had been strung out for a while, they had even put the girl in rehab once or twice. He wanted me to know that my sister was dead and he wanted me and my brother at the funeral. Toni, I wanted to tell that man to kiss my sanctified ass. He wouldn't even send a flower to my mama when she got killed, not even a sympathy card to the woman who had been ridiculed for having two babies for him."

Toni had stopped chewing now and laid her sandwich down because Kim had never told her this story before.

"Now wait a minute, Kim, had you ever met his daughter before?" she asked.

"Did you meet her?"

"Hell no." Toni snapped.

"Anyway my aunt just said to give him the number. At first I got mad with my aunt. But the joker called later on that night, my aunt talked to him and got all the information. I wouldn't talk to him and neither would Neal. My aunt left the information on the table and never said another word. Neal and I looked at the information; then Neal came up with this idea. See, Neal said let's go to New York and go to the funeral, but let's not tell him who we are. Neal just wanted to see whether he would recognize us. Girl, I thought that was the most brilliant idea in the world. So we took the train to Brooklyn then took a cab to the funeral home. They had never taken the child to church or anything like that. I sure thank my aunt for taking me and Neal, girl. Tee, Neal and me sat about in the middle of the funeral home. We could tell who our daddy was by where he and his wife were sitting. Girl, that fool didn't know who Neal and I were anymore than the man in the moon. We walked up front with everybody else, to view the body. Neal put a sympathy card right in the hand of our daddy's wife and he was standing next to her and the man did not recognize us."

Toni's eyes were the size of saucers by now. "Wait, please tell me that you and Neal made yourselves known to the man, Kim."

Kim let out a haunting laugh and brushed the hair away from her face. She continued to laugh as she reached for a cigarette and lit it.

"Talk to me, Kim, did you let him know who you were?"

Again Kim laughed and took the edge of the matchbook and picked her teeth. "Hell no, a father should know his children. Just like Neal had said when we planned to go to the funeral, if he knows who we are, then we'd talk to him. But, if he did not recognize us we wouldn't make ourselves known to him and would never have anything to do with him. Now wait a minute before you open your mouth, Tee. In the card that Neal gave our daddy, he told him that it seemed like the death of our mother had caused him to believe that his first-born son and daughter had also died with their mother. But the death of his daughter caused him to remember his two first born were alive but he could not recognize them when they stood before him. I gave him a card as well with a copy of my mother's obituary notice in it and a note. I told him that his children had been orphaned and abandoned by him before our mama died and totally rejected when she did. But he could not replace the loss of the child he had taken care of with the two he had abandoned and rejected. I asked him never to even contact us again."

"Oh, my goodness. I bet you he almost had a heart attack when he read those two cards and realized that his oldest children were at the funeral and he didn't know who they were. But I would have paid a king's ransom to see his face, girl when he opened that card with your mother's obituary in it."

"I would have paid a double king's ransom to see his face. He left my mama with both of us claiming that he was coming back to get her and us. He came back alright, with his wife and new baby."

"Did he try to call you and Neal, again?"

"No, mam. If he did my aunt didn't tell us. Now that Neal is such a college superstar in basketball, can you imagine what our daddy must do each and every time Neal shows up on television and slamming."

Toni started to leap like a little lamb. "Oh girl, that's right, I forgot about that. You and Neal got his last name."

"Tee he can't even tell his friends, that is, if he got any sense, that Neal Sanders is his son. You see what Neal does every time they interview him after a game, 'I love you Aunt Sylvia, hey Kim and Toni, love y'all'." Kim said, acting like she was Neal at a post-game interview.

Toni lit a cigarette and sat down at the table, again.

"Now, Kim, I can't say exactly how that would make your daddy feel, but I really don't think that he sleeps well at night."

"Girl, God don't like ugly and very little He cares for pretty." Kim said. "The one thing my aunt told Neal was to stay in school and get his degree. In a few months he'll have it and them NBA scouts hounding him, too. He made it Tony in spite of the fact that he never knew our daddy. Neal was a baby when he left our mama. Neal saw the man for the first time where he could remember a few years ago at the man's daughter's funeral. But, the loving father didn't recognize either of his children. Come on girl, let's get started for the airport. Remember, Toni, pray before you do anything down there. I'll be praying the whole time and call me after you get there."

8

Toni had tired herself out from the morning's activities. When she took her seat on the plane it was as if she inhaled a sleeping pill and fell asleep almost instantly. She did not have time to think about what had happened, or what she was going to do; she slept the entire flight. The flight attendant had to wake her so that she could bring her seat forward and prepare for landing. It was nearly dark when Toni walked through the terminal. She prayed that Alma, her girlfriend, had gotten her message to pick her up from the airport in Charleston.

As she began the walk to the baggage claim area, Toni's eyes spanned the small terminal trying to catch a glimpse of Alma. She breathed a sigh of relief when she heard her name being called.

"Hey Miss Legs." Alma said as she ran to catch up to Toni. "I had to go to the bathroom so bad that I couldn't wait so I couldn't meet you when you got off the plane. You looking good, girl, college life sure nough agree with you."

"Me? Look at you. Alma, you gotta a new man or somebody in your life? Girl, look at you, you look like a model, honey. Oh, girl, I love the color of your hair. Don't keep no secrets, Alma, what color is that? I'm gonna get mine that color when I get back to Connecticut."

"This is that new burgundy, child. You like it?" Alma asked.

"Girl, I love it. It look as good as collard greens and fried chicken and I'm gonna get a tad for myself." Toni responded.

The friends hugged and kissed each other on the cheek. They were such good friends that long ago they had shed any and all inhibitions about what people would say if they saw two females kiss each other on the cheek.

"Alma how your mama and them doing, and Mr. Troy Pierre?"

"Mama and them doing fine. I forgot to tell you, my brother, Tony, graduated from South Carolina State last year and he went into the officer program for the Marines. But he always asks about you. Girl, I don't know what it is about him and you, he really, really likes you, Toni. Anyway, he asked for your address, again, and this time I gave it to him, so expect a call from him."

"Alma, you know, Tony just playing around. He just had this thing about both of us being called Tony, and besides, he couldn't get none from me. He knew that he was cute and all those other little heifers couldn't resist him, but he had his hands full when it came to me."

"Yep, but he always liked himself some Legs. That's why he started calling you that, he was into you and your legs, sister." Alma said as she laughed.

"Yep, right, Tony wanted to get between my legs."

The women laughed at Toni's statement and watched as the carousel began moving and the bags began to fall off and roll around. Toni spotted her luggage and reached over to pick it up. The two friends walked out of the terminal into the warm night air.

"Alma, how is my little gentleman, Troy Pierre?"

"Oh girl, please. Mr. Man is just too much. He started kindergarten last year, as you know. He don't want nobody calling him just Troy. They have to call him by his whole name, honey, Troy Pierre. Boyfriend came from school one day and told me that I better go talk to the teacher and make her do like he said, call him Troy Pierre."

"Come on, girl. So what did you do?" Toni asked.

"I went to the school and I asked the teacher to please call him by his name, Troy Pierre because that's what we called him and he did not like people just calling him Troy. She said okay and that was the end of that. But Toni you started that with that boy."

"Heck, that's his name and people should respect other people's name. Start them when they're young and they'll know and appreciate special things like their name."

"So, Miss Legs, what are you this year in college? A junior or senior?"

"I am officially a junior now and I'm also taking senior credits. Girl I don't plan to be in college for five years. I'm going almost all year round. The school is set up whereby you can take the same class at two different hours of the day from the same professor, so you know that works fine for me."

"I've been looking at the Registered Nurse's program. With my L.P.N., I can go another two years and get my bachelor's degree in nursing. I also saw these specialized areas for degreed nurses like midwife. I like that, so I've been trying to situate myself so that I can go in the evening and get my degree. Shoot, girl I may not ever get a husband so I've got to do as much and all that I can for me and Mr. Troy Pierre."

"You got that right. I remember you wanted to be a doctor, what happened to that dream?"

"It's still there, but I don't know how to get the dream into reality. So, for now I do the best that I can to take care of me."

"And you know what, even if you get married, Alma, you've got something to bring to the table. All that stuff about women getting married and never having to work anymore is old and it's a lie. You'll need two incomes for a while, even if one person works full time and the other one works part time. Besides, if the poor brother have to work all the time you can't even enjoy him for who he is because he's too tired from working. With two people working for a while you can get what you want quicker and pay it off, then move into cruise for the long haul."

"That's the way I've been looking at things Toni. But the Lord know that if an opportunity for me to go to medical school comes up, I'm gonna take it, even if I have to leave Troy Pierre with you until I'm done. I had that baby before we got out of high school and the Lord blessed me anyway. I was able to finish high school and go to school for my L.P.N. I'm not even twenty-three yet, but I believe that God is just establishing my foundation for where I am going. I want to get started on a little more education and training. I want to build a decent resume. I got to show my son that all women just don't have babies and stop wanting or trying to do better. Girl, I don't want my son to grow up and grab just any old female out there and get stuck with a liability."

"And you know for us, Alma, the country girls, people think that we're supposed to just stay in the country and other people come into our neighborhood and get the good paying jobs and we're supposed to accept that. Girl, we can do whatever we want to."

The car was heading out of the airport parking lot and onto the interstate. The friends continued to talk about their future.

"You still smoke, Toni?"

"Yes, I have to stop that, too, it makes your teeth yellow and brown."

Toni opened her purse and took out two cigarettes and lit them. She handed one to Alma, then cracked the window.

"Thanks." Alma said as she took the already lit cigarette. "Toni, you still want to be a lawyer?"

"Yes, mam, I do. And I'm going to be a lawyer."

"I'm looking forward to the day when we can toss that graduation hat in the air like they do." Alma said.

"I'm looking forward to the same thing for you, girl. What kind of bachelor's degree is that for nurses?" Toni asked Alma.

"It is called a B.N.S., Bachelor's of Nursing Science, madam."

"Well, it sure does sound impressive. Go get it girl. I still like the sound of M.D.- Medical Doctor better."

The friends chuckled; then silence fell over the car as they drove. Alma was thinking about the reason that Toni was there, but had not figured out how she would introduce the subject. She had hoped that Toni would have said something by now.

"Toni, have you heard anymore about Miss Trudy?"

"Just before I left home, Margaret called me with the latest on everything. I'm getting a little tired, Alma, of having to come down here and clean up other people's mess. I wish that I could just have a life of my own without all of the mess. Margaret told me that that fool had the nerve to call the house and tell Henry that he was next."

"No, he didn't. Oh, Jesus, he thinks he's real bad, huh? He can shoot the mama and then start on the kids. What the old folks used to say, when you dig a grave for somebody else, you might as well dig one for yourself, too. He better watch his tail, honey, he could be the 'next' one. Mr. Isiah thinks he's so bad that he's running for who tied the bear. But he had better watch out because there're a few folks out there who quietly go for who loosed the bear. Why this fool ain't in jail, yet? Ain't the police looking for him or something?" Alma asked.

Toni cut her eyes toward Alma. "See, Alma, that's what I was thinking, too. But, Kim, my girlfriend in Connecticut, said something that made me think. Suppose mama didn't tell the police who shot her. You know what I mean, trying to protect this fool."

Alma began waving her one hand while driving with the other. "You cannot protect people like that, especially when you got children. Remember that girl, I can't think of what her name is now, but she was in elementary school with us? Her step daddy was molesting her and her mama knew it. The poor girl told her mama, the teacher and you and me, remember? But the mama lied and said that she was just lying. But, you remember she stabbed her step daddy to death at three o'clock in the morning, right in her room. Mama couldn't lie anymore."

"Oh yeah, Maxine." Toni said. "Her mama couldn't tell a lie why he was dead in Maxine's bedroom."

"Yeah, that's right, Maxine. She was closer with you than she was with me." Alma said.

"You and she liked the same boy, Miss girl."

"I should have let her have him, I wouldn't have gotten pregnant with Troy."

The two friends started laughing. The conversation had triggered old memories and they were overwhelmed with laughter. Finally they were able to contain themselves and continue their conversation.

"That's not how you got pregnant with Troy Pierre, liar. Liking a boy don't get you pregnant. I knew you was sneaking a piece with Troy Pierre's daddy. But you kept lying." The friends laughed about those teenage years.

"Toni, you know me and Albert had been boyfriend and girlfriend for a long time before that. I was so stupid, that fool told me to just let him put the head in. When it was over and done with, I had the head, the shoulder, the chest and feet of Troy Pierre coming out of me. And that hurt more than losing my cherry to Albert, girl."

Toni and Alma laughed at the old line the boys were using at that time.

"Toni, mama couldn't tell me anything for a minute then. I remember the minute when I got pregnant, too!"

"Girl, how can you remember the minute about something like that?" Toni asked as she laughed at Alma.

"For real, Toni, no kidding. I conceived Troy Pierre standing up against the wall in the kitchen. Me and Albert was in the kitchen and I was looking out the window so I could see when daddy was coming. I could hear something and I told Albert to stop but he said wait a minute he was almost finished. He was finished alright. I felt a little lump right here in my side, just like that, girl." Alma snapped her finger. "And Toni, I slid down the wall and had to sit on the floor for a minute before I could get up. Then here you come, Miss Legs, asking me whether Albert had knocked me to the floor."

Toni let out a loud laugh and clapped her hands.

"He had knocked me alright, knocked me up, pregnant, big time going into my junior year of high school. That lump never went away until I pushed out the head, shoulder, chest and legs of Mr. Troy Pierre."

The two women laughed as they rode down the highway. Toni teased Alma a little bit about what she had said.

"Oh hush your mouth, Toni, you couldn't even tell that me and Albert had just done something."

"Well how was I supposed to know? I hadn't had the experience yet of having my fruits plucked." Toni and Alma laughed.

"Now, I can tell them young girls, don't believe that old craziness about letting them boys put the head in, or that you got to be laying down and butt naked to get pregnant. I tell them now, honey, you don't even have to take your panties off to get pregnant. I'm a living example of that." Alma said.

"Do you ever hear from Albert, girl?" Toni asked.

"Yeah, he's stationed out in California on a ship. He went in the Navy. That support check comes on time every month. He said that he's making the Navy a career." Alma said.

"That's good. You think you ever want to get with him again, Alma? You know, marry him?"

"Now Toni, I don't know what I ever saw in Albert in the first place. No, girl, I don't think that I could see myself married to him. You never see all the flaws and everything on a person when you're in love."

Alma was now turning off of the main highway and heading down the local street to the neighborhood they lived in. As she turned the corner into the street where Toni's family lived, she could see a car parked in front of the house. Alma pulled in just behind the car and immediately Lloyd and Margaret came out to meet them.

"Hey Toni, how you doing, how was your flight? How you doing Alma?" Lloyd asked.

"I'm okay, Lloyd, how you doing? How your sister and them?" Toni asked.

"They all doing fine, just fine. She just started a new job with the county and making more money now so she really feeling good about herself." Lloyd said.

"That's good. More money and the potential for promotion can make you feel better."

"Lloyd, you know Troy Pierre said he gonna sue you." Alma said.

As Lloyd removed the suitcase from the trunk of the car, he began laughing. Toni laughed as well, although she didn't know why.

"Why Troy Pierre gonna sue Lloyd?" Toni asked.

56

"Well he's not old enough or big enough for the pony league, which is where he wants to play. Lloyd told him that he possibly could play there in another year or two. But that was not the answer Troy Pierre wanted to hear. So he told me that he wanted me to lend him twenty dollars so he could get a lawyer to sue Lloyd because Lloyd disseminating against him." Alma said as she began laughing.

"Oh so Lloyd ain't discriminating against him, he's disseminating against?" Toni said as she again began laughing.

"Maybe that's why all he needed was twenty dollars for a lawyer, cause I was disseminating against him. See discrimination would require a whole lot more money." Lloyd said as he laughed. "You bring Mr. Troy Pierre out to the field next week when I'm practicing the subs, and we'll see what he can do."

"I sure will. Troy Pierre wants to be where all of the bigger boys are and he can't compete with them, yet. But he thinks he can." Alma replied.

Margaret just threw her arms around Toni. Margaret had a deep sadness in her eyes. Sleep looked it had not found its way to Margaret, yet. Toni sensed a sadness and confusion within Margaret as she hugged her.

As she walked into the house, for the first time Toni noticed the wear and tear of the house. Soon, she thought, they would have to think about doing some fixing up and general repairs to the house.

The house was quiet. The same sadness Toni had sensed within Margaret seemed to be throughout the house. She kicked off her shoes and sat at the kitchen table. Jeremiah came running down the steps and jumped right in Toni's lap.

"I knew you was coming, Toni, so I stayed up." Jeremiah said.

"Who told you that I was coming, Margaret?"

"No, nobody told me. Isiah shot Mama so I knew you would come. You always come when something happen."

Alma looked at Toni and lowered her head. Alma's eyes began to fill with tears and she made an excuse of having to use the bathroom. Toni was hurt because even a child was beginning to know and associate the pattern of her coming to town.

Margaret was at the counter trying to figure out something on a box.

"What are you doing Margaret?" Toni asked.

"Trying to figure out something quick to cook for everybody before it gets too late."

"Don't worry about that, if you and Lloyd will go and pick it up, I'll buy us dinner from Burger King." Toni said.

Lloyd and Margaret went upstairs to find out what everybody wanted. Tony handed the money to Lloyd and told him to make sure that he got some extras so they would have leftovers, just in case.

"Jeremiah what do you want? A hamburger, or a cheeseburger?" Lloyd asked.

"I want some chicken. Get me mashed potatoes, macaroni and Cole slaw, oh and a biscuit." Jeremiah said.

"Jerry, you gonna eat all of that?" Lloyd asked.

"Uh, huh."

"Okay. Let's go Margaret." Lloyd said.

"I wanna go with y'all." Jeremiah said.

Lloyd picked Jeremiah up and carried him to the car with him and Margaret. Lloyd had always been fond of Jeremiah and had kept him pretty busy with after school things.

Lloyd and Margaret began dating after Margaret began taking Jeremiah to little league and soccer practices where Lloyd and another fellow taught community kids to

57

play. Jeremiah was quite fond of Lloyd as well. Once Lloyd drove to Virginia to visit an Army buddy and took Jeremiah with him. Jeremiah had talked about that trip in his sleep. Lloyd could do no wrong, as far as Jeremiah was concerned.

Henry and Wilson, at first, had been concerned about Lloyd and Margaret's relationship because Lloyd was a little bit older than Margaret, but it did not take long for them to change their opinion. Lloyd was older than Toni and Aaron Junior. The seven years age difference did not bother Aaron Junior at all.

Joyce came downstairs and after squeezing Alma's shoulders and touching her cheek to Alma's cheek; Joyce sat in Toni's lap and hugged her.

"Oh girlie, girlie, you getting a little heavy ain't you." Toni said, patting Joyce's hip.

"No, I think I might have lost a few pounds." Joyce said. "How long you been here?"

"I haven't been here long, I sent Margaret and Lloyd to get some food from Burger King so that Margaret wouldn't have to cook." Toni said.

"You first have to know how to cook so you wouldn't have to cook. Margaret don't know nothing about cooking. I cook better than she does. But you just might have saved our lives by sending them to Burger King." Joyce said.

Henry, who had been taking a nap when Toni and Alma arrived, was now awake and stomping as he came down the stairs.

"I thought the aroma in the place had changed." Henry said as he saw Alma. "Miss Magnolia in the house. What's up girl?"

Alma started laughing immediately; she and Henry had always been in the habit of teasing each other. "I knew this house was too quiet for a reason. The giant was sleeping, but he's up now. What's going on Henry?"

"I'm doing the best I can with what I've got, Miss Magnolia. You look like you doing great with all that fabulous hair."

Alma started laughing again. "What you call it, Henry, fabulous hair? Now that's the right name."

"I turned that corner and seen all of that fabulous hair, I thought I was looking at sparkling burgundy wine." Henry said as he and Alma began laughing. "Girl, how that little bad boy of yours, Troy Pierre?"

"Henry, that boy is too much. He want to sue Lloyd now for disseminating, not discriminating against him because Lloyd won't let him play in the pony league. He asked me to lend him twenty dollars to get a lawyer." Alma and Henry burst into laughter.

"I bet you Troy Pierre was serious, too. Girl, that boy of yours reminds me of your mama brother, Mr. Grady. That's your Uncle Grady back from the dead."

"Tell the truth now, Henry. I declare that's exactly who Troy Pierre reminds me of." Alma said.

"Girl, Troy kind of scary sometimes. I think that was last week or the week before, I was coming out the little store up the road with the gas station. I heard this voice, sound like a man voice say 'hey, Henry, how you doing?' I looked around and recognized that it was your cousin, Lawrence car, but I didn't see him. I walked over to the car and here Troy Pierre sitting up in there. So I asked him how he was doing and how was school. Alma, this child asked me whether I was still seeing that girl round there on Ratcliff Road. Well I couldn't lie. He only seen me with that girl one or two times at the ball diamond. I told him no. Guess what he said to me?" Henry asked, as he looked Alma in the eye.

58

"Uh, uh, what he say? Alma asked.

"He told me that was good cause the girl was no good for me, she had too many boys she was already seeing. I said to myself, if he know that much, I better not ask him how he knew, he just might tell me. But he was telling the truth, though." Henry said.

Just about that time, Lloyd Margaret and Jeremiah walked in the front door.

"Jerry, who that chicken for?" Henry asked.

"It's for me, that's who."

"I thought that you like Whoppers." Henry said as he began going through the bags.

"I do, but I felt like some chicken." Jeremiah replied.

"Oh you felt like some chicken? What kind of chicken you felt like, a rooster or hen?"

"Oh leave me alone, you hog. I'll get some of Toni's Whopper tomorrow." Jeremiah replied.

"See, that's daddy right there, just come back to life. He gonna always try and get the most mileage out of a freebie."

Lloyd looked at Henry and handed him a Whopper and a fish sandwich.

"You got me some French fries, too? Henry asked Lloyd.

"Yes sir, I do, and a chocolate shake, right?" Lloyd asked.

"Man you know me, I don't have to worry about my food if Lloyd on the case." Henry said.

Lloyd held up a large bag of onion rings and said, "me and you got to split these cause I know you like just a few and I like a few, so I just got one large order."

Henry's eyes lit up like a light bulb. "See, my man know what we like. Come on, let's go out here on the porch so nobody can imitate our good manners." Henry said as he and Lloyd walked out of the front door.

Lloyd yelled back to Toni that Margaret had her change from the food. Margaret laid the change on the table and took her food from the bag. Toni walked over to the cabinet to get a plate for Jeremiah, but he said that he wanted to eat his food from the box. Everybody else came and got what they wanted and went back upstairs to watch television.

Everybody had gotten what they wanted and several Whoppers and other things were left over. Wilson came downstairs to throw away the wrappers and saw the remaining items and took another Whopper.

"Wilson, didn't you have a Whopper and a fish sandwich, with fries and a milk shake?" Alma asked.

"Yeah, but I got some fries and a soda left, I need something to go with them." Wilson responded.

Toni and Alma looked at each other and started laughing.

"Toni, I wouldn't want to be the one who had to feed Wilson. Feeding him would send me to the poor house." Alma said.

"Wilson just a old hog." Jeremiah said.

Toni laughed and told Jeremiah not to call his brother names. But Jeremiah insisted that Wilson was a human hog.

After everybody had eaten as much as they wanted, Toni began putting the food in the refrigerator. Joyce made sure that Jeremiah took a bath and put his pajamas on. Toni insisted that Jeremiah stay up a little while longer so that his food could properly digest.

Toni and Alma sat in the kitchen talking about old times and the times ahead of them regarding their career focus. Jeremiah came downstairs and crawled up on Toni's lap. She held him like an infant and rocked him. She could feel the sadness within the little confused boy. Jeremiah had suffered a lot because he was the youngest and her mother had led a very fast paced life style of drinking and partying since he was less than three years old. Jeremiah had not really known his father because he died while Jeremiah was only a toddler. Therefore, other than his brothers and Lloyd, Jeremiah had not been exposed to an adult male figure. The various men that their mother had brought home, Margaret, Joyce and the boys had kept Jeremiah far from.

Lloyd came inside to go to the bathroom and Jeremiah asked if he could sit with Lloyd on the front porch. Lloyd did not refuse Jeremiah much, and told him that he could, but the minute he started nodding, he would put him to bed and did not want any argument. Jeremiah agreed to Lloyd's terms and when Lloyd returned from the bathroom, he picked Jeremiah up took him outside where he and Henry were sitting.

The house was relatively quiet now. Everybody was either sleeping or watching television. Toni could tell that her siblings had been awake for quite some time and now they felt a little more secure with her in the house. Alma did not have to be at work again until Monday afternoon so she did not have to rush home. She still lived with her mother which was very convenient for her and Troy Pierre always had a relative at home with him while she worked.

9

"Seriously, though, Toni, I have been thinking about leaving South Carolina. You know, go somewhere else for a while; see what the other side of the state line is all about. Other than visiting you in Connecticut and Tony, my brother, in California, I have not been anywhere at all."

"Why don't you move to Connecticut for a while with me and Kim. You met Kim and she is a real good person. Hey, you could get your degree there."

"Oh girl, yes, I like Kim. The sister has survived a lot, just like us. She got her head on straight. When does she graduate?" Alma asked.

Before Toni could answer Alma's question shots rang out piercing the night's silence. The shots were so close that Alma fell to the floor and crawled into a corner. Toni jumped up from the table and ran to the front door without regard for her safety. There was no one on the front porch. Her heart quickly sank. Then she saw Henry at the edge of the house shining almost like he had been drenched in a semi-golden light or yellow oil, with a pistol in his hand. Just as Toni spotted Henry she heard two or three more shots fired and she ran to grab Henry. Toni reached up and could only get a hold on Henry's arm between his wrist and elbow and dragged him into the house slamming the door behind them. Henry's arm had seemed to be locked with the pistol in his hand.

Things were moving very fast, now. Toni did not see Lloyd or Jeremiah and grabbed the pistol from Henry and ran out of the house to look for them. As she got to the corner of the street from where they lived she saw Lloyd carrying Jeremiah.

"Lloyd, y'all alright, did you or Jeremiah get hit?" Toni asked.

"No, no, me and Jerry okay. Is Henry okay?" Lloyd asked.

"Yeah, he's in the house."

Toni tried to take Jeremiah from Lloyd but he told her that he had Jeremiah and to go on to the house. The three of them walked quickly back to the house. People had started turning on their porch lights.

"Toni, my ears feel funny." Jeremiah said. "The bullets was going by my head."

"It's okay, baby, you're gonna be alright. Everything's gonna be alright." Toni said, trying to reassure Jeremiah.

Jeremiah was clutching Lloyd as though he were holding on for dear life. The little boy in his pajamas was frightened and began to cry as they entered the living room. While Toni was looking for Lloyd and Jeremiah, Alma called the police and told Toni that they were on the way there.

"Henry what was all of that out there?"

"That was that crazy ass Isiah Henderson."

"You mean to tell me that he came over here?" Toni wanted Isiah Henderson dead so badly that she was ready to go out and look for him with the pistol she was still holding.

"Give me that Toni, before the police get here." Henry said. Henry looked at Lloyd and asked him to put the pistol upstairs.

"I was sitting in the chair leaning on the banister talking to Lloyd when all of a sudden somebody grabbed me by the neck and started pulling me over the banister and out of the chair. I got the jump on him because I leaned into him and fell on top of him. That's when I saw it was Isiah. All I could say to Lloyd was go, so he could get Jerry out of there. While we were both down I hit him a couple of times in his face. When I straightened up the joker had his pistol out and tried to get a shot off, but he missed. He tried to run but I think I hit him a couple of times."

"You think you might have hit Isiah?" Toni asked.

"Yeah, I think I got him a couple of times."

Toni began checking Henry to make sure that he had not been hit by the gunfire. Lloyd had put Jerry to bed and he came downstairs and checked Henry for himself. Margaret then said that the police were there and some of them had circled the back of the house. From the corner of her eye, Toni could see Henry and Lloyd whispering. Then she saw, or thought she saw, Henry nod his head in a motion to say yes.

The police knocked on the door and Lloyd took Henry into the kitchen as Toni went to answer the door. Tony opened the door to let the policeman in. She explained to the policeman what had happened. She told the policeman that Isiah Henderson had shot her mother and had called the house, prior to her arrival from Connecticut, and told Henry that he was next. While Toni and the policeman were talking another officer ran up and said, "we got a body in the back on the other side between the houses."

Toni's heart sank because she knew that the body was that of Isiah Henderson and he was dead. If he was not dead, he would have been gone, she thought. Toni did not want Henry to have to go to jail, after all, Isiah had come to their house and his intent was to kill Henry. The room began to spend and Toni's head felt light. She couldn't think clearly, Toni looked back at Henry and watched Lloyd, with both hands on Henry's shoulders and their foreheads touching. It looked like Lloyd and Henry were praying.

The officer told Toni and her family to remain inside the house until they returned. Jerry had gotten out of his bed and come downstairs. He went over to Henry and clung to his leg as Lloyd prayed.

"I know Isiah was dead, Henry." Jeremiah said.

"Jeremiah, you got to be quiet now, baby. You cannot say anything because the police will switch it around and try to use it against Henry, so go back upstairs with Margaret, okay?" Lloyd said to Jeremiah.

Jeremiah just said "okay" and went back upstairs. Henry stood in the kitchen and waited for the policemen to return. Every now and then, Henry would look at Lloyd and shake his head up and down. The policeman returned and asked Toni if she could recognize Isiah if she saw him. She told the policeman that she had seen him maybe three or four times but she believed that she could recognize him. Toni turned and looked at Henry and walked out of the door with the policeman.

Everything seemed to go into slow motion as Toni and the policeman walked around the side of their house and toward the houses in the back. Toni could see a heap on the ground as she got closer to Helen Baker and Mayfield Johnson's house. As she approached the heap with the policeman shining his flashlight, she could see the pistol in Isiah's hand. The policeman guided Toni away from the direction of the pistol in Isiah's hand was pointing. He did not want the pistol to go off as the body cooled down he said. The policeman shined the light directly in Isiah's face. Isiah's eyes were open wide, he had died too quickly, she thought, to close them.

Toni could see several bloodstains on the front of Isiah's shirt, his shoelaces were untied and he didn't have on any socks. There was a silver chain around his waist, the kind of chain that people used to put keys on. There was also a chain around his neck with a strange looking medallion on it. Then Toni saw the ring on his pinkie finger. It was a gold ring that she had given her mother several years ago. She reached down to take the ring off of his finger. But the policeman told her that she could not take anything off of the body. Toni did not stop, she just told the officer that the ring was one that she had bought and given to her mother a few years prior and Isiah must have taken it off of her finger when he shot her. But Toni took the ring off of the dead man's finger and walked away.

"He might have died with my mama's ring on his finger but he sure as hell won't be buried with it on his finger." Toni told the policeman. "That's Isiah Henderson, officer." Toni said. "Why couldn't he just put that pistol to his head and pull the trigger rather than coming over here messing with my family and getting other people involved with his craziness?"

Tony walked back into the house and looked at Henry and Lloyd. "He's dead." Toni said, so matter-of-factly and sat down. "The policeman's going to take you to jail tonight. Don't talk to anybody unless it's a lawyer. No matter how nice these guys try to be, just don't say anything at all, until I get you a lawyer down there. You hear me, Henry?" Toni asked.

"Yes." Henry said as he looked at Lloyd and Wilson. Then Toni saw the three men holding hands.

The police officer returned to the house and asked Henry and Lloyd what had happened. They told what had happened. The policeman asked where was the weapon Henry had used. Henry told him that it was upstairs on top of the dresser in his mother's bedroom. Another officer went upstairs and got the pistol. Toni looked at the pistol and thought that it was not the same one that she had taken from Henry. She had also held the pistol when she went out to look for Lloyd and Jeremiah. Toni stared at the pistol and thought that maybe she was just confused but something inside of her would not allow her to accept that as truth. Then she remembered that she had had to reach up and grab Henry's arm, but could only reach his forearm. Something crazy was going on Toni thought.

"Son, how old are you." The officer asked Henry.

"Eighteen, almost nineteen."

"Have you ever been arrested before?"

"No sir."

"Son, I'm sorry about your mother and everything, but I'm gonna have to arrest you for this. We can see that you didn't go out looking for this trouble and I don't believe a jury will convict you, this look like straight self-defense to me. But it's routine and I have to take you in now."

"Uh, huh." Henry said.

Lloyd's eyes spanned the room as though he were seeing it for the first time. It was a warm night but Lloyd and Henry appeared to be sweating as though they both had just run the Boston Marathon. Lloyd leaned his head forward as the policeman spoke to Henry and Toni, grasping every word with his ears and eyes and making verbatim mental notes or audio recording of everything that was said.

Wilson had tears in his eyes as the officer read Henry his rights and told him that he would have to place handcuffs on him. Lloyd laid his hand on Henry's shoulder and told him to be strong and continue to pray, just as he had told him. Toni just watched as the policeman put the handcuffs on Henry and took him out to the car.

Her anger was rekindled, but with a greater fury. She walked out to the police car with Henry and reassured him that she would have an attorney there to see him as soon as she could. Henry nodded his head. Toni saw the tears in Henry's eyes, but he did not let one roll down.

Lloyd stood on the side of the street and watched until the police car turned the corner. Then he walked around to the side of the house and watched from the distance as the other officers completed their work. Toni walked back to where Lloyd was standing. Lloyd seemed to be so focused on what the policemen were doing that he had not seen when Toni came and stood next to him, her presence startled him causing him to jump.

Toni did not know what to do now, it was only eleven o'clock, a man was dead and a young boy had been carried off to jail for killing him. Several of the neighbors began to come over to where Lloyd and Toni were standing and watching.

"Toni, how you doing sugar?" a voice said. Toni turned to see who it was and recognized Lena Cunningham.

"Hi Miss Lena, how you doing?" Toni responded.

"I'm okay sugar. Was that Henry the police took away from here?" Lena asked.

"Yes, mam. Henry killed Isiah and they took him to jail."

"Well, I seed Isiah myself sneak up on Henry, honey and you can tell the police that cause I'll say it again, anytime and anywhere. I had just walked out there on my front porch and I seen Henry and Lloyd and Jerry out there. So I said to myself, I'll just sit out here a little while till I gets sleepy. So I went back in the house to get my cigarettes and just as I got there to my door, I wasn't quite out the door, but just before I put my foot on the porch to walk completely out the door. I seed this here person on the side of the house and before I knew what was going on, I seed this man grab Henry around the neck and starting pulling him over the banister. I couldn't move for a minute, then Henry was off the porch and on the ground on top the man. Next thing I know they was shooting and I just hauled tail back in my house. Bullets ain't got no names, just intentions."

"Miss Lena I was sitting right there on the steps with Jerry and at first I didn't know what was happening." Lloyd said.

"I know it, son, cause it just seemed like things was happening so fast. I never heard a word or anything until they started shooting." Lena said.

"I realized something was happening behind me when I heard the chair fall over and I seen Henry going cross the banister." Lloyd said.

Toni couldn't say anything. She just watched and listened to Lena and Lloyd.

"I run back up in the house and called the police." Lena said. "Now that's a God in heaven shame for Isiah to come all the way over here and cause so much trouble. But you see what happen when you do wrong? Oh yes sir, he thought he was gonna come over here and cause more harm, but God put a stop to his mess. I just pray for God mercy on Henry."

"Mercy, mercy, mercy. That's what we need now more than anything Miss Lena, mercy. Now I gotta tell mama that not only is her crazy boyfriend dead, but that her son killed him when he came here to try and kill her son." Toni said.

Lloyd looked at Toni and put his arms around her. "Toni, we gonna get through this too, God don't make junk, we gonna get through this and we gonna get Henry through this, too."

"Toni, I'm scared. Where they took Henry, Toni?" Jeremiah asked.

Toni thought that Jeremiah was in the bed, but somehow he slipped out of the house without anyone seeing or stopping him. Lloyd picked up Jeremiah and held him in his arms. Jeremiah laid his head on Lloyd's shoulder and hugged him. Lloyd walked back into the house carrying Jeremiah. Toni stood outside and talked with Lena for a little while then sat on the steps.

Alma came outside and sat on the steps next to Toni. Alma lit two cigarettes and gave one to Toni. The two friends sat on the steps in silence for a long time. Then Toni broke the silence.

"Alma, you know before I left Connecticut I was thinking how I could track down Isiah and kill him before the sun rose. But look at what happened. Before the sun rose I identified his dead body. Now ain't that something girl?"

"Yes, it is, girlfriend. I'm just so sorry that it was Henry who did it. But, if anybody was likely to do it, it was one of your brothers, cause Isiah hurt your mama. I know it don't look good right now, Toni, but ain't no jury gonna convict Henry for this. I just don't see it."

Joyce came out on the porch to tell Toni that their Uncle Clifford had called and said that he was on his way there. Joyce sat down on the step below Toni and rested her head on Toni's knee. Toni could feel the tears saturating her pant leg. She began to caress Joyce's cheek and head. The family was in a shamble now with their mother shot and in the hospital and Henry in jail for just having killed the man who had shot her.

"Joyce, did you get any sleep today, sweetie?" Toni asked.

"I got a little bit. Toni, what you think gonna happen to Henry." Joyce asked.

"Well, he's got to go before a judge, first. So he'll be in jail overnight or for a few days. Just as soon as I can, I'll bail him out so that he can be home with us until the trial."

"You think Henry going to prison, Toni?"

"I pray to God not, Joyce, but lets not think about that tonight, sweetie, okay?" Toni said.

Toni sat in silence with Alma at her side and Joyce sitting between her legs with her head on Toni's knee. Toni did not know what to do, but was inspired to get her siblings away from the house for the night so that they could get some rest.

"Joyce how would you like to go over to Lloyd's house for the night and get some sleep, then come back in the morning?" Toni asked.

"You going, too?" Joyce asked.

"No, I'm gonna stay here and get some business straight, but I want you guys to get away from here for the night, okay?"

"Okay, if that's what you want." Joyce said.

"Go in there and tell Lloyd to come here for a minute, please." Toni said to Joyce.

Joyce stood up and went inside and shortly Lloyd came outside.

"Toni, you wanted to see me?" Lloyd asked.

"Yeah, Lloyd, I really need you to do me a favor tonight. Can you take all the kids over to your house so they can be away from here for the night and at least get a good night's sleep? So much has happened today, I just think they need to get away from here, at least for the night."

"You and I thinking on the same wave length, Toni. I can put them in beds and on my pull out sofa in the den. I'll take them with me now, you gonna be okay right?" Lloyd asked.

"Yeah, Alma's gonna be here with me for a while and Uncle Clifford is on his way here. I just wonder where in the world is Aaron Junior?"

"Only God knows, but I know he'll be alright though. It's a good thing A.J. wasn't here, Toni, ain't no telling what else would have been going on." Lloyd said.

"Yeah, you're right about that, Lloyd. Here, take this money with you Lloyd so you can get something for their breakfast in the morning."

"Toni put that money away. I keep plenty of food in my house; these kids ain't gonna starve, or go hungry. I'll leave my phone number on the table in the kitchen so you'll have it, but I'm in the book just in case you miss and throw it out." Lloyd said as he walked back into the house.

Toni and Alma went into the house so that Toni could talk to her brothers and sisters. As Toni looked around and about she could see that the lights were on in every house on the street and people were sitting on their porch watching their house.

"Wilson, Margaret, Jeremiah, Joyce, I want y'all to go home with Lloyd for tonight, okay? I don't want y'all fretting about anything, I'll try and get Henry bailed out of jail just as soon as they set bail. So get something to sleep in and something to put on tomorrow, okay?"

The children went upstairs and began getting the things that they needed. Margaret got Jeremiah's clothes and came downstairs. As she sat at the table, Margaret hung her head down and the tears began to flow.

"We all told mama to stop messing with that dam Isiah. Everybody else told mama the same thing, but no, she thought that everybody was jealous of her or trying to run her life. When Isiah hit her the first time that I know about, cause I seen it with my own two eyes, I begged mama to call the police and stop messing with that man. Now look at all of the trouble she done cause. Poor Henry got to sit in jail and everything is just messed up. I wish daddy was here. Why daddy had to die and leave us?"

Margaret was in pain and Toni could not answer her question. Toni just walked over and hugged Margaret and assured her that everything would be alright. Lloyd came into the kitchen and took Margaret by the arm and told her to come on so she could get some rest because her nerves were shot. Toni walked them out to Lloyd's car. Wilson still had not spoken a word and continued to avoid eye contact with anyone.

Alma was sitting on the sofa in the living room comforting Joyce who had heard everything Margaret had said. Jeremiah stood in the middle of the floor and appeared to be lost. The little boy looked like he did not know which way was up. The day's events had managed to suck what confidence he had had out of him. Toni walked over to Jeremiah and picked him up and kissed him.

"Don't be afraid pooh, everything's gonna be okay. I'm here. I want you to go with Lloyd and get a good night's sleep and I'll see you in the morning, okay?"

"You not gonna leave, Toni? You gonna be here when I come back?" Jeremiah asked.

"I'll be right here, sweetie, and if you want to talk to me ask Lloyd if you can use the phone and you can call me right here." Toni said.

Lloyd came up and took Jeremiah out of Toni's arms and told him that he would dial the number for him just as soon as they got to Lloyd's house so he could talk to Toni and say good night. With a sparkle in his eyes, Jeremiah leaned forward in Lloyd's arms so that he could kiss Toni again. Then he wanted Alma to kiss him as well. Alma hugged his neck and kissed him several times.

Toni and Alma stood on the porch and watched as Lloyd drove away.

"I think you made a wise decision, Toni, to get them away from the house for tonight." Alma said.

"Alma, I didn't know anything else to do, right then. But they have been hurt so bad by all of this and I just wasn't sure that I had the answers needed to make them understand what was happening or to make them feel better."

Alma put her arms around her friend and they walked back into the house and closed the door.

"Uncle Clifford's coming over here, isn't he?" Alma asked.

"Yeah. I guess Uncle Clifford is wondering what in the hell we've gotten ourselves into now."

"I need a cup of coffee, Toni, you want me to fix some for you, too?"

"Please, mama always keep some coffee around here. Henry and Margaret are coffee drinkers so look up there in the pantry, some should be there."

"I already had spotted the coffee, girl. We in for the long haul, tonight, so we might as well get ready." Alma said.

As Alma poured the water into the coffee maker, Toni sat at the kitchen table in unbelief. In a matter of hours so much had happened, she thought. Her mind was on Henry and how he was doing at the jail. Henry had never been in trouble before and had never spent a night in jail. Toni's heart pained inside because she had seen the fear in Henry's eyes as he got into the police car.

Toni's anger was rekindled against her mother. Margaret had been angry before she left, but Toni was angrier. How could her mother put her family in a position to suffer like this because she wanted to have a good time? Toni had had as much as she could take of her mother's life style. How could a woman who once got up before sunrise and pray and spoke in tongues, become so out of control? Toni wanted to tell her mother off, but she had never spoken harshly to her mother or said exactly what was on her mind to her mother. But she thought, 'there's a first time for everything.'

"Hey girl, you study long, you study wrong, the old folks say. Try not to think too much Toni. You gotta wait until Monday morning to try and get in touch with a lawyer. Take my car tomorrow and go see your mama at the hospital. While you're there, I'll call to see whether we can see Henry at the jail. How's that?" Alma asked.

"That's a good plan, Alma. Thanks a lot girl."

There was a knock at the door and Toni knew that it was her uncle so she got up and opened the door. Clifford hugged his niece and patted her on the back. Clifford walked into the kitchen where Alma was putting out the cups for the coffee.

"How you, Miss Gardenia?" Clifford said.

Alma started laughing. "You see that, Henry got all of y'all calling me Miss Gardenia. I'm okay Uncle Clifford, how you doing?"

"Sweetheart I'm doing okay. How you mama and them and that little old man of yours?"

"They all doing just fine. You want some coffee, Uncle Clifford? I made a whole pot full." Alma said.

"Yes, mam. I need a little something to perk me up, or calm me down." Clifford responded.

Toni and Alma filled Clifford in on what had happened since she got to town. The mood was rather somber. Toni was so distracted most of the time that she found herself asking Clifford or Alma to repeat something that they had said five minutes earlier. Clifford could see that his niece was tired and not in the right frame of mind to comprehend much of anything. Clifford told Toni that he would come there the next morning so they could go to the hospital to see her mother. Clifford got into his car and left.

Alma called her mother, again, to let her know that she was still at the house with Toni. Alma was tired as well because she had had to work earlier that day, so she and Toni checked the doors to make sure all of the doors and windows were locked. Toni went into the girls' room and took off her clothes and laid across the bed. She was asleep before her head came to rest on the pillows. Alma placed the sheet across her friend and crawled into the next bed and fell asleep almost instantly.

10

Toni awoke just before eight o'clock that Sunday morning. Alma was asleep and snoring just a bit. Toni thought that if she had a tape recording she could record Alma's snoring and let her listen to it. Alma swore that she didn't snore.

Toni went downstairs and started the coffee. As she sat at the kitchen table she looked into the dining room for the first time since she had been in the house. She saw her image in the mirror on the wall and looked as though she was seeing herself for the first time. Everything that had happened the prior day and night had not been undone, and she knew that it wouldn't be.

As she sipped the hot coffee, Toni shifted the curtain at the kitchen window just a little so that she could see out. As she began to think about all that she had to do and the impact that all that had happened was having on her brothers and sisters, Toni began to cry. The tears slowly and silently began rolling down her face. Toni felt the cold tears as they made their way down her face, over her chin and down her neck coming to rest in her bosom. Jeremiah had almost witnessed what could have been the death of his older brother, but God was merciful, Toni thought. Yes, God had been merciful even though Henry now sat in jail, he was alive.

Drying her eyes became an effort in futility. Suddenly, Toni remembered that she had not called Kim. Reaching for the phone, Toni dried her face in a paper towel and dialed Kim's number.

"Hello, this is Kim."

"Hey Kim, you must have thought that you were at work." Toni said.

"Girl, it seems like I spend so much time there sometime it's hard to break the habit. But tell me what's going on down, there. How's your mama?" Kim asked.

"I guess she's doing okay, I haven't been to the hospital yet. Henry's in jail, he killed Isiah Henderson last night." Toni said.

"What the hell are you talking about Toni? Henry your younger brother killed the man that shot your mama?"

"Yep, right here at the house, well just behind the house."

"Henry was the one that he called yesterday and said that he was next, didn't he? That fool didn't figure God a possibility in his evil equation. How is Henry?"

"Well, the police took him to jail about eleven o'clock last night. Me and Alma and the other kids were right here in the house and I had just bought Whoppers and shakes and stuff like that for everybody. Henry and Lloyd, Margaret's boyfriend, were sitting out on the porch and Jeremiah was out there with them. Henry said that he was sitting with the chair leaning against the banister when suddenly he was pulled up out of the chair. Lloyd was sitting on the steps just in front of Henry, holding Jeremiah and he said that he didn't realize that Isiah had sneaked up on them until he heard the chair fall."

"Toni, you mean to tell me that that fool sneaked up on your brother and them."

"He sure did, Kim."

"Toni, I'm sorry that Henry gotta sit in jail for this mess. But I am thankful that it is not Henry whose laying in the morgue this morning. You see, Toni, that fool could have just open fire on Henry and them and they would never have known who did it. But it was the grace of God that allowed it to go the other way. Isiah was too bold, girl.

The devil wanted a soul last night, but people right here in Connecticut was praying for you and your family, so the devil got back that which was his to begin with."

"Kim, now I've got to get a lawyer for Henry, bail him out of jail until the trial as soon as the judge set bail for him. Me and Uncle Clifford going to the hospital this morning to see mama and I've gotta tell her that her boyfriend is dead. Besides her boyfriend being dead, her son killed him when he tried to kill her son. Now, you tell me how am I supposed to do all of that?"

"Remember what you just said?"

"Yeah."

"Say the same thing when you get to the hospital. You need any money or anything?" Kim asked.

"No, I'm okay, I think, at least until I see how much this bail is gonna be."

"Well let me know and I'll send you what I've got. I'm gonna ask Pastor and the church to pray for y'all again in light of what happened last night."

"Ask Pastor to pray for my mama. The truth be told, Kim, I don't even think this is going to make her change. I pray to God that it does, but I just don't feel it in me that it will."

"Toni, we don't understand a whole lot of stuff, but if we could understand everything about God, He wouldn't be God. But let's just hope for the best but prepared for the worse. I'm going to church but I'll call you later tonight, okay?"

"Okay, and thanks Kim."

"Toni, we gonna get through this, too. I'll be praying for Henry, too."

The friends hung up. Toni sipped her coffee and looked out of the window. She could see her godmother and two other people near the spot where Isiah had fallen when he died. Toni wanted to go out and say something to her godmother, but she decided that it was better to sit in the kitchen and be still.

Toni knew that her brothers and sisters needed a good meal so she looked in the freezer to see what was there. Everything was frozen so she decided to take Alma's car and go to the grocery store before she woke up. As she got to the top of the stairs she could hear Alma snoring and knew she was out for a little while longer. Toni put on the same outfit she had worn the night before and took the keys from Alma's purse. She went to the store and picked out a nice big pork roast, one big enough for leftovers. After picking up a few other things, and a couple of packs of cigarettes for herself and for Alma she headed back home.

Alma was still asleep and did not know that Toni had even left the house. Toni washed the meat and put it in a large pot. She knew that the food would not be completely finished by the time her uncle came, but she continued to prepare Sunday dinner for her family, anyway. She cut up the potatoes for potato salad and put the water on to boil for the macaroni and cheese. Toni decided that she would cook several different things so that there would be plenty of cooked food in the house for the children. As she was putting the macaroni and cheese in the oven, Alma came downstairs.

"Girl, please tell me you got some coffee made, Toni."

"Girl, you know I got some coffee on up in here. After hearing you snore, I knew I'd need something to keep me alert and I wouldn't have to come up there and kick the bed to quiet you down."

"Now Tonitia Renee, I like lively people, but a liar I cannot stand. Why you wanna stand there on a Sunday morning and lie on one of the Lord's angel?"

70

"Lie, I'm speaking the truth. I wish I had a tape recorder so you can hear for yourself."

"Toni, you lying, I have never ever snored. You lie, and everybody in my house lying about that. I ain't never heard me snore."

The two women burst into laughter at the statement. Alma reached up in the cabinet and got a large coffee cup. After fixing herself a cup of coffee, Alma sat at the table and watched Toni cut up sweet potatoes.

"Toni, me and Troy Pierre coming over here today for dinner, I just want you to know that right now."

"Girl, you know I don't cook no slack pot, so you and Troy Pierre and your mama can rest your feet under my table."

"What all are you fixing, Toni, it's a lot of stuff on that stove?"

"I went to the store and got a fresh pork roast. I got a nice big one girl, so everybody can eat off of it a couple of times. I also bought some stew beef so there would be some other kind of meat for meals later in the week. I got macaroni and cheese, potato salad, candied yams, cabbage, corn bread and I'll fix a nice big peach cobbler when I get back from the hospital."

"I didn't hear you say anything about some rice, you gonna cook some rice ain't you?"

"Girl, you know the rice was first. I know how all of us like them swamp seeds, girl. You should have just asked what I was cooking with the rice." Toni said as she and Alma laughed.

Alma told Toni that she was going home to check on her son and mother but she would be back. Alone in the house now, Toni, sat at the table and wondered how her brother was doing in jail. She began to wonder if her moments of wanting to kill Isiah had somehow found its way to a place where it was acted on it.

As she sat at the kitchen table Toni's mind seemed to have been transported back to the night before. She saw Henry with the gun in his hand, he seemed to be glowing. But why was he so tall? She thought. Henry appeared to be very tall as she struggled to bring his arm down with the gun in his hand. The mental picture caused Toni to spring forward in the chair. Everything about Henry was different she remembered. If she didn't know any better, Toni thought, she could swear that it was not Henry who was holding the gun in his hand. Henry was dark skinned, but she remembered that he appeared to have a lighter complexion.

A cold chill ran through Toni's body and she shivered as she tried to analyze what she had seen the night before. Henry was about five foot eight or nine inches tall. She was five foot eleven inches tall. Then she remembered Henry's eyes as she had brought his arm down. Almost as in slow motion, Henry had turned his head to the right and his eyes had locked with hers. The eyes were very gentle, full of love and compassion, yet filled with what Toni could only see as innocence. The face was stern and the lips to the face were drawn taut. As she saw the eyes again in her mind, Toni saw the face of her cousin, Joseph. There were the freckles just lightly across the bridge of his nose, the light brown, almost hazel eyes and the little fuzz across his top lip. Toni's body shook as she stared into the face of a person who had died when she was only about Jeremiah's age.

Toni jumped up from the table and grabbed her cigarettes from her purse. She had broken out in a cold sweat, her armpits itched, and her hands shook uncontrollably. "How could that be?" she asked herself aloud. How could a dead man be standing before her holding a gun and kill another person. She poured herself another cup of coffee and wasted some of it on the counter because her hands were shaking violently by now.

Joseph was very tall as she remembered. He had always talked about playing professional basketball and was the star player for the local high school, before his death. People for many miles around and in several counties remembered Joseph Keith Spann.

Toni turned the eyes down low under the pots on the stove and leaned against the counter. As she tried to compose herself, all that she could see was the face of her cousin, Joseph. The light brown-skinned face with the freckles across the nose, the light eyes and the naturally even teeth, there was no doubt, it was Joseph she had seen and touched the night before. She could still see the wavy hair that lay flat around his head. Joseph would put some kind of pomade on his head then place a stocking cap made from the top of an old pair of their mother's stockings on his head to make the waves lie flat.

The kitchen seemed to get brighter and brighter and Toni's head felt light. She began to see little spots and became weak in the knees. Toni had forgotten to breathe as she relived the scenes from the night before. As she now panted for breath, the face of Joseph stayed before her mind's eyes and would not go away. Joseph had just turned seventeen when he died. He had lived with Toni and her family for as long as she could remember. Joseph's mother had left his father when he was just a toddler and moved to New York. Trudy, Toni's mother had watched over Joseph and took the responsibility of raising him because he did not have a mother. Even after Joseph's father had remarried, Joseph preferred to live with Toni's parents and no one had ever tried to make him move in with his father and stepmother.

Joseph had always been very close to Trudy and she had shown more than a little favoritism with him, but it didn't make anyone jealous. It was almost as though Joseph was Gertrude's first born, although he was just her nephew.

Joseph had been killed the summer before his senior year in high school in a car wreck with one of his friends. Joseph had told her father that he was just going up to the ball diamond with a few of his friends to watch a community baseball game. One of Joseph's friends came to the ball diamond driving his father's new Chevrolet Impala. Joseph and four other boys got into the car and they all went for a joy ride. Joseph was sitting in the backseat of the car as the boys enjoyed their ride in a new and popular car. Somehow the driver while speeding, did not slow down enough to manipulate the curve in the road. The car left the road hit several trees, flipped over killing the driver, Joseph and two of the other boys. The two survivors received numerous broken bones and lived only by the "grace of God," Toni's father had said.

When the telephone rang and the caller told Gertrude that they had heard that there had been a car wreck and they believed that Joseph had been in the car with the other boys, Gertrude had dropped the phone and began praying in tongues. Toni was a little girl, but she remembered how her mother had walked the floor praying and crying that Joseph was not in the car. Then the police came to their house, where Joseph's father and stepmother had come to await news. The police said that the wreck was bad and he believed that when the car flipped over, Joseph and the other boys were thrown from it and died almost instantly.

The entire community, Toni remembered was silent that night after the wreck. Four families were in mourning and an entire neighborhood in shock. Gertrude sat in the living room looking at all of Joseph's trophies, rocking back and forth and crying. She had never seen her mother so pitiful before. Even as a young girl, she remembered

72

trying to comfort her mother. Toni knew what the police meant when he had told her parents that Joseph was dead, she would never see him alive anymore.

At the wake, Toni remembered her mother getting up in the middle of the night after everyone had left the house and others were sleep. Wakes were still held in the home of the dead person. The casket holding Joseph's body stood along the wall just under the window. Toni looked in the living room and could see the casket holding Joseph's body. She saw the standing floral arrangement with the clock on it showing the time of Joseph's death. Trudy leaned over the casket to hug Joseph, then she saw her mother reach down and lift the stiff cold body of Joseph almost up out of the casket and held him in her arms like a baby and cried as she rocked him back and forth.

Toni realized that her mother's love for Joseph was the result of her own experience as a child. Trudy had been abandoned by her father and Joseph had been abandoned by his mother. Toni believed that her mother had also felt abandoned by her mother but because her mother had died and not walked away and left her, she could fully understand the abandonment. Toni remembered sitting on the floor that night watching her mother as she held Joseph talking to him and rocking his cold body back and forth in her arms. Her mother had laid Joseph's body back in the casket and smoothed the continental suit on his body. Trudy had insisted that Joseph's Stacy Adams shoes, which he had loved so much, be placed on his feet in the casket. The entire casket was open and no one had dared to speak against anything that Trudy had said, not even Joseph's father.

As Toni sat on the floor near the staircase her mother had walked past her as though she had not even seen her. Toni wondered, as she stood in the kitchen looking into the living room, had her mother been in her right mind that night. She wondered whether her mother's right mind had started its slow departure with the death of Joseph. But Toni was sure of one thing; she had seen and touched Joseph last night. For more than fifteen years she had not even had a dream of Joseph but she had both seen and touched him as he held a gun in his hand the night before.

For what seemed like hours, Toni stood and watched the spot in the living room where Joseph's casket had set so many years ago. Could Joseph have loved Trudy and them so much that his spirit would avenge what had been done to her? Toni did not understand it, but she did not question whether it was Joseph whom she had touched the night before, she knew that it was. She only questioned how could it have been so. Could a bond between the living and the dead be so strong that not even death could break it?

Toni was not confused about what she had seen and experienced the night before. She completely believed what she had experienced but did not understand her belief in the unbelievable. Tony also knew full well that no one would ever believe what she had witnessed. It was Joseph who held the pistol last night, it was his arm that she had pulled down from its position, and no one could ever make her believe differently.

The telephone startled Toni and she had to scramble to bring her mind back to where her body stood. It was Jeremiah calling to find out what she was doing. She assured her little brother that she was doing okay. She told Jeremiah that she was cooking dinner for him and when he came home that day he would have a big dinner waiting for him. Jeremiah wanted to know whether Henry would be there, too. Toni had to tell him the truth, that Henry would not be there with them for dinner, but soon he would be. The little boy sounded disappointed, but Toni did not want to give him false hopes.

Shortly Toni's Uncle Clifford was knocking on the door.

"Girl, you stinking the house, what time everything gonna be finished?" Clifford asked his niece.

"I'm gonna turn everything off while we're gone but it shouldn't be too long after we get back."

"That's one thing I can say about my nieces, you girls can cook just like your mama and grandmama. All of my brothers been blessed, though, they married women who can cook and their daughters can cook just as good as they mama."

"Jeremiah just called, he wanted to know whether Henry was gonna be here when he come home. I wasn't about to tell that little boy something that wasn't true, Uncle Clifford."

"That's right, babe, don't start lying and you won't have to apologize or try to explain it. Jeremiah has been through a lot in his young life. He wasn't three years old when my bubba died and Lord knows he couldn't understand that. Then with everything else that's happened, the little fellow probably so confused he don't know what's going on."

"Uncle Clifford, do you understand mama? I mean, you remember her from the first time she and daddy met and over the years could you really see her living a life like she living now?"

"No, babe, I don't understand it and I could never see this coming. Uh, huh, if somebody had told me that Trudy would do some of the things she's done, or even be involved with some of the people she's been involved with, I would've called them a liar to their face and probably smacked 'em."

"I've been trying to make heads or tails of all of this, Uncle Clifford and for the life of me I can't figure this thing out. Uncle Clifford, I'm tired of having to come home every time something goes wrong, and it's always something that mama has caused. Uncle Clifford, I work everyday and go to school at night, other than church, I don't have a social life. I want to get my education, I want to be a lawyer, Uncle Clifford, but I get all uptight and start wondering when is the next Gertrude fiasco gonna come."

As her uncle poured the coffee into his cup and began stirring in the sugar, he looked at his niece with eyes that were so sympathetic that they would have made trees bow down and weep their tears into milk bottles.

"Toni, there comes a time in our life when we have to know the things that we can change and the things that we cannot. Baby girl, all that we can do is the possible, God is the only one Who can do the impossible. You hear me? I ain't much on preaching the word of God, but there are things that I have read in that Bible that I know are true, well all of it's true, but I mean things that I have come to know from experience, is true. The Lord didn't assign nobody but Jesus on this earth to save other people. We have to just pray for people and make sure that we don't lose ourselves trying to save them. The devil is a tricky fellow and he'll do all he can to make sure that you and I don't do what God wants us to do, and he'll use even our family to do that. Trudy used to trust the Lord, babe, I don't know what happened. I used to envy the way she trusted the Lord. Trudy used pray with me and I couldn't believe the way that she was changing right before my eyes. Did you know that Trudy led me to the Lord and for that I will always be grateful, so I won't ever walk away from her and I'll always pray that she will find her way back to the Lord."

Toni sat and allowed the words of her uncle to enter her mind. No one had believed or had even imagined that her mother would become the person that she now was.

"Uncle Clifford, you know yesterday I called granddaddy before I left Connecticut, and I let him know what was going on. Granddaddy said that mama had this in her all of the time and that daddy was the person who had kept it from coming forward. Granddaddy said that he was not coming here because mama had told him not to darken her door, again."

"Well babe, I don't know what your granddaddy know, but I know he and your mama had some terrible arguments from the time I knew both of them. Trudy seemed to hate her daddy and couldn't forgive him for everything that she blamed him for, including her mama's death. I never understood that, but your granddaddy was always kind to me, and everybody else that I knew. I think he just got tired of trying to make things better between him and Trudy cause it was just one sided. When you've asked for forgiveness and done all you know to do, babe you can't do no more. Some of the things that I heard Trudy say to your granddaddy was so hurtful that I almost cried. But the old man just took it and walked away, and he took it for a long time, too. I don't think that the average person could have taken it that long, but for true he tried. So don't hold anything against him. Unforgiveness and bitterness more destructive than any force on earth, and your mama, I believe just got eaten up by what she wouldn't lay down. "

"No, I ain't holding nothing against granddaddy, I wish that I could understand mama more."

"Toni, there are some things we will never understand in this life. But I'm a firm believer that God will let us understand, one day. I know some things happened to me, right in my own family, it made me leave here and say that I would never come back. During those years, God prepared me to get an understanding. Sometime we ain't ready to know or understand, you know what I mean?"

"I think so."

"So God just let us go off somewhere so He can get us to the place where we can understand what happened. But I'm gonna tell you this much, child, you follow your dream and let the Lord handle all of this. I know you concerned about your brothers and sisters, but the Lord can take better care of them than you and me. Sometimes we just gotta go through some stuff in order to be what the Lord want us to be. Iron sharp iron, babe, don't you ever forget that, God toughen us according to His plan, not somebody else's. I'm here and I'll look after Jeremiah and the other kids, but you get your education and don't let nothing turn you around. You hear me, Toni?"

As the young woman looked at her uncle she could see the tears in his eyes. Toni knew that there was wisdom in what her uncle had said and if she ever wanted to see her dreams come true she would have to follow his advice.

"Baby girl, sometimes we just have to leave things alone and let them ride itself out. Things sometimes, not just sometimes, but most of the time, will die out if we just learn how to let them pass. You just remember that you cannot bottle up a hurricane, just get out of the way, grab hold of something until it passes, then try to salvage what it left behind."

11

The uncle and niece sat in quiet for a few minutes then Toni turned off the stove and went upstairs to get dressed to go to the hospital to see her mother.

As she walked down the hospital corridor to where she had been told her mother's room was, Toni remembered why she did not like hospitals. Hospitals had a smell that she could not get out of her system for days. A sterile smell, but a peculiar smell that was so different from any smell in the world.

Clifford walked quietly just to the side of his niece with his hat in his hand, twisting it around. As they entered the room, Trudy was turned toward the window looking out.

"Well, oh girl, the doctor said you can get up and go home and cook dinner." Clifford said.

Trudy rolled over and smiled shyly at Clifford and Toni, but avoiding eye contact with them.

"How you feeling?" Toni coyly asked her mother.

"I'm okay, but I don't think I can cook dinner, today."

"Well I've taken care of that." Toni said as she drew closer to her mother's bed.

Clifford pulled up a chair so that he could be closer. Toni looked at her mother and for a few seconds was overtaken with doubt about whether she should even tell her about what had happened. Toni looked over at her uncle and widened her eyes. Clifford sat with his hat in his hand twirling it around and around like it was a top. He appeared to be as nervous as Toni. Trudy was not able to maintain eye contact with either of them. But Toni knew that she had to do what she and Clifford had come to do.

"Mama, Henry is in jail, the police arrested him last night."

Trudy looked at Toni in shock. "In jail for what?" She snapped.

"Henry killed Isiah Henderson last night behind the house."

Trudy looked like she had seen a ghost or had been hit in the stomach by an unseen boxer, then groaned. The tears rushed forth from her eyes like two small geysers. Clifford got up and touched her hand.

"What do you mean, Henry killed him?" She asked.

"Isiah sneaked up on Henry while he, Lloyd and Jeremiah were sitting on the front porch. Isiah tried to kill Henry. Henry fought with Isiah. Isiah tried to shoot Henry, but Henry shot back and killed him as he was running away."

"Now I told all of y'all that if something happened between me and somebody else that it was my business and I would handle it. If Isiah was trying to get away, why Henry just didn't let him go on about his business?"

"Mama, did you hear me, Isiah sneaked up on Henry, he was trying to kill Henry." Toni tried to explain.

"Didn't you just say he was trying to get away and that's when Henry shot him?" Trudy asked.

Toni felt the fury of a million waves of anger rise up within her. For the first time in her life she wanted to slap her mother. Angry, Toni stood at the bedside waiting for her mother to ask about Henry. But all that she heard was the whimper of her tears for a dead man.

"Trudy, Isiah called the house yesterday and told Henry that he was 'next.' It would have been one thing if he had not shown up at the house. But it became another something when he sneaked up on Henry in the dark with a pistol." Clifford said.

"But he didn't shoot Henry, all Henry had to do was let him go, if he was already leaving." Trudy rationalized.

"He should not have even come there in the first place, Trudy." Clifford said. "If I had been there when he sneaked up round there, I would have killed him my dam self before I let him kill my nephew." Clifford said angrily, and left the room.

Toni stood at her mother's bedside, waiting, but not exactly sure of what she was waiting for. Her mother never asked about Henry and cried instead for the man who had tried to kill her and her son. Toni was angry, but she would not leave, she seemed to be waiting to give her mother an opportunity to redeem herself, but there seemed not to be a moment of redemption forthcoming. But anger made Toni wait even longer, staring at her mother and in silent demanding that she say something that would show that she loved her son more than the man who had tried to kill her. Toni waited because she needed to hear something from her mother that would give her hope that they, all of the children meant more to her mother than a man that she had slept with and who had tried to kill her and her son.

Toni felt a sharp pain in her jaw. She had clenched her teeth so tightly in anger that she did not realize that she was also grinding them. Not only had she gritted her teeth, Toni tasted the blood in her mouth and realized that she bitten the sides of her cheek and tongue. The anger that had flared up within her was so great that it took every bit of restraint that she could muster to keep from slapping her mother. Toni heard herself speak, but the voice was not hers.

"Lord, help me Jesus."

"The Lord ain't got nothing to do with this, Henry did this on his own." She heard her mother say. "Where Henry got a gun from anyway. If he didn't have a gun none of this would've happened."

"I for one am glad that he did have a gun. If he didn't he would be the one laying on a cooling board this morning rather than Isiah. Did you tell the police who shot you, mama?" Toni asked. "Maybe if you had, Henry wouldn't be in jail this morning. But I'm glad he's in jail rather than in the morgue. Let Isiah just go to hell where he belongs anyway. I thank God that he didn't take anybody there with him. We could have been making funeral arrangements today for you, as well. I got to go take care of your children so I'll see you tomorrow." Toni said as she walked out of the hospital room.

Clifford was sitting in the waiting area with his head down. Toni walked over to her uncle and sat down.

"Uncle Clifford, I was so mad at mama that I could have slapped the hot pee out of her. Mama done lost her mind, Uncle Clifford. You know she never asked me how Henry was or anything. She didn't even ask about Jeremiah or any of the kids."

"I know, babe. That boy did something evil to Trudy, and now he's gone to wherever people like him go to. She put that Isiah ahead of her own flesh and blood. My skin crawled listening to Trudy just now. Oh yes, something is wrong here. I don't like this one bit and I'm sure God ain't please either. I wanted to grab Trudy and shake her back to her natural senses. That's why I had to walk out of that room. Trudy in her own little messed up world."

"Uncle Clifford, if I was to say to Henry or any of the kids what I just saw, they would all probably just leave home and never come back. I don't understand how a mother can forget about her children. Mama ain't the least bit concerned about Henry. When Henry get out of jail he's got to come back there and live in the same house with a person who probably so mad at him that she won't stand for him to be around."

"Well Henry ain't got to worry about where he'll live, as long as I got a place to live, he got one, too. Trudy got to get herself together. That boy done took another man's life for her and she's got the nerve to be mad at him. Isiah could have killed Henry, or Henry could have been laid up in a bed in this hospital, too. But Trudy mind so messed up now that she can't even see anything. Only God can take care of this, babe. Do the best you can, but don't stop living, don't stop living cause anybody else done stop. God hold you accountable for what you do, not what other people around you do, or what they do to you. Go on back to Connecticut and get your education. When Trudy ready to change, she'll have to do it, not you, me or anybody else."

Toni knew in her heart that what she was hearing was true. It didn't matter what she or the kids did or suffered, her mother was a strong-willed person and she alone was responsible for her actions.

As Toni and her uncle walked down the corridor to the elevator, she was filled with a new resolve about her family situation. The urge to cry no longer surfaced. Toni's will seemed to stiffen under the pressure of the circumstance. It started to bubble up in her that she had to stop running up and down the road trying to resolve or assist in any and everything that came up regarding her mother. She realized that she just might be aiding and abetting her mother because she jumped on the first thing smoking headed south when there was any difficulty. This, Toni thought, just might be another form of attention that her mother enjoyed and it did nothing to eliminate the potential for more of the same.

By the time Toni and her uncle pulled up at the house, she could see Wilson sitting on the porch and knew that Lloyd had brought them all back home. Alma pulled up right behind Clifford's car.

"I timed myself just right." Alma said as she got out of the car. "How you doing Uncle Clifford?" she asked.

"I'm just doing right now, Miss Magnolia. How you doing?"

"I'm okay, sir."

Alma walked ahead of Clifford and Toni and sat on the banister talking to Wilson. Wilson seemed to be so saddened by everything that had happened. Clifford looked at Wilson and laid his hand on Wilson's shoulder and told him that they were Spanns, and Spann men stood strong through the storms. Wilson said "yes, sir," with his mouth, but his tone and demeanor said something far from what his mouth had.

As Toni walked into the living room Jeremiah was sitting on the sofa with his school book bag.

"What you doing sweetie?" Toni asked.

"I got to do my homework for school tomorrow. The teacher say we have to do these words cause we gonna have a spelling contest. You'll help me, Toni?" he asked.

"Yeah, I'll help you. When you're through studying or doing whatever you got to do, let me know and we can start practicing, okay."

"Okay, cause I wanna get a hundred. You gonna get me something to wear to school tomorrow, too?" He asked.

"Yes, pumpkin, I'll get you something to wear to school. You wanna wear anything in particular?"

"No, just something nice. Toni, if the teacher ask me about mama, what you think I should say?"

Toni was stunned for a few seconds. Jeremiah's mind had been concentrating on all of the things that had happened. Toni had hoped that her little brother would not think about those things. But she determined that she would answer any questions truthfully to the point of understanding for a seven-year old.

"If she ask you anything Jeremiah, just tell her your mama's doing okay, she's still in the hospital but she can call me here at the house. Okay?"

"Okay, but what if she ask me about Henry?"

"You just tell her to call me. Don't even try to answer any of her questions, baby. I don't think that your teacher will ask you anything, at all. But if she does, Jeremiah, I want you to tell her to call me."

"Okay, whatever you say."

Alma had been standing in the door while Toni and Jeremiah were talking. Alma just looked at Jeremiah and smiled. Toni went into the kitchen and turned the stove on to complete her cooking. Alma began helping Jeremiah with his homework.

"Hi darling, did you enjoy spending the night over at Lloyd's house?" Alma asked.

"Oh yeah, but I fell asleep and couldn't see the rest of the late movie. Now that made me mad, cause it was a good movie, Alma."

"I bet it was. I don't get a hug from you, today, Jerry? You know I gotta have my kiss from you so I can feel better."

Jeremiah stood up and wrapped his arms around Alma's neck. Alma was on her knees so that she could stand about as tall as Jeremiah. She hugged the little boy and rocked him from side to side in her arms. Jeremiah just kept his arms wrapped around Alma's neck. It looked like it gave him a lot of comfort. Toni smiled, she knew that Jeremiah would be okay when she was not around. Since Alma's son was about the same age as Jeremiah, Toni felt confident that Alma would include him in the things that she did with her own son.

Alma walked into the kitchen and started a fresh pot of coffee.

"Where's Uncle Clifford?" Toni asked Alma.

"He and Wilson got in the car and left. He said to call him at his house just before you serve dinner. Wilson seems to be taking this hard, Toni and there ain't nothing we can do about it but pray and ask the Lord to ease the pain on his heart. I want to tell you this here, because the telephone call came to my mama just before I walked out the door."

Alma had a serious, but an angry look on her face as she drew a little closer to where Toni was standing. Toni's heart seemed to drop a little lower from the place where hearts usually sit.

"Mama got this call from Miss Anna who live next door to your mama friend, Miss Clara. Miss Anna must have been at Miss Clara's house getting her little Sunday nip. But anyway, Miss Trudy called Miss Clara to get some more information about what happened last night. Miss Anna, who you know mama cannot stand, told mama that she couldn't believe that Miss Trudy was trying to find out about last night."

"Girl, you mean to tell me that she called Miss Clara and can't even call her own house to check on her kids?" Toni was getting angrier by the seconds.

"Wait a minute Toni. So mama asked Miss Anna why was she calling her and that she should let what she got in other people's house stay right there. Then mama went on tell her that she should be trying to learn from what happened to Miss Trudy and get her life in perfect order. Mama told her that she didn't have no room to be pointing fingers cause if Miss Roberta caught her with Deacon Hill she could be the one in the hospital next or dead. Girl, I don't know whether Miss Anna hung up the phone first or mama. Mama was hot under the collar, honey and started cussing and saying something about all of them backdoor whores making her sick."

Toni and Alma laughed at Alma's mother's comments. But Toni was still hurt about her mother's behavior.

"Alma, you know we tried to tell mama about last night and mama mad with Henry."

"What the hell she mad with Henry about? Henry sitting in jail today because of her."

"That's what I said, too. But mama said that she told everybody that if anything happened between her and somebody else that she would take care of it. Then she said that if Isiah was running away, Henry should have just let him go on about his business."

Alma had the coffee cup up to her mouth, but she couldn't take a sip because she was almost in shock. Margaret was standing in the kitchen and heard what Toni had said.

"You mean to tell me that she think more about the sucker that tried to kill her ass than she did about the child that she pushed out of her womb? Now ain't that bitch for you?" Margaret said as the tears ran down her face. "My brother sitting in jail for killing a man who hurt his mama and all she can say is that Henry should have let him go on about his business. Isiah's business was to kill Henry. Did you tell her that he called here to tell Henry that he was next?" Margaret asked.

"Yeah, Uncle Clifford told her."

"And what did she have to say about that?"

"She wanted to know where Henry had gotten the gun, cause if he didn't have the gun none of this would have happened."

"Did you slap her ass, Toni?" Margaret asked.

"No, Margaret, but I came dam close to knocking mama on her ass, today. Uncle Clifford had to walk out of the room. But before he left, he told mama that if he had been here, he would have killed Isiah his dam self before he allowed him to kill his nephew. I just told mama that I was glad that Henry had a gun because if he didn't he could have been the one on the cooling board in the morgue today rather than in jail. At least in jail we don't have to sing over his body and plan a funeral."

"Then what she say?" Margaret asked.

"I don't know, Margaret, I left and told her that I would see her tomorrow because I had to go take care of her children."

Alma was shaking her head in disbelief. She sat the coffee cup down and walked to the back door. She asked if she could open the back door because she felt like she couldn't breathe. Margaret walked over and opened the door and patted Alma on the back.

"You okay, girl? I don't want you flaking out on us now." Margaret said.

"I'm okay, Margaret, but I ain't okay with what I'm hearing. I had a pain to hit me right in my heart. Toni, Margaret, I'm telling y'all, that Isiah put roots on Miss Trudy. I know something is devilish about all of this." Alma looked like she was going to faint.

"Alma, I've been watching mama going on like this for more than five years now and it's getting worse. I'm just sick of it; I'm telling you I'm just sick and tired of all this mess with mama. Since she hooked up with that Isiah, man I'm telling you, she's gotten down right ridiculous." Margaret said.

"Y'all know Lorraine and them over there by the schoolhouse? You see what happened to their mama and daddy; they divorced now because of Isiah. But guess what, Lorraine mama ain't never had nothing to do with Isiah. Everybody whisper about what happened but all of them know that Isiah did something to break that family up." Alma said, almost in a whisper.

"Sure you right, Alma, tell the truth." Margaret said. "Now I know something devilish went on there. Miss Frances stopped mama one time when we were in the shopping center and she asked mama if she was seeing Isiah. Mama got all huffy and acting like she had all the answers to life in her bosom. But, y'all, I remember Miss Frances saying to mama, 'Trudy, I ain't trying to get all in your business, but you deserve better. Isiah got a black heart and he don't care about nobody but himself, he is the devil personified. She almost begged mama to cut him loose before it was too late. I heard it y'all, then Miss Frances went on to tell mama about how Isiah had messed up Lorraine and them family. Isiah wanted their mama to have an affair with him and she put him in his place and told him to not ever disrespect her husband or approach her again."

"Margaret, you mean to tell me that Miss Frances told mama, as well, and she just kept right on messing with that fool?" Toni asked.

"Toni, this is the God in heaven truth, mama think everybody is jealous of her, or she just got to be the person with the spotlight on her. Toni, sometimes I'm so ashamed when I go to work that I just hold my head down and go on and do what they pay me for. We can't really go nowhere cause mama already been there and acted a fool."

Alma hung her head as Margaret spoke to Toni through flowing tears.

"Toni, one night me and one of my old elementary school buddies hooked up and decided that we would go out and have us a good time. So we decided to drive a little piece down the road and across the bridge. We stopped in the joint for about five minutes and scoped it out and decided that we would drive to Charleston and go to the Merchant Seaman Lounge, on East Bay Street. Girl, as we walked out the door, this crazy looking Negro grabbed me by the neck and put this pistol in my face. I thought that I was dead. This fool claimed that me and some red girlfriend of mine were at the club and told his girlfriend some mess about him."

"Margaret you never told me this before. How long ago was this?" Toni asked.

"It was right around the Christmas holidays. Well, anyway, I tried to explain to this fool that I did not know who he was talking about. He just kept saying 'that old red girlfriend of yours with the big titties.' Toni, I knew he was talking about mama and Miss Clara, and even though I'm way younger than mama, I look like her. He thought that I was mama. Alma's cousin, Lil John came up about that time and asked this fool what was he doing? Lil John explained to him that he definitely had the wrong person. Lil John told the guy that he was getting ready to go to jail cause I was a high school girl and he knew who I was. Lil John told him to take a good look at me, cause he had me pegged wrong. The guy started apologizing and asking me to forgive him. But Toni, I knew that it was mama and Miss Clara he was talking about. I came on back home."

Toni was so angry by now that she could barely see. Her brothers and sisters were going through hell because of their mother.

"Margaret, did you tell mama about that?"

"Yes, I did, and she acted like it wasn't nothing. The next thing I knew, she was on the telephone with Miss Clara laughing and telling her that they had gotten this guy."

"Say what?" Alma snapped. "She thought that it was funny that this guy had put a pistol in your face because of what she and that Clara had done?"

"She sure did, Alma. Mama didn't seem to care that I had almost gotten killed because of her and Miss Clara. Toni, I hate to say this but it's how I feel, I almost hate mama. I can't stay here with her anymore. Henry in jail now because of her, Wilson has had to jump into fights because of her, only God knows where Aaron Junior is now, he just got so tired of it he just left and didn't tell anybody where he was going. And still, mama can't cool down and see what she's causing for everybody. I got to get out of here. I hate to leave the rest of the kids, but Toni, I feel like I'll hurt mama or she'll hurt me if I stay here any longer. Lloyd and me getting married tomorrow."

Toni didn't just sit in the chair she dropped into it when she heard Margaret. Alma couldn't close her mouth. Alma tried to tell Margaret not to get married just to get out of her mother's house but to just get a small place of her own. But Margaret assured Alma that she and Lloyd had talked about getting married before and now was just as good a time as any, but she was definitely not going to be there when her mother came home from the hospital.

There were no words that Toni could utter from her lips. She sat in the chair and looked out the backdoor. She stretched out her legs so that the warm sun could penetrate her skin and warm up the blood that had begun to run cold in her veins. It was as though the world had stopped turning on its axis. Toni could no longer hear any sounds. She could not even see Alma and Margaret who were in the same room with her; everything seemed to have just stopped. Then she felt someone tugging on her hand.

"Toni, Toni, you hear me, Toni?" Jeremiah asked.

It took Toni a little while to refocus and remember where she was. "What you need, Jeremiah?" she finally asked.

"I'm ready for you to help me with my words for tomorrow."

"Okay, sweetie, just give me about ten minutes, okay." Toni replied.

"Okay. When we gonna eat, Toni?" Jeremiah asked.

"It won't be too much longer Jerry. We'll spell some words before we eat and we'll spell some more when we're finished, how's that?"

"All right. Sound like a winner to me."

The little boy walked away happy. But Alma and Margaret were staring at Toni like she had just landed on earth from another planet.

"Toni," Alma asked, staring at her, "are you okay?"

"Yeah, why?" Toni asked.

"For a while you looked like you had stopped breathing. We were talking to you and you just had a blank stare on your face. Jerry kept talking to you and you acted like you didn't hear him either. I was about to dial 9-1-1." Alma said.

"No, I'm okay, really, I'm okay." Toni said. But even she was not fully convinced that she was okay. Toni knew that something had happened to her but she didn't know what. Things were a little strange in her mind and she did not know what was happening to her.

"I'm going upstairs and pack my stuff, Toni. I'll look out for the kids when you leave. Wilson is out of school now, this is Joyce's last year and Jeremiah is the only left who can't defend himself, but I'll take him with me and Lloyd, so mama can do whatever she wants to. If she wanna drink herself to death that's her business."

"Okay, I'm gonna finish cooking so I can feed everybody. Where is Joyce now?" Toni asked Margaret.

"She's upstairs in her room looking at television. You want me to tell her come down here?"

"No, just let her alone."

Alma was staring at her friend. She was more than a little concerned now about Toni's mental health. Alma thought that the situation had worn Toni down. More than anything, Alma wanted for her friend, was peace of mind. Alma decided that the best thing that she could do for her friend now was just to be there. If Toni wanted to talk or just to blow off some steam, she decided that she would be there to listen.

Toni checked the pots and the oven and began turning the jets on the stove even lower than before. Alma knew that things were near done and it wouldn't be long before Toni would set the table for her family. Alma reached up on the wall for the phone and called her mother to let her know that she was still with Toni. Alma told her mother that Toni had cooked up a lot of food. Alma gave Toni the phone.

"How you doing sweetie?" Toni said to Alma's mother. "I'm hanging right in there. Oh I cooked some of everything, candied sweets, pork roast, stew beef, macaroni and cheese, potato salad, cabbage, cornbread, peach cobbler, rice and a few other things. You can have whatever your little heart desire, sweetie, cause I cooked enough to feed the Naval Base. Okay, I'll send you and Troy a plate right now. No mam, just send my bowls right back. Get out your bowls so you can pour the stuff in them and send the bowls right back. You want to Cole slaw, too? Okay girlfriend, I know everything mean everything, I'm getting older and just a little slower." Toni laughed with Alma's mother and hung up.

"Girl, mama was determined that she wasn't cooking today, but get herself a meal anyway." Alma laughed.

"Well she said to tell you not to let her food get cold before you brought it to her."

Toni fixed several containers and put them in a large Winn Dixie bag for transport to Alma's mother. Alma hurriedly took the large bag to her car. Toni called her uncle and told him that it was time to eat and that he and Wilson should start for the house.

As Toni checked the oven once again to see whether the second pan of corn bread was browning, Jeremiah came behind her and tapped her on the shoulder.

"Can I eat now Toni? I'm hungry."

"Yeah sweetie, you can eat now. What you want on your plate?" she asked the little boy.

"I want a spoonful of everything."

"Okay, sir, wash your hands and a plate with a spoonful of everything will be ready by the time you get back."

Jeremiah went around the corner to the bathroom to wash his hands and Toni began fixing a plate for him and one for herself. Jeremiah sat at the table swinging his legs and watching his big sister.

"I love you, Toni."

"I love you, more." She replied.

"Nope, I love you three times more." Jeremiah said.

"Well, I love you three times more than that. What you got to say about that?"

Jeremiah laughed and pinched Toni on the arm as she placed the plate in front of him. She set her place as well and went to the refrigerator to get them something to drink. Toni asked Jeremiah to say the grace and the two of them sat at the table eating and talking. She asked Jeremiah to get his spelling words so they could go over them while they ate. So they ate and spelled words until Alma walked back into the house. Within minutes of Alma walking in, Clifford and Wilson walked through the living room.

"It sure smell good up in here." Wilson said as he headed to the bathroom to wash his hands.

Soon everybody was downstairs fixing a plate. Alma took off her shoes and loosened the buttons on her shorts. Everybody was glad that Toni had cooked.

"Toni, you must have cooked ten pounds of potatoes to make all of this potato salad." Wilson said. "You must be expecting the U.S.S. Everglades over here."

"No, I knew you and that long belly of yours would be here." Toni laughed.

"Yes, mam, you fixed Wilson this time, he's got to look at the food because it's too much for him to eat in one day." Joyce said.

Joyce pointed her nose at Margaret and smiled. "I guess a certain party can't talk because she's too glad that she don't have to eat her own cooking today."

Everybody started laughing and looked at Margaret. Margaret raised her head from her plate and cut her eyes at Joyce.

"I ain't studying you today, Joyce, I'm gonna enjoy my dinner. You better talk to the girl, Uncle Clifford before she mess up our good thing." Margaret said.

Clifford looked over at Joyce and laughed. "I can't do too much talking right now because Wilson didn't say that he was finished yet. If I slow down for conversation there might not be enough left for me to take a plate home for later."

Everybody, including Jeremiah laughed.

"I told you Wilson was hog, Toni, and everybody know it."

Toni smiled at Jeremiah, "no, he's not a hog, he's got a real healthy appetite, that's all."

"Yeah, his appetite is so healthy that he eat until he get sick." Margaret responded.

The laughter rang out around the table. Wilson had to laugh as well, although he was the brunt of the joke.

"Y'all just jealous cause you can't digest the food as fast as I do." Wilson snapped back.

"That's the problem with you, the food don't digest, it just pass straight through you." Joyce said. "Look, if you don't mind, tonight please use the bathroom at the Shell service station, we want to sleep without being suffocated." Joyce said. Everybody burst into laughter. Alma laughed until tears rolled out of her eyes. Wilson looked at Alma and asked why she thought that was so funny. But she continued to laugh as though her tickle box had tipped over. Wilson began to tease Alma about her silent and lethal passing of gas which made her laugh even more.

Everybody had eaten as much as they wanted. Toni asked Margaret and Joyce to put the food away and wash the dishes. Toni and Alma sat out on the back steps and just talked about the future. Toni heard Lloyd come and she told him that there was plenty food and to fix himself a plate. Wilson heard Lloyd downstairs and he came downstairs and fixed himself another plate; he said that he was being polite so Lloyd wouldn't have to eat alone.

Toni made sure that everybody was in bed and she sat downstairs and watched television, alone. She knew that tomorrow she would be busy trying to get an attorney for Henry. As she lay on the sofa in the den watching television, Toni began to cry softly. First she cried for herself, then her siblings. Soon, Toni found herself crying for her mother who seemed not to have a clue about what her children were going through. She prayed that God would protect her family and keep them healthy and alive. She thought about Aaron Junior and wondered where he might be. He had been so ashamed of his mother's behavior and life style that he left and did not tell anyone where he was going. Toni remembered one of her older cousins saying that boys were different than girls in how they accepted the behavior of their mothers, and that Aaron was sensitive.

The television wasn't really being watched by Toni, she just had it on so she would not have to listen to the voice of silence. Other than the television, the house was silent.

Toni prayed that daylight would come soon or sleep would overtake her and when she awoke no darkness would be seen. But for now all that she could do is stare at the television or in the direction from where it sat and think. How she wished that her father had not died. Toni thought that if her father was alive none of the problems they had encountered since the day of his burial would have arisen. Maybe, just maybe, she thought, her father's spirit was somewhere around them and his love for them would keep him there.

Toni felt the room closing in on her and the loneliness of having to do what needed to be done became so overwhelming that she slammed her face into the pillow and cried.

The telephone woke Toni from her sleep. The last thing she remembered was slamming her face into the pillow to cry after a feeling of loneliness and despair overtook her. She didn't remember falling asleep but now was in a bit of a panic as the telephone rang again. As she got up from the sofa to answer the telephone she saw that it was daylight, that which she had last hoped for. It was Alma calling to wake her up so that she could get the kids up and ready for school. Alma was already at work.

12

Toni looked in the pantry to see whether there was grits so that she could prepare a hot and wholesome breakfast for Jeremiah and Joyce before they left for school. There was the blue and white bag sitting in the back like it had been hiding. Toni grabbed a small pot and poured the grits in and took it to the sink to add water and salt. After covering the pot and turning the eye on the stove down low, Toni called upstairs to wake Jeremiah and Joyce.

After a few minutes of silence, Toni decided to go upstairs and wake the children. There was Jeremiah curled up in a fetal position in his mother's bed. He must have gotten out of his own bed during the night and gotten into hers. Before Toni could start down the hall, Joyce came out of her room and walked across the hall to the bathroom.

"Good morning, Missy, how you doing today?" Toni asked.

"Morning. I'm so-so, how about yourself?" Joyce replied.

"Well, I've seen better days, darling, hopefully, more of them are ahead of me."

As she walked into the bathroom, Joyce stopped and looked at her big sister. "Toni, I don't wanna go to school today, can I stay home?" She asked.

"How many weeks of school do you have left, Joyce?"

"About two and a half."

"Please try to hang on for that time, Joyce. You've got one more year before you graduate, then you don't have to go through it anymore. I know it's not easy, especially since everybody knows what happened. But put your head up and your chest out, this too shall pass."

"You know what, Toni?" Joyce said as she leaned against the wall.

"Uh, uh, what, sweetie?"

"I'm beginning to lose my feelings. All of that that happened this weekend, Henry is the only one that I really feel sorry for. No mother should do things that would get her children locked up or even hurt. You know what I mean?"

"Yes, I do, Joyce. But something in my spirit is telling me that mama got a problem that none of us know anything about. What we might be seeing ain't really the problem, although it's causing a lot of problems for us. But there is something deep down inside mama that she needs to get out before it kills her or get somebody else killed."

"Toni, I'm just afraid that mama's gonna be the one that dies next, if she don't straighten up. When is she coming home from the hospital, anyway?"

"I don't know, maybe today or tomorrow."

"I'm sorry to say it, Toni, but this house has had a different feeling in it with mama gone."

"How do you mean, Joyce?"

"Well, I haven't felt that feeling of things closing in on me, or like being in the middle of a lot evil. I didn't have to inch around the house trying to avoid mama getting mad at me about something and getting all up in my face then slapping me in it."

"If it gets too bad Joyce and you just can't take anymore, let me know and I'll send for you to come to Connecticut with me and finish school. Okay?"

Joyce walked into the bathroom and sat on the side of the bathtub. Toni could see the tears falling from her eyes and hitting the floor. Joyce rested her chin on her chest and stared down at the floor. Toni's heart was broken because she did not know what to do and she was hurting just as much as Joyce and the other children. Toni walked into the bathroom and sat beside Joyce on the edge of the bathtub. No words were spoken between the baby sister and the big sister. Toni just placed her hand on Joyce's back and rubbed it.

Joyce's face bore all of the signs of a teenager who had seen and been through more than she could bear. Toni knew that she had to become and look like the rock of Gibraltar for her siblings. No words of comfort or reassurance would come from her lips so Toni told Joyce she had to check the pot and went downstairs where she shed a few tears in private. Toni then went back upstairs to her mother's bedroom to get Jeremiah up.

"Jeremiah, get up sweetie, its time for school."

The tired little boy opened his eyes and looked around the room before he spoke. "Where you sleep at Toni?"

"I fell asleep downstairs watching television. Why?"

"I tried to wait for you to come upstairs, but I went to sleep." Jeremiah said as he crawled off the bed. "I gotta pee, wait a minute." He scampered off to the bathroom ignoring Joyce who was in the shower.

Toni went downstairs to get breakfast ready. She had almost forgotten about Wilson and had not thought to knock on his door. Maybe he would hear the others and get up. As she pulled out the frying pan, Toni thought about Margaret. She had packed her things the night before and went home with Lloyd. There wasn't much that Toni could do about that, Margaret was an adult.

No one had spoken to Henry since he was arrested Saturday night, now Toni had to get an attorney and get his defense started. As she thought about the many things that she had to do today, Toni grew angry. She was angry with her mother, she was angry with Isiah, although he was dead, she was angry with her father who was also dead, why did he have to die and leave them.

As she stared out of the window and wondered again about Aaron Junior, she got angry with him for just leaving and not telling anyone where he was. It had been more than a year since anyone had heard from or seen Aaron Junior. He just got up one day and left, no hints about where he was going or anything. No one knew or suspected anything. Aaron just said that he could not stand it anymore. He could not bear to see his mother destroy her life and maybe his, anymore. Many times Aaron Junior had said that he felt like just beating his mother until she came to her natural senses. But he knew that if he raised his hand to his mother his life would be doomed.

As Toni fried the bacon, she felt like she was not alone in the kitchen. She turned around to see whether Wilson had come downstairs and she had not heard him, but no one was there. Still, there was a feeling of someone being present. The feeling did not frighten Tony, but the sense of someone being there in the kitchen with her was very strong. As Tony turned the bacon she smelled the scent of Old Spice, the after shave lotion her father used. Maybe, she thought, it was Wilson who had gotten up and also used Old Spice. As she walked toward the refrigerator, Toni saw a flash of light, then what looked like a person who had just run swiftly past. She missed the handle on the refrigerator door. Toni stood and stared at the spot where she thought that she had seen someone run past.

Toni thought that her mind was playing tricks on her this morning. So she began to pray silently and compose herself so that she could get Joyce and Jeremiah fed and off to school. This was Monday and she had to see Henry, as well as get an attorney for him. She also had to get to the hospital and see her mother. She began to feel just a little overwhelmed by all that she had to do. How would she go about choosing a lawyer for

Henry, how would she know that she had the right one? The questions began to flood her mind and failure began to overtake her.

"Hello."

"Toni, how you doing, this morning?" Kim asked.

"For a moment, girl, I thought that I was being pulled under by all that I gotta do today." Toni replied.

"Oh, no, girlfriend, don't go under. Henry needs you now. I got the whole church praying and you know I'm praying for you guys, anyway."

"Thanks, Kim. I'm getting Joyce and Jeremiah some breakfast before they go to school this morning. Alma called earlier to make sure that I was up, so I'm doing the best I can."

"Well that's all you can do, Toni, and don't let nobody tell you that you can do more. You can only do the possible, God specializes in the impossible."

"You know what, Kim, something strange has been going on here, girl. You gonna think I'm crazy if I tell it to you, but when I get back there, I'll tell you."

"I'm learning, Toni, that real life is more eerie than make believe, so I don't think you're crazy. But don't forget to just trust the Lord in everything, even when you don't understand. Pastor said yesterday that there'll be many things that we don't understand in this life, but at the time we just ain't prepared to understand. But God will reveal it to us when He has prepared our hearts to receive the truth. So don't spend a lot of time, like Pastor said, trying to figure something out because God in those situations has already worked it out."

"I guess I understand that part of not understanding. But like the old folks used to say, 'we'll understand it better, by and by.' Thanks Kim for being my friend, I really appreciate having you and Alma there with me."

"Toni, I told you before, not only can you lean on me, I'll carry you too, when you can't walk. I mean that, girl, God knows I do, so don't fret about things, just do what you can do and let God's plan work itself. Look, I love girl, but I got to go to work, okay?"

"Love you, too, Kim, have a good day now. By."

Toni felt a little more strengthened inside now that she talked to both of her dearest friends. She felt almost assured that if she had not had friends praying for her that she would have lost her mind by now.

Wilson came downstairs and asked whether Toni had cooked enough for him to have a little breakfast before he went to work.

"A little breakfast? Boy you know you don't eat a little bit of anything. I made enough for all of us, sit down and I'll fix you a plate."

As Toni fixed Wilson's breakfast she asked him what kind of cologne he was wearing. Wilson said that he wasn't wearing any cologne or after-shave lotion. Toni was curious and wondered what she had smelled.

"Wilson, I was standing here in the kitchen and smelled that old spice after-shave that daddy used to wear. I'm telling you the smell was so strong that I thought I felt somebody in here with me."

Wilson looked at Toni without any astonishment in his eyes. "I was in my room, just a few minutes ago and I smelled daddy, too. It was like he was standing right there in the room with me."

"Come on, Wilson, you too?" Toni said.

"I ain't kidding you, Toni. I was like trying to decide whether I was going to work or stay around here and you know, help you do what needed to be done. Then all of a sudden it was like somebody came right past me and I smelled that cologne daddy used to wear. Then something just said go to work. I can't explain it, Toni, but I felt daddy so strong up there, I knew he was close. The dead got a way of knowing when things ain't right with their own on earth, I think daddy know that and he trying to protect us."

Toni put the plate before Wilson and poured herself some coffee. The two sat at the kitchen table in silence for a few minutes before Jeremiah came downstairs.

"I'm so hungry, Toni, I can eat a cow, if Wilson ain't eat it yet." Jeremiah said.

They laughed at Jeremiah's little joke and Wilson massaged Jeremiah's head.

"Well I ate the cow, so it look like you gonna starve little boy." Wilson said.

"No I ain't, I'll get a fork and eat some of what's on your plate, Mr. Pig."

"Oh so that's how you gonna live, Jerry, dangerous, huh? Eat off of my plate and expect to keep both of your hands?"

"Oh, Lord, I forgot, Wilson, you could eat my hand, too." Jeremiah said as he began laughing with his older brother. "That's alright, you can have all of everything on your plate."

"You studied all of your spelling words last night, Jerry?" Wilson asked.

"Uh, huh. Toni helped me, I can spell everything the teacher had on the paper. You'll see my grade when I come home today. Toni, you fixing me lunch, today?" Jeremiah asked.

"Here, buy some lunch from the cafeteria today." Wilson said as he gave Jeremiah a dollar bill.

"Keep the change, Wilson?" Jeremiah asked.

"Yeah, you can keep the change, but don't buy a lot of candy with it either, you hear me?"

"Uh, huh, but I can buy one candy?" Jeremiah asked.

"Yep, you can buy one little candy, after school."

"Thank you, sir, Mr. Wilson Spann." Jeremiah said as he smiled and ate his breakfast.

Toni was relieved that the little boy was in such good spirits this morning. The dollar that Wilson had given him to buy hot lunch at school was a royal treat. It was even more of a treat because he could keep the change and buy candy after school.

"Toni, what we gonna have for supper, today?" Jeremiah asked.

"Boy you're not finished with breakfast yet and asking about supper. You can't talk about Wilson being a pig anymore."

Jeremiah closed his eyes and smiled as he chewed. He was such a handsome little guy, Toni thought. All of the older siblings had assumed the role of parent in Jeremiah's life since their father died and their mother's life style seemed not to include being mother to a toddler. Toni prepared Joyce's plate and her own. The brothers and sisters sat at the kitchen table that morning eating breakfast and drilling Jeremiah on his spelling words. Jeremiah only missed one word, but Wilson made him say and spell the word seven times so that he would not forget it again.

Margaret, Henry and Aaron Junior were the only ones missing that morning. Joyce seemed to have perked up since Toni first talked to her that morning.

"It sure feels better in the house this morning. I don't mean that it's really okay, but there's a different atmosphere here. I wish that Margaret, A.J., and Henry were here, then everything would be good." Joyce said.

"How about mama, Joyce?" Jeremiah asked. No one looked up from their plate or answered Jeremiah's question. But Toni knew what Joyce meant. The years following their father's death had impacted all of their lives in ways that they could never have imagined. The change in their mother could not have been perceived by anything that they had seen or could have imagined.

This morning the children of Aaron Spann, Senior sat in different places, some known, others not, even one that now sat in jail, a murderer. A sudden and deep sadness fell upon the kitchen like a blanket of darkness. The temperature in the room even seemed to drop. Wilson got up and kissed Jeremiah and Joyce on their foreheads. He kissed Toni on the cheek and thanked her for breakfast.

Shortly after that, the house was silent and empty. Toni washed the dishes and cleaned the counters and the stove. She went upstairs to take a quick shower before her uncle came over. As she showered, a deep sorrow seemed to penetrate her and she cried as the water ran over body. She did not understand the sorrow and prayed that God would not allow any hurt, harm, or danger to come to her family, or herself. As she dried herself the phone rang. It was Clifford calling to let Toni know that he was on his way and for her to put on some coffee because he was stopping by Krispy Crème to pick up donuts.

Toni pulled out her suitcase and took out a blue pantsuit and matching shoes. She looked at the outfit trying to decide whether she really needed to iron it. It was a little wrinkled but she decided that no one could tell after she had put it on whether the wrinkles were from the beginning or had come after she had put it on.

Toni grabbed the telephone book and began to look in the yellow pages for lawyers. There were so many to choose from. Henry needed someone who handled criminal cases and would help to get him free. Clifford arrived with the donuts after Toni had showered and put on makeup. Usually, Toni made sure that her eyebrows were arched and put on lipstick and she was ready. But today she decided to do something extra, she did not want to look like she had been beaten down by the events of the weekend. She determined that anyone who saw her as she represented her family would see a near flawless young woman.

"You seen anybody in the phone book you want to get in touch with, baby girl?" Clifford asked.

"No sir. I don't really know who to call, Uncle Clifford, but I know that I need to call somebody quick so Henry can get out of that jail cell."

"Well, I ran into Roy Lucas, boy, Jimmy, this morning at the donut shop."

"Wait a minute, he's the one that shot and paralyzed that fellow from James Island?" Toni asked.

"Yes, that's the one. He gave me this here card." Clifford pulled the card out of his pocket. "He walked right up to me and asked whether we had a lawyer yet for Henry. I told that we hadn't because everything happened Saturday night. He said to give this lawyer a call and tell him that Jimmy recommended us. Jimmy said that this lawyer is a God-fearing man and got him off."

"Well, at least I got a place to start. Let me call him right now."

Toni looked at the clock and picked up the telephone. Within minutes she was making arrangements with the lawyer. Toni told the lawyer that she had some money saved up but that she would pay him everything he charged, if he would accept payments when the retainer ran out. The lawyer told Toni to come by his office now and bring a check so that he could get started working. He told her that he would make a telephone call to arrange bail for Henry before he did anything else, because Henry shouldn't be in jail any longer.

When Toni had finished her conversation with the lawyer, she called her bank in Connecticut and asked them to transfer all of her five thousand dollars into the checking account because she would be writing a check later that day.

As they drove Clifford asked whether Toni had talked to Trudy.

"No, Uncle Clifford. I really don't want to talk to mama. Right now I'm more concerned about Henry. Mama put herself in that position, Uncle Clifford, then she put Henry in the position where he had to either kill that fool or let himself be killed. I know where mama is, I just don't want Henry where he is any longer than necessary."

"I understand, babe. We'll do whatever we gotta do and get pass this, too. I was sitting in the bathroom this morning and I tell you, babe, I sensed the presence of my bubba, your daddy, so strong I just expected him to appear any minute. I said 'Aaron, get out this bathroom and let me have my privacy.' I can't explain it, but I know Aaron was there with me."

"You too, Uncle Clifford? Wilson and me had the same experience this morning, too. I smelled daddy's Old Spice after-shave cologne in the kitchen so strong, then I thought I saw a reflection or a flash of somebody passing by real fast. It was like a flash or something. Then Wilson came downstairs and told me that he had sensed daddy's presence in his room."

"It's almost like Big Aaron got the news that his children in danger and he letting his presence be known. You know, it's like he wants us all to know that he's protecting his own. I believe that those relatives who die before us still somehow can know when things ain't right with us. Somehow, or another, they still protect us."

"Uncle Clifford, I just don't know what went wrong with mama after daddy died. She just ain't been the same since."

"I don't know, babe. All we can do is just pray for your mama. I just think that Big Aaron's death was kind of like the straw that broke the camel's back for her, truthfully. Whatever happened to Trudy didn't just happen when Big Aaron died. As I think back, little by little, I think something was happening in her. I just pray to God that whatever it is just runs its course and she get it together before anything else happens. Nobody knows where Aaron Junior is, or whether he's even alive. Aaron Junior left more than a year ago with a swollen heart and we ain't heard from him since. Lord have mercy."

Clifford began to cry as he drove, he was so overwhelmed that he could no longer drive and had to pull the car over on the side of the road. Toni sat and cried as well because everybody seemed to have been overtaken with an unexplainable grief as a result of the things that had happened.

"Hey babe, I don't make no excuses anymore about crying. When I hurt, I will cry now and let the Lord have His way. I just feel helpless to do anything for my family right now. My nephew is sitting in jail, I don't know where another one is, the rest of my nieces and nephews are being dragged through shame and humiliation. Trudy done all but lost her mind, it seems and I don't know whether things gonna get better before they get worse. Lord help me, Jesus, we don't know what else to do." Clifford prayed.

Toni had never seen her uncle like this before and she felt helpless. In spite of the circumstance, Toni felt a sense of pride and an even greater respect for her uncle because he did not make an excuse, or apologize for crying. She saw her uncle as a bigger man for crying and saying that he did not know what else to do, then to ask God to help. This, Toni thought was a real man. He did not have the answers, but he called out to God for guidance. A fool would have denied that he did not know what to do. But this man knew that what he did not know that God had the answer.

Clifford dried his eyes and pulled the car back onto the highway. As Toni and her uncle pulled in front of the lawyer's office her uncle reminded her that she could only do the possible because God had cornered the market on the impossible. As she got out of the car Toni nodded her head and clutched her purse. Almost every cent that she had was about to be given up for Henry's defense. She never flinched or had a second thought about what she was about to do.

David Kingsley, the attorney, was on the telephone when Clifford and Toni walked into his office. The receptionist was very courteous and told Toni and her uncle that Mr. Kingsley was working on getting Henry's bail reduced. Nearly ten minutes had elapsed when Mr. Kingsley walked out of his office and apologized for being on the telephone so long. Mr. Kingsley took Toni and Clifford into his office and explained that he was trying to get Henry out on a Personal Recognizance bond. If that was not possible he was shooting for bail as low as he could get it, so that they could bail Henry out that day.

Toni stood up and reached for her purse. As she took her checkbook from the purse she looked the attorney in the eye as though she were looking straight through him. Toni informed the lawyer that she was writing a check for all the money that she had in the world. But, that she would pay as much as she could each month to pay for Henry's defense, she just wanted her brother set free so that he could make amends with God and go on, as best that he could with his life. The agreement was made and all of the paperwork signed. Toni never asked her uncle or anyone else for a dollar to help pay for Henry's defense, and no one offered her any help.

The lawyer looked at Toni and accepted the check humbly. He promised her that he would do his best to see that Henry did not spend anymore time in jail. The old lawyer's eyes held a sincerity that could not be shaken. It was as though he too, felt the pain and knew the situation that Toni was facing as though he too, had personally experienced it.

The old lawyer and the young woman shook hands. The lawyer asked whether Toni had any money left for bail or whether the check that she had written included the bail. Toni turned and looked at the lawyer with eyes of brown steel, "sir, I have given to you all that I presently have, and I want my brother free today. Can you understand that, sir?" The lawyer nodded his head and without blinking an eye said, "then I lift it up and it is done."

The lawyer told Toni to stay close to the telephone because he would be calling just as soon as he heard from his bail bondsman and had arranged for a hearing. Someone, the lawyer said, would have to pick Henry up from the jail. Toni told the lawyer that she would call if she was away from home because she still had to go to the hospital where her mother was still a patient. The lawyer apologized for his failing memory, but Toni smiled and walked over and shook his hand before leaving his office.

As Clifford and Toni walked to the car it was as though Toni had gotten an internal revival notice with evidence. Inside she felt as tall as one of the pine trees across the highway. Her determination seemed to have steeled up and she did not feel alone anymore or that she was fighting the battle by herself.

"That's a good thing you did, babe." Clifford said, referring to what Toni had done with her savings.

"No, Uncle Clifford, that was the right thing that I did. Who else was going to do it for Henry? Henry doesn't have anyone to fight for him now but God and me. Can you imagine what he's been through since Saturday night? I can't Uncle Clifford. Henry's got blood on his hands and people just ain't gonna let him live that down soon, regardless of how the blood got on his hand."

"I pray that this lawyer can get him out and Henry don't have to spend no more time in jail." Clifford said.

"That's my prayer too, Uncle Clifford. Henry ain't never been in any trouble before and I don't know what prison would do to him. I pray for God's mercy. I just got to make sure that I have enough money to pay for everything."

The uncle and niece drove to the hospital in almost silence to see Trudy. As they walked onto the floor after getting out of the elevator, Clifford began to scratch his head. He had been so angry with his sister-in-law the day before that he was a little reluctant to see her this day. Toni walked in the room and asked whether the doctor had given her mother a time when she could go home.

"Well, the doctor just left here, just before y'all came in. He said that I could go home today, but he was gonna write a couple of prescriptions for me to get." Trudy said.

"Well how you feeling?" Clifford asked. "Ain't no need in rushing it if you ain't feeling up to par, yet. Stay right here until you feel like you can come home."

"No, I feel okay, Cliff, just a little sore, but I feel good enough to go home and rest there." Trudy said.

Toni sat in the chair and bit her lower lip, trying to remove a piece of chapped skin from the corners of her mouth. She tried as hard as she could to soften her looks at her mother but she was angry.

"How you today Tonitia?" Trudy asked.

"Fine, how are you?" Toni responded.

Toni hoped silently that her voice was not gruff or showed any sign of angry. But as she waited for the next words to be spoken, Toni noticed that her mother had a telephone directory under the covers. Toni determined that she was not going to get into a confrontation with her mother and she would just pretend that she had not seen the telephone book under the covers.

"What time did the doctor say you could go home, mama?"

"He said he would be back, but I can go today."

"I better go to the house and get you some clothes to wear."

"Babe that's quite a drive to go all the back to the house and come back here to the hospital. We can go to one of the stores on King Street and get Trudy a dress or pair of pants to wear home. She just gonna get in the car and go right in the house and go to bed, anyway."

"Yeah, we could do that. We might as well go do that now so when the doctor get back mama can get dressed and be home before Jeremiah gets home."

Toni waited to hear whether her mother would ask about any of the children but Trudy just looked past her out of the window. Toni felt the anger rise quickly and furiously within her and she wanted to go over to the bed and slap her mother. But as she looked she could see tears begin to flow from her mother's eyes. But Toni could not feel any sympathy for her mother because she knew the tears flowing down her face were not for Henry, or any of her mother's children. Toni's lack of compassion frightened her more than the anger raging inside of her.

"Mama, are you hurting somewhere?"

Trudy shook her head that she was not, but did not speak a word. She sat up in the bed and just stared out of the window as though Clifford and Toni were no longer there.

Toni picked up her purse and walked out of the hospital room with her uncle in tow. As they got to the elevator Clifford grabbed Toni by the arm.

"Tonitia, that's still your mama, regardless of what has happened. So don't destroy yourself or your blessings by being angry. Don't let that anger build up like a volcano, babe, cause it'll only hurt you and those you love."

Toni did not even want to be lectured now. Her thoughts were on her siblings and how they were going to deal with their mother after this. Maybe her mother was feeling some shame about what had happened, Toni thought. It wasn't the easiest thing in the world to face for a woman her mother's age. Her mother had a son in jail for killing her younger lover and now two families were in pain, but only one had a son who was still living. Then Toni decided that if she had to choose which son lived, it would have been her mother's son, after all, he was the innocent one. The hell with the dead one, she thought.

Toni and Clifford made their way to the store and found a dress and a pair of underwear for her mother to wear home. It wasn't really a dress but a tent styled cotton dress that zipped up the front that Trudy could wear around the house after she got well.

Toni decided to call the lawyer's office while she and Clifford were out and before they returned to the hospital. Toni was shocked when the lawyer told her that he had spoken to Henry and that Henry said he did not want to stay in the same house with his mother. The lawyer said that he needed to know where Henry would stay because he was going to court later that day and had to have an address where Henry would be living. Toni muffled the telephone and told Clifford what the lawyer said. Clifford took the telephone and told the lawyer what his address was and that Henry would stay with him.

When Clifford got off of the telephone, he told Toni to put Henry's clothes in a suitcase and put it in his car when they got to the house so that Henry would have all that he needed. Toni was relieved that Henry would be with Clifford, but she was concerned why Henry did not want to return to his own house. Toni began to worry about Henry's psychological state and whether he was having feelings of hatred for their mother.

Clifford began to look like as though he was wilting under the pressures of the situation before them. Several times Toni had watched as her uncle stared into space as though he had stopped breathing or was not aware of anyone else who might be breathing. Clifford had had only one child and he had drowned when he was only nine. But here was Clifford, concerned about his brother's children and even his brother's wife. If no one had known differently, they would have thought that Clifford was Trudy's brother, not her husband's. Toni felt guilty and like she was imposing on her uncle with her family's problems. But Clifford had always said that come hell or high water Toni and her siblings would always be his family. Well, Toni thought, now they had a little of each, high water to go with all of the hell that had broken loose and things looked like they may just be steaming up.

Trudy was sitting on the side of the bed, almost in the same spot where Toni and Clifford had left her. But they could see that she had packed what things that she was taking home with her from the hospital in a little plastic bag. Toni showed her mother the housedress and told her that it was something that she could always wear again and again. Trudy seemed to be pleased with the dress and asked for help to get to the bathroom and get dressed.

Toni seemed to have been caught in a fog of some sort because she at first did not think that her mother needed any help getting to the bathroom. Her mother's request for help seemed to just go over her head. When Toni realized that she had asked for her assistance she was embarrassed because she had not heard the request at first and it appeared as though she was distant from her mother. As quickly as she could recover, Toni helped her mother into the small bathroom.

As Toni helped her mother remove the hospital gown, she saw the swelling around the top of her chest just a short distance from her breast. The bullet had struck Trudy in the back just under her shoulder blade and exited just above her right breast. Her mother seemed to be a little embarrassed by her condition. Toni realized that if her mother could have helped herself she would not have asked Toni to help her. Trudy truly did not have the strength necessary to even stand up alone and snap up the housedress.

Toni pulled the lid down on the commode in the bathroom and gave her mother the new underwear and told her to sit on the commode and put her legs in so she would not fall. Trudy did as her daughter instructed her, but she appeared to be so far away from the spot where she and her daughter stood. Toni had hoped that her mother would take this time to ask about Henry or Jeremiah or one of the other kids, but she did not. While Trudy sat on the commode, Toni just placed the dress around her mother so that she could put one arm in at a time and she zipped it up.

Clifford sat in the chair waiting for the two women to emerge from the bathroom.

"Y'all got it together?" Clifford asked.

"Yes sir, we're about ready to go now, aren't we, mama?" Toni said as she helped her mother to the bed.

"Well, I guess so. I just got to get the prescriptions filled before we get home."

"Where the prescriptions at?" Clifford asked.

"The doctor said that he would have them up at the nurse's station when we leave."

"I'll go ahead of y'all and see whether they ready and where I can get them filled at." Clifford said as he walked out of the door.

Tony was alone now in the hospital room with her mother. Still, Toni questioned herself as to why she could not feel enough sympathy for her mother to hug her, or even a true desire to do for her what her mother was unable to do.

There was a very present feeling of distance within Toni for her mother. She was doing things now because they had to be done, but her heart was not in it. This was her mother, yet nothing inside of Toni resembled compassion. She knew that Trudy also needed the assurance of someone she could lean on now. But there seemed to be a wall that would not allow Toni to tell her mother that all was well between them and that they would get through this situation, as well. Toni knew that she needed to say something, anything, to her mother, but she could not speak a word.

Trudy watched her eldest daughter with the eyes of a child as Toni made sure that everything that belonged to her mother was packed. Even as Toni knelt on the floor in front of the bed and her mother and placed the socks on her mother's feet, she did so out of obligation but with no compassion.

Trudy sat quietly, watching, as Toni placed the socks on each foot and rolled them down to her ankle. The act appeared to be loving, but Toni questioned her own heart because she did not feel love in her heart, just a need to get this over and done with.

"Thank you." Trudy said as Toni finished and patted the tops of the socks.

"You're welcome." Toni responded.

Trudy's eyes followed Toni as she walked over to the window and looked out. The silence between the two women was deafening. The tension in the room could be cut only with a very sharp knife. Trudy dropped her head as a little child would when it knew that it had done something very bad. Trudy cleared her throat, making Toni turn to face her.

"If you got something you want to say to me Tonitia, go on. I know everybody thinking all of this is my fault."

Toni looked at her mother and sighed before speaking.

"Mama, like you said before, this is your life and you can live your life however you want. Not me, not Margaret, not one of us got the right to tell you how you should live your life; you were grown before any of us were born. Do what you wanna do, mama."

Before Toni could say another word, Clifford walked in the door with several pieces of paper in his hand and a large brown bag.

"Man, you know who one of the nurses out there is?" Clifford asked.

"No, who?" Trudy asked, as Toni stood staring and waiting for the answer.

"You remember Lucky Boy Jackson?"

"Yeah."

"You remember that woman he married who used to be married to the sailor that got killed up there on Remount Road in that car wreck with a couple of fellows off one of those ships at the Navy Base?"

"Uh, huh. Wait a minute, is she the tall brown skin nurse?"

"Yeah. That's her." Clifford said.

"I thought that woman looked familiar when she was in here, but I couldn't place her. She acted like she knew me, but she didn't say anything to help me remember who she was."

"Well she remember all of us. She already got your prescriptions filled and these are the prescriptions for later on. She said that she didn't want you to have to go round and round to get the stuff you needed so she had everything sitting right up there."

"I got to tell her thank you, cause she didn't have to do that for me." Trudy said.

"Hey, babe, the Lord still got some good people down here. She said that the baby she and Lucky Boy had is in high school now and the two she and her first husband had just about to graduate from college. She said they live in Mount Pleasant now down the street from the television station."

"Is that right? She sure looks good. I knew I recognized her, but couldn't remember from where." Trudy replied.

Toni was thankful that she did not have to stop again before getting home and silently thanked God for His intervention.

Toni told her mother to sit still until she got a wheelchair to take her to the car and walked out of the room leaving her mother and uncle talking. As she walked down the hall to the nurse's station, Toni began to feel very tired and longed for a good night's sleep, but realized that her work was not finished. As she approached the nurse's station she saw the tall brown skin lady coming from around the corner smiling.

"Mrs. Jackson, I'm Tonitia Spann. Thank you, mam, for helping my mama and for getting her prescriptions filled."

"Oh sweetheart, it was no more than your mama would have done for me. It was your mama who prayed for me and lifted my spirits honey when I wanted to die. You don't remember it, but your mama laid down some prayers for me and my children years ago, that's the least I could do."

"Well mama, want to tell you thank you herself before she leave. I just need to know where to get a wheelchair so we can take her downstairs."

"I'll get a wheelchair and bring it down there in a minute. Honey, if my son was to see you, he would be beside himself, you just as pretty as you can be."

"Thank you, mam."

"Tonitia, what you doing with yourself?"

"I live in Connecticut, work for the government and go to college fulltime at night."

"Oh baby bless you, don't stop, keep going until you finish and don't forget the Lord."

"No mam, I can't forget God, I don't want Him to forget me."

"How your brother holding up, Tonitia?"

"I don't know yet, mam. I just retained a lawyer for him and the lawyer is working on getting him bailed out today. I believe he'll be out today, so I need to get out of here so that I can pick him up."

"Hold your head high, Tonitia, this too shall pass and know this that I'll keep you and your family in my prayers."

"Thank you, Mrs. Jackson, we can use plenty of prayers."

As Toni walked back down the hall to her mother's room she felt a need to go somewhere and just let the tears that she felt welling up inside of her come out. Maybe, she thought, just maybe God will now make her mother walk a straight and narrow path and make amends with her family. But Toni knew that her mother had to make the decision to do that in order for God to help. Toni felt just a little bit frustrated that God would not force her mother to live a better life, but remembered that people had free will.

"I saw Mrs. Jackson and told her that you thanked her for getting those prescriptions for you, mama. She's bringing a wheelchair down here for you."

"Oh that's good, I can tell her thank you myself, too."

There was a thump on the door and Mrs. Jackson came in with the wheelchair in front of her.

"Gertrude, forgive me for not making myself known to you before, but when I saw Clifford, here, I couldn't keep myself unknown."

"You have to forgive me as well, girl, cause I knew you looked familiar but I couldn't place your face with a name. But I knew for sure that somehow we had made one another's acqaintance before."

"I'm Sally. I'm the same way, Gertrude, I might forget the name but I never forget the face. As many times as you prayed for me girl, I could never forget you and I didn't. When my first husband brought me here when he was in the Navy, honey I didn't know a soul when he got killed. I couldn't go back to mama and daddy with two kids and I didn't know what I should do. But girl you saw me sitting in the front room looking out the window and stopped and knocked on the door. Gertrude, I'll never forget that day, girl you told me that if I could just hold on, God was gonna turn it around for me and you prayed a powerful prayer over me."

As Mrs. Jackson talked the tears in her eyes welled up and began to run down her cheeks. As she cried, so did Trudy. Toni watched as the two women shared.

"Sally, how the kids doing?" Trudy asked.

"The two oldest ones are in college, my oldest boy he'll graduate in another two weeks and my daughter got one more year left, she'll graduate next year this time. My baby boy, that's mine and Lucky's, he's in the tenth grade going to the eleventh. Gertrude, you gotta see that boy, he look so much like Lucky, you'd think Lucky spit that boy out."

"How Lucky doing, Sally?" Trudy asked.

"He's doing so-so, Gertrude. Kind of like your Aaron. But I'm praying and believing that God will heal him. Come on let me get you out of here."

Toni could see the pain as it tried to set upon Mrs. Jackson. Toni remembered how the cancer had taken her father down like a piece of ice in the scorching hot sun. Toni knew well the pain Mrs. Jackson must have been suffering knowing that one day, any day, cancer would make her a widow, again.

Clifford looked at Mrs. Jackson and assured her that God had everything under control and that he would be sure to come to Mount Pleasant and visit his old friend Lucky Boy.

Tony thought to herself, what a name to have yet have the unlucky posture and disease of cancer. In her heart Toni prayed for a miracle for Mrs. Jackson and her family because the death of her own father seemed to have precipitated a ghostly nightmare for Toni and her siblings. How wicked cancer was, Toni thought. Although cancer was wicked, Toni knew that there were other things that were just as deadly and could eat away the structure of a family as quickly as the dreaded disease.

The time was quickly passing and Toni's mind again was turned to her siblings. She wanted to be home when Jeremiah got there and to have time to pack a suitcase for Henry. Toni had not seen Henry since Saturday night, and she needed to talk to him. Still, Trudy had not even asked about her son. Toni was angry about this but determined that it was better not to say anything more. It seemed obvious that her mother had indeed made a choice, Isiah was and had been more important to her than her children. Trudy had asked about Isiah, but had not whispered an inquiry about Henry. All that had seemed to matter to her was that Henry did not have to shoot Isiah, even when she was told that Isiah had called the house threatening to kill Henry and showed up there with a pistol.

"Uncle Clifford, I need to get a start on, Jeremiah and Joyce will be coming home soon, and I still got some other business to take care of." Toni said.

Mrs. Jackson apologized for staying so long but Toni reassured her that she hadn't stayed long enough to get reacquainted with her old friends. Mrs. Jackson told Trudy that she would also include her and her family in her prayers. Trudy thanked her and tried to get down from the side of the bed. Toni and Mrs. Jackson seated her in the wheelchair and Clifford opened the door so that Toni could push the chair out. Clifford went ahead of them to get the car and instructed Toni to meet him the front of the hospital.

As Toni pushed the wheelchair down the hallway to the elevator she became completely unaware of other people around her. As she stood at the elevator, Toni just stared at the wall with her hands locked securely around the handles on the wheelchair. She was oblivious to her mother trying to reach the button. Toni just held onto the handles on the wheelchair and stared into space. When the elevator opened Toni had to be asked twice by the man and woman remaining on it whether they were going down. Toni realized that she, again, had blanked out and became concerned about her own wellbeing, mentally.

The ride down on the elevator seemed to take forever, but it was only a minute or two because it had not stopped on another floor. Trudy was silent and did not want to say anything to Toni. There was still tension between them and their conversation started in the hospital room had been interrupted by Clifford's return with the medication.

Toni began to move and act like she was in some kind of trance; all of her movements seemed mechanical and she tried extra hard to maintain her focus. Her brothers and sisters remained her major and only concern.

Clifford pulled up in front of the hospital and got out. Toni opened the backdoor of the car and moved the footrests on the wheelchair to the side. Clifford and Toni helped Trudy into the car and placed the bags beside her on the backseat. Toni walked back into the hospital and placed the wheelchair to one side and got in the car.

13

The ride to the house was one of the most silent rides that had ever been taken by the trio. Clifford turned the radio on so that there would not be absolute silent. Trudy sat in the backseat and looked out the window.

When Clifford pulled up in the front of the house Joyce walked out to the car to meet them.

"How you doing, mama?" she asked as she opened the door.

"I'm okay, baby, how you doing?" Trudy replied.

"I'm okay, too." Joyce responded.

Jeremiah stayed in the house and watched from the front door as Clifford and Toni helped Trudy from the car. The neighbor from across the street stood on her porch waving and watched as Trudy was helped into the house.

"Lemme just sit down here for a while and get my breath." Trudy said, referring to the sofa in the living room. Joyce had the bags from the backseat in her hand and asked whether her mother wanted them beside her in the living room.

"Mama, you gonna live?" Jeremiah asked.

"Yeah, baby, I'm gonna live, I'm here with you."

"Mama where Isiah shoot you at?" Jeremiah asked.

"Jeremiah," Toni said, "stop asking mama so many questions, she ain't feeling too good right now, okay?"

"That's okay, mama, Henry kill Isiah for shooting you." Jeremiah said.

The room suddenly began to spend and everybody became absolutely silent. Trudy began to cry and the tears rushed forward like little lakes filled to their capacity. The little boy did not realize what he had said; he thought it a good thing to tell his mother that his big brother had gotten even with the person who had hurt her. But Toni's jaws tightened like drying paint on a car. Toni knew that the tears were not for Henry, they were for a man who had abused her mother and sought to control and intimidate the rest of the family with his violence and boldness.

Toni walked away because the urge to ask her mother what or who she was shedding tears for became overwhelming. Toni went upstairs to pack Henry's belongings, but called the lawyer to find out whether Henry was going to be released. The secretary told Toni that the lawyer was meeting with the judge, but it did look like Henry would be getting out of jail on a personal recognizance bond. The secretary told Toni that from what she had heard that day, because Henry had shot and killed a man who had tried to kill his mother and had come after him in his own home the judge did not deem him violent. Toni was pleased to hear that because she did not have anymore money. The secretary made sure that she had the right telephone number to reach Tony when she heard anything more from her boss about Henry.

Toni looked under the bed where she knew the suitcases were kept and pulled one out to start packing Henry's things. Toni packed the one suitcase and went back for another. Henry had a job and had only missed one day of work so far, Toni decided, maybe he would not be fired and would need more clothes to wear to work, so she packed more clothes for him. Toni went into her mother's room and turned the covers back. She raised the window just a little so that some fresh air could come in and circulate in the room.

As she walked back downstairs Toni heard her uncle talking to her mother. She was glad that there was someone that her mother could talk to because she wasn't sure that she could talk to her, not even about the weather.

As she entered the room, Trudy looked up at Toni and asked whether Toni had called her father. Toni lied and said that she had not. Before Toni or Clifford could say anything else, Joyce began to speak.

"We called granddaddy right after Miss Clara came here to tell us that Isiah had shot you and that you were in the hospital." Joyce said.

Trudy looked at Joyce as though she were waiting for more information. But Joyce was silent and turned to watch the television. Realizing that Joyce had nothing else to say, Trudy decided that she wanted to go upstairs and lie down. Toni helped her mother upstairs and helped her get into a nightgown.

The telephone began ringing while Toni was putting Trudy to bed so Joyce answered.

"Toni, pick up the phone, it's the lawyer for Henry." Joyce said.

Trudy's eyes widened when she heard that it was a lawyer for Henry. Toni reached down and unplugged the telephone next to her mother's bed, and went downstairs. Toni believed that her mother would pick up the telephone upstairs and eave drop on the conversation. The lawyer told Toni that Henry had been released and was at his office with him. Toni said that she and her uncle would be right over.

Toni went upstairs and asked Trudy whether it was time for her to take any medication. Trudy had pulled the covers up over her legs and asked Toni to turn the television on before leaving the room. Toni walked down the hall and picked up the two suitcases and carried them downstairs and out of the door to Clifford's car before anyone realized what had happened. Toni looked at her uncle and nodded her head to signal to him that it was time for them to leave.

Jeremiah went upstairs to be with his mother and Joyce sat in the den staring at the television, it was uncertain whether she was actually watching. Toni walked into the room and told Joyce that she and Clifford were going to pick up Henry and would return as soon as possible. The sadness that masked Joyce's face was so hard and tight, Toni could not imagine that her mother would not change her lifestyle if she could have seen it.

Clifford walked over and sat beside Joyce. Toni's heart seemed to faint as she too, briefly sat in the chair beside the sofa. It seemed like Joyce's sadness had drained every ounce of strength out of Toni. Clifford told Joyce that trouble didn't last always and one day peace would come again. But the words seemed not to mean anything to Joyce. The tears just flowed down her face like streams of hot steamy water. Joyce's heart was broken and there was nothing that either Toni or her uncle could do to immediately mend it.

"Y'all go on and get Henry, I'll be okay. If mama want to eat I'll warm up something for her and Jeremiah. I know Henry ain't coming back here, Toni, and I don't blame him. Wouldn't make no sense in him coming here so mama can tell him to get out." Joyce said.

"Joyce, come on, your mama would never say that to her own child." Clifford said.

"You mean she wouldn't say it again, while you were in hearing distance. But mama has said it to Henry before about that old Isiah, and now that he's dead and Henry killed him, please, Uncle Clifford."

Joyce took her hand and tried to dry her eyes. Clifford could say nothing else and got up from the sofa. Toni leaned over and kissed her baby sister on the forehead.

14

Henry was sitting in the chair near the window in the lawyer's office when Clifford and Toni arrived. Henry jumped up and hugged his big sister.

"Toni thank you. I know you put up all of your money for me and I appreciate that. I'll try to pay you back. I called my boss this morning and he told me to just take the rest of the week off and come on back to work next week, so I'll have some money to help."

"We're family, Henry, I'm not gonna see you sitting in jail, if I can do something to help. Mr. Kingsley is the one with the know how, though. Thank you sir." Toni said as she walked over to shake the lawyer's hand.

"We're gonna git through this here mess, Ms. Spann and put it behind us so far that only God will know where it's really hidden. Now take Old Henry here home and feed him."

Clifford shook Mr. Kingsley's hand asked whether he had his telephone number if he needed to talk to Henry. After writing the number down on a piece of paper, the trio walked out of the lawyer's office and got into Clifford's car.

"Henry how they treat you in that jail?" Clifford asked his nephew.

"Nobody bothered me. The fellows just said that they would have done the same thing but they probably would have gone out and hunt him down. But nobody bothered me. I just don't want to spend no more time in jail, though."

"Well, don't worry about that now, just pray and ask the Lord to help you, son. Me and your sister gonna be right here by your side."

"How's mama doing?" Henry asked.

"She 's okay. They let her out of the hospital today so I brought her home and put her to bed." Toni replied.

"How Jeremiah doing? He ain't fretting or anything like that, is he?"

"No, he seem to be okay. I left him upstairs with mama when me and Uncle Clifford left the house. Joyce is the one that I'm concerned about, Henry. I mean, I'm concerned about all of y'all, but Joyce just seem to be so sad."

"I just didn't have anything that I could say to that baby today before me and Toni left to pick you up. That child's heart is broken and I pray to God that she can just release all of that pent up pain and hurt inside." Clifford said.

Henry hung his head down, then looked out the window. "I guess there ain't much of anything that anybody can do right now. It seems like if one thing bad happens, there's something else and then something else to add to that, it's like it never stops." Henry said.

"It stops Henry, but sometimes things just have to run its course. It's like having the flu. It don't matter how much cough syrup you drink, or pills you swallow, once the flu hit you that's it until it runs its course. You gonna be weak, stuffy headed, coughing, fever and sweating, but after a few days of that, you just work on getting your strength back. We just gotta work on getting our strength back now." Clifford said.

Toni wasn't buying any of that, she hadn't seen too many good days since her father passed. She had to get back to Connecticut but dreaded having to leave her siblings who really needed her. But she had Henry's defense to pay for, her education to finish and so many things that seemed nearly impossible for her to do.

Clifford turned the car down the little lane where he lived. The house was such a cute one, Toni had thought. Clifford had bought the house for his second wife, Sylvia. Sylvia was a few years older than Clifford was but, she certainly did not look like it. Sylvia and Clifford had met while Clifford was stationed at the Air Force Base in Texas. Sylvia and Clifford bought the house before Clifford retired and began decorating. Sylvia became sick in Texas after they had married and died of a blood clot on the brain. She never got an opportunity to live in the home she was decorating for her and Clifford.

Clifford pulled into the carport and turned the car's engine off. Henry got out and grabbed the suitcases in the back seat. Toni took one of the suitcases and they walked up to the backdoor and waited for Clifford to unlock the door. As they were getting ready to step into the house, Clifford's neighbor across the street called out to let him know that the mailman had left a package for him at her house.

"Henry take one of them rooms and put your stuff in the drawers and closets." Clifford said.

"Yes sir." Henry said as he walked into the kitchen.

Toni went into the little den and turned the television on. Clifford walked in and set the small box on the table in the kitchen. He opened the refrigerator door and took out a bottle of beer.

"Toni." Clifford shouted.

"Sir?"

"You want a cool beer, babe? I got some Falstaff and some Schlitz in here." Clifford said.

"No, Uncle Clifford, I'd just go to sleep if I drank one."

"Well, I'll drink Toni's." Henry said. "I need to get that jailhouse dust out of my throat."

"Go on, get what you want, Henry. There some cold cuts and stuff to make sandwich with in there if you want something to eat."

As Toni sat on the sofa she thought of how she would approach the topic of Henry's defense and the events of the past weekend. She did not want to dredge up the memories of that fateful moment when Henry pulled the trigger of the gun that ended the life and times of Isiah, but knew that she had to before she left South Carolina.

Henry stood in the kitchen holding the beer bottle and looking out of the window. He was staring as though seeing something. He lifted the bottle to his mouth and looked down at the counter before him. Toni wondered what he was thinking about. If only she could get inside his mind and know what he was feeling or thinking. How did it feel to know that you had taken the life of another person? Did the scene of that moment play over and over in your mind, when, if ever, did you stop seeing that moment? Toni did not want Henry to be tortured in his mind about what had happened. The only relief she could find in all of this was the fact that Henry was home, sitting on his porch when Isiah came looking for him. Henry had done nothing to provoke Isiah. But like Kim had said, Isiah did not figure God in his equation, he had not anticipated the possibility of his being the one to die when he came to the house that night.

Toni's thoughts were interrupted by Henry's voice.

"Did mama say anything when y'all brought her home?"

"No, she didn't say anything, Henry." Toni replied.

"Y'all told her about Isiah?"

"Yes, we told her, but she hasn't said anything about it yet." Toni said.

"I don't think she really know what to say." Clifford said. "She look like she's still a little confused, or in unbelief. But I don't think she really know what she should be thinking or saying right now."

"Henry, tell me why you didn't want to go home." Toni asked.

A hush fell over the room, Clifford and Toni waited for Henry to respond. Henry walked out of the kitchen and sat down in the den with his sister and uncle. He looked at each of them and twirled the bottle in his hand as though it were a stick or baton.

"I knew mama would be mad at me and I didn't want her to feel uncomfortable with me in the same house." Henry said.

"Why would she be mad with you, Henry. If you hadn't got Isiah, he would have got you." Clifford said.

"I know that, and you know that, Uncle Clifford, but I don't think mama know that or even care. I live in the same house with mama everyday, and she live and breath Isiah, he comes before all of us. I remember one time Isiah told her that she should put me out and let me get my own place and mama was ready to do that. I had to remind mama that she couldn't put me out because daddy made that clear in his will, the house belongs to all of his children, not just her. Man there was so much going on in that house with mama because of Isiah. I bet you mama sitting there right now just hating me. You know what, the sad thing about all of what's happened is that people think that I did that because of what Isiah did to mama. But the truth is, I did that to save my own life. When I looked in that man's eyes when he was trying to drag me over the banister, y'all I'm telling you, it was like I was looking straight in the devil's eyes. Isiah was frothing at the mouth and dribbling like somebody getting ready to eat a meal."

Toni was almost in shock listening to Henry tell of his struggle with Isiah the night he shot him. As she listened to her younger brother, Toni felt the hairs on her body stand on end and goose bumps formed on her skin. Clifford looked at his nephew in awe and listened intently to what he was saying. Clifford's hands were folded as he listened as though he was in prayer.

"Uncle Clifford, Toni, I'm telling y'all the God in heaven truth. None of us even heard Isiah coming. Usually Miss Lizzie old dog, Buckshot, would bark up a storm anytime somebody cut through the back, but the dog didn't even whimper. I didn't even see a shadow or anything. All I felt is this icy grip around my neck, then I was being lifted in the air. Have y'all ever smelled blood?" Henry asked.

"No." Toni responded.

"I think I know what you talking about, Henry. I hit the ground so hard one time it seemed like I smelled blood." Clifford responded.

"Well, I could smell blood. Then it was like I realized in my mind that I was going to die and I got so scared that I almost didn't have any strength. I mean things were happening real fast, but while I was laying in that bunk in the jailhouse, I could see the whole thing clearer and slower."

Toni and her uncle were listening to Henry with the intensity of receiving instructions for their own lives. The silence in the room when Henry would pause made it seem like no one was even breathing.

"The whole time that I was scuffling with Isiah, it was like he was trying to keep me from facing him, he kept trying to get me from behind. When you real close to another human being, they're usually warm, but I'm telling y'all, Isiah was cold. His arm was around my neck and it felt like a piece of ice and he was choking me so tight that I could feel myself kind of fading away. Look here." Henry said, as he showed Clifford and Toni the finger marks around his neck.

Toni's eyes became the size of saucers, because she had checked Henry's body for marks that Saturday night and had not seen those marks. Clifford could not believe what he was seeing.

"What the hell?" Clifford said as he touched the scars. "Look at this. Did you show that to the police or the lawyer?"

"Yes sir. The police also told the guards at the jail that if I should have a sore throat or feel like I needed to go to the emergency room to take me there immediately. All of the guards came by and kept asking me if I was alright, though." Henry said.

"It look like Isiah had spikes in his fingers trying to tear your goozle pipe out or something." Clifford said.

"Anyway," Henry said, "something inside of me said 'fight, fight, live, you can beat him.' When I heard that I believed that I could beat Isiah and I started to fight him like my life depended on it. Isiah was strong, too. Suddenly I got strength from somewhere and broke his hold on me. The next thing I knew me and Isiah was on the ground and I was on top of him but with my back on his chest. Then something happened that I still can't figure out or explain. But I wasn't scared any more, I was just determined to kill him, not hurt him, kill him. It was either Isiah, or me, and I thank God that I was the one that lived. I still got some things that I need to straighten out in my head about that night, I just don't understand it all."

Toni had a very good idea about what Henry was referring to. She too, had seen and experienced something that night that she was still trying to figure out.

"Something was going on that we are yet to understand." Clifford said as he clapped his hands. "Oh but God don't let us sit in the dark forever, He'll reveal it to us when we can receive it."

Toni wished that she could understand it all right then. But in her heart of hearts, she knew that what her uncle said bore truth. Although she knew there was truth in what he had said she found it difficult to accept because she thought that she needed an explanation and understanding right then in order to move on.

"I've learned in this life that sometimes we just have to wait on God to tell us why some things happen in our life. The truth is like a secret agent in a place where we're going. We don't know who it is yet, but somehow we know it when we meet it. We just have to keep moving so we can get to the place where truth is, that's God's truth, so it all can be understood. Truth is sometimes ahead of us, we just have to keep moving with an open heart to receive it when we get to the right place. We don't always know exactly what the truth is, but something in us always let us know what it's not." Clifford said as he stared at something past his nephew.

Toni was almost in shock as her uncle spoke. The words seemed to have been an answer to her questions earlier. Somehow she knew that the answer was not immediately available to her but it would not be forever that she would be in the dark about it.

"I know you're right, Uncle Clifford." Henry said, as he took another swallow of the beer. "I believe that there is something about everything that's happened that none of us even know about, yet. But I got to face the music about what happened, too. Now that's kind of scary to me because I don't know what's gonna happen. But right now, it's almost as if something inside of me is saying stand up."

The telephone's ringing interrupted the conversation. Clifford walked over to the counter and picked up the phone. Toni and Henry watched the look on Clifford's face as he listened to the person on the other end.

"Don't say anything, we'll be there in a few minutes." Clifford said.

Toni wondered what the conversation was all about, but could tell from the look on her uncle's face that it was not anything good.

"Henry, you stay right here until I get back. Come on Toni, let's get over to the house and see about things there." Clifford said as he walked to his bedroom. Clifford returned and grabbed for his car keys.

Toni hurriedly followed her uncle out of the door. She stopped and looked back at Henry and said that she would see him later. Henry nodded his head as he watched her walk away. As Toni got into the front seat with her uncle she knew that something was wrong but kept silent so he could speak.

"That was Joyce on the phone. She said that she heard Trudy on the phone talking to somebody and she thinks it's Isiah's people. Trudy gave them directions to the house, Joyce said, then she said that she was sorry all of this happened. Joyce said that she believe that those people are coming to the house."

"Say what? Uncle Clifford, you believe mama could be that stupid? Why would she invite those people to the house knowing that her son was the one who killed those people's relative. Those people could come in that house and kill everybody in there." Toni said.

"If those people got war on their mind then they'll get a fight, you hear me? I don't know what's wrong with Trudy, but I ain't fooled by them people. I tell you that man had something on Trudy, but they ain't got nothing on me and you." Clifford responded.

Toni's head felt light and started to spin. Her armpits began to sting and she felt a heat begin to blaze inside and she felt the sweat begin to run down the side of her body. Toni had hoped that she would not have to fight with Isiah's people, or her mother, but suddenly was filled with an anger that not even she understood. Toni thought that once and for all she had to put an end to this madness her mother was suffering from. She also prayed that maybe, just maybe, Joyce had over reacted to what she had heard. Now she could deal with that, just let it be an over reaction.

"Toni, are you afraid of guns?" her uncle asked as he drove.

"No sir, I'm not afraid of guns, especially if I'm the one holding it."

"Okay, when we get to the house, I want you to sit in the kitchen and I'll sit in the living room so we can have those people in the middle of us. If any crap go down they'll be in the crossfire. I've got another pistol in the trunk of my car, it's a thirty-eight, just put it in your pocketbook until we get in the house. But keep it right by you at all times if those people are crazy enough to come to the house and think about starting anything."

Toni was ready and willing, even if it meant that she would have to shoot or kill one of Isiah's relatives, she was willing to do that. Since her uncle was willing to put his life on the line for her and her family, she would do no less. It was still somewhat of a mystery why her mother was behaving the way she was. What was it about this man that she would put her family's safety and wellbeing in jeopardy? Maybe there was something to what the people said about witchcraft, her mother was not operating in her right mind and had not done so since her father's death. But, Toni was not willing to let her mother's state of mind jeopardize the safety of her siblings.

"Uncle Clifford, do you believe that Isiah had something on mama? What I mean is, do you think mama got something on her?"

"Babe, I don't know for sure, but I believe there is. But if she got something on her, I ain't about to let it get on the rest you. Uh, uh, no sir, buddy, even if it gotta be another funeral or two in that family, cause it ain't gonna be one in this family."

The conviction in Clifford's voice was eerie to Toni, but she was feeling the same thing in her heart.

"I'll tell Joyce and Jeremiah to stay upstairs while those people are there. Wilson should be home by now, too. I just hope those people don't get there before we do and mistake Wilson for Henry." Toni said.

Clifford hit the gas when Toni made her statement. It was as though he had forgotten about Wilson. As the two of them speeded down the road, Toni prayed that they would reach the house without being stopped by the police and get there before anyone from Isiah's family. Clifford turned the corner and came to an abrupt stop in front of the house. Toni was glad and a little relieved that there were no other cars in front of the house.

When Clifford and Toni walked into the front door Trudy was downstairs sitting on the sofa. There seemed to be a peculiar glow about her as she looked up at Clifford and Toni. Toni could sense that something was amiss. The look in her mother's eyes was almost eerie, there was a glare and her eyes did not move from side to side as they followed Toni and Clifford. Trudy's eyes seemed to dart and get to the place where Toni and Clifford were going before they did. There did not appear to be sickness or any form of weakness showing in Trudy's eyes. The look on her mother's face nearly matched the glare in her eyes, Toni thought. Something was not right about this situation, Toni thought.

"Mama, you want something to eat now?" Joyce asked.

"No, I thought I was a little hungry before, but I guess I ain't as hungry as I first thought I was." She responded.

Toni looked around the room for Jeremiah. Then Wilson walked in the door. Her first thought was to pull Wilson aside and tell him what she thought was about to happen. But Toni did not want to start a panic needlessly.

"Mama I thought the doctor said you should stay in the bed and rest for a few more days. Why you going up and down the stairs? Come on, let me take you back upstairs so you can rest." Toni said as she walked over to the sofa to help her mother back to her room.

Clifford watched the two women and the door. It seemed as though Clifford knew in his heart that Toni's ploy was to find out for sure whether her mother was sitting downstairs to be with her family or waiting for someone else to arrive.

"No, I want to stay here for a while cause some people gonna come by here and drop off something to me. They should be here any minute." Trudy responded.

"What people gonna drop off something to you and what are they going to drop off, mama?" Toni asked, almost innocently.

"Well there was some stuff of mine left in the car when I went to the hospital and the people want to bring them to me."

"What car, mama was something of yours left in?" Toni asked, knowing what her mother was talking about.

"My clothes and stuff was in Isiah's car," Trudy said, sheepishly as she lowered her head, "and his mama and them wanted to bring them to me."

"Mama, you mean that those people are coming here to this house to drop off some clothes that you might not ever wear again?" Toni asked.

Wilson stopped and leaned against the arch between the dining room and the living room as he watched his mother. Wilson looked like he was in shock but waited for his mother to answer the question. All eyes were now on Trudy and she knew it. It was if everyone had stopped breathing while they waited for her answer.

107

"Well, they my stuff and I want them back. They was kind enough to stop by here and bring them to me on their way home. They ain't gonna be here long, no how." Trudy said.

"Mama how Isiah's people know where to find you to get those clothes to you?" Toni asked.

"I talked to them on the telephone."

"Mama, for the love of Jesus, please tell me how you talked to them on the telephone? Did they have the number here?" Toni asked.

"No, I called over to the funeral home and left my number for them to call me so I could get my things." She replied.

"Mama couldn't you just let those few pieces of cloth just be put in the garbage or something, rather than have those people come here to the place where their relative was killed?" Toni asked as she stared at her mother with a look that could cut a fat man to shreds.

"My God, Toni, all they gonna do is drop off my stuff to me, it ain't like they coming for dinner or something like that." Trudy said.

"Mama, your son killed those people's son. He killed him right out there just a piece from the door of this house and you think that they are so forgiving that they can walk up in here and smile and not think about doing harm to anybody else up in here. Mama, what if Henry was in here when those people come, what do you think they would do, or even try to do?" Toni said as the anger began to rise in her voice.

"Oh Toni, please, everybody ain't as bad as you think they are." Trudy said.

"Mama, you done lost your dam mind." Wilson angrily said. "Those people can walk up in here with pistols and kill everyone of us and what we gonna do then, huh, what we can do, mama? They don't know whether I'm Henry or not and I could get hurt or killed. Mama you ain't thinking about nobody but yourself." Wilson said, as the tears rolled down his cheek.

"That's a dam lie if anybody in this family gonna get hurt or killed." Clifford said. "Trudy you ain't thinking clear, but I ain't gonna let you jeopardize my brother's children, not today, not tomorrow. You can mess up your own life if you want to, but you ain't gonna bring danger right in here to them."

"What the hell you talking about, Clifford? Them people just dropping something off here to me, they ain't coming here to kill nobody." Trudy said.

"You don't know what they coming here to do, Trudy. Isiah got your mind all messed up. You ain't asked one question about Henry and you birthed him. Not one word have you asked about how Henry was doing, he could have been in the hospital with you just floors away and you wouldn't have known, cause your dam mind was on Isiah. Your children watching things go on now that they really don't understand. And all that you can do is play detective trying to find Isiah people and bring them right here. You know they could be snakes, but you would let them snakes loose right in your own house so they could bite your kids. What if Henry was here, Trudy, suppose like Wilson said, they mistake him for Henry? How would you feel then? Tell the truth, how would you feel? Ain't it enough that your behavior done cause one of your kids to leave and nobody know where he is, another has blood on his hand and now you putting the rest of them in danger? What's it gonna take Trudy for you to operate in your right mind?" Clifford asked.

"I love my kids, Clifford and nobody can love them more than me. So don't come here telling me how to treat my kids." Trudy said.

"Somebody need to tell you, mama." Wilson said. "You ain't showing no love to nobody but yourself. If this is the way you show love for me or any of us, then, mama keep your so-called love to yourself. I got to get out of here before the next death is me killing you, mama."

Wilson walked out of the backdoor and slammed it so hard that Toni thought for sure that the hinges had been broken. Trudy sat up so straight on the sofa that no one would have thought that she had even been shot. Joyce walked back into the kitchen and started running water in the sink. Toni went into the kitchen and asked Joyce where Jeremiah was. Joyce said that he was upstairs asleep. Toni told Joyce to go upstairs and to keep Jeremiah there until after Isiah's family had left. Joyce went upstairs and Clifford continued to stand at the door.

Toni wondered where Wilson would go, but prayed that he would stay wherever it was until Isiah's people had come and left. It was unbelievable that Trudy would even think about allowing the family of the man her son had just killed to come into their home just two days after the killing. Toni could feel anger and pity rising up in her at the same time. She was angry with her mother for her actions but felt sorry for her because she was no longer in her right mind. What had gone wrong? Toni asked. What was it that had taken control of her mother? Isiah had tried to kill her mother, but her mother seemed to be more in love with him than ever. Even in death Isiah seemed to be controlling Trudy.

Clifford lit a cigarette and walked out to the front porch. His mind was on survival, survival of his family at any cost. Clifford sat in the chair where Henry had sat just nights before when Isiah had tried to pull him over the rail in an attempt to kill him. His head was half down and half up, his eyes searched the streets for anything. As people passed they waved their hands at Clifford and said, "how you?" Clifford finished his cigarette and called to Toni to join him on the porch.

Trudy leaned against the pillows on the sofa and acted as though she was watching the television. Toni knew that she was not, but decided not to entertain the obvious. The darkness was taking over and the only light that could be seen was that of the streetlights and the houses. Clifford asked Toni whether she had her pistol and gave her further instructions. Toni, surprisingly, was as determined or more determined than Clifford to preserve her family, regardless of the cost.

Jeremiah came downstairs and stood at the door while Toni and Clifford talked on the porch. Toni turned and saw the little boy standing there looking through the screen door at them. He remained quiet, not saying anything, just watching. It was as though he knew that they were talking about something and that he should not disturb them.

As Toni and Clifford talked Jeremiah turned and walked away from the door. Toni walked inside to see where the little boy was. There was Jeremiah sitting in the chair across from his mother with his feet hanging down not touching the floor. Jeremiah's hands were folded in his lap and he just watched his mother. Jeremiah got down from the chair, looked at Toni and told her that he was tired and was going to bed. Toni kissed him goodnight and walked him to the stairway.

Clifford walked inside and sat in the chair where Jeremiah had sat. The look in his eyes revealed that something else was going on. Toni told Jeremiah to go upstairs and stay there. Toni then walked to the kitchen, grabbed the newspaper that Joyce had been reading and pretended to read it herself. There was a knock on the door and Clifford got up to open the door. Trudy sat up with a gleam in her eyes that could have provided light for the entire state of South Carolina on a dark night. Toni could again feel that

109

anger rise up inside of her. But this was no time for her to be angry because she did not know what plan these people had in their mind and heart.

Toni never stood up from the table as the five people walked in the front door. Toni had laid the pistol on the windowsill behind her so that she would only have to reach over and get it, if there was any trouble. Toni saw the black plastic bag being carried by the only male in the group. Toni's eyes followed the bag without seeing the hand of the person that was carrying it. After a few words of introductions, Clifford offered his chair to one of the people. The old lady half walked and half shuffled to the sofa where Trudy was now sitting up.

Toni watched as the others seemed to move aside making a clear path for the old woman to get to the sofa. Her anger was kindled again, but Toni stiffened her back and determined that she would act like a soldier. Although there were no artillery tanks or weapons she knew that she and her family were in a war. The war, Toni thought, had to be won by her and her family, so she had to put aside the anger so that she would not miss anything.

Clifford stood at the front door watching as the people feigned their kindness. As Toni watched she felt a heat come before her. The heat felt like she was standing in front of a hot oven, but this heat was moist and different. Toni felt and heard herself exhaling through her nose like a dog would do. She could not and would not inhale until after she had blown through her nose. The atmosphere in the house seemed to change. Toni began to pray in her mind, asking God to keep all hurt, harm and danger from her family and to make their enemies their footstool. She did not know why those words had come to her but she sat at the table watching and repeating the words over and over in her mind, but never taking her eyes off of the bag being held by the man.

"That's my brother-in-law, Clifford Spann, and my oldest daughter, Tonitia, who live in Connecticut." Trudy said.

Toni looked in the living room and spoke to the people. Trudy, somehow was inspired to add that Toni was very tired because she had not had any sleep since arriving from Connecticut and needed to just let some things go and get herself a good nights rest. One of the ladies in the group commented that rest was important because "whatever will be, will be." Toni smiled at the lady and was inspired to say, "I'll get some sleep, Jesus never sleeps so ain't no need in me staying up." The statement seemed to slap the five people in the face. Toni watched them as the words seemed to silently circle the room, but not one soul commented. Everybody was staring at Toni, now. It was as though the statement had shocked every hearer.

Toni soon felt like she was in charge of the situation. Toni offered the five people something cold to drink. She knew in her spirit that they would not accept, but she was almost shocked by the resounding "no thank, you." They had all said the same thing at the same time. Toni almost laughed to herself, because southern people who were suspicious of witchcraft did not eat or drink anything from other people. Toni watched from the table as the man reached in his pocket and pulled out a handkerchief and wiped his face even though there was no sweat and no heat in the room. Toni thought it strange as they chit chatted about nothing how the man waved the handkerchief. As the handkerchief waved back and forth Toni was compelled to do something to stop it.

"Sir do you want me to take that bag? Jesus knows how plastic can hold heat." Toni said as she walked forward and almost took it out of his hand.

"Oh, yeah, you mama things are in here, she might want to check to make sure everything is there." He said.

"That's okay, I'm sure everything is there, who would want to take under garments that's already been worn by somebody?" Toni said as she walked away with the bag.

The old woman watched Toni as she walked back into the kitchen. The old woman was not the only one watching. It seemed like the bag might have held something. Toni tied the top of the bag as she set it on the floor near the backdoor. Clifford also noticed the look on the faces of the five people as Toni tied the top of the bag. Toni knew then that there was something wrong and that the folks sitting in her mother's living room were up to no good.

"Mama, I think it's time for you to go upstairs and rest like the doctor said. These people got a distance to drive yet tonight in the dark." Toni heard herself saying.

There was some quiet agreement to what Toni had said. The people slowly began to move, but they understood that they were no longer welcome. Clifford stood on the porch holding the door open and waited for the first of them to come out. It had become more than obvious that Toni and Clifford wanted them out of the house in spite of what Trudy may have wanted. Trudy had been allowed to have her way because no one had been there to keep an eye on her. Now, Toni thought, Trudy had seen the family of Isiah and it was time for them to leave.

15

After the five people left the house, Clifford commented about the strange smell that had been left behind. Toni had also smelled it, a mixture of garlic and onions and something else that she could not recognize. Clifford opened the front and back doors so that the breeze could clear the air. Trudy sat up on the sofa and stated that she couldn't smell anything. Joyce came downstairs and looked around the room.

"Jesus Christ, those people sure left an odor in here. I started smelling something just before I got down here. I pray to God that whatever it is it just disappear or get out of here and catch up with them people." Joyce said.

Trudy looked at Joyce with a bit of anger. Everybody was smelling something strange except her. Clifford told Trudy to wrap the covers around herself if she was going to sit downstairs because he was going to leave the doors open for a while to get rid of the odor. Trudy did not respond, she sat back on the sofa and watched as everybody else commented about the smell.

Joyce went back upstairs saying that she had something that she wanted to get. Quickly Joyce returned with a thin package in her hand.

"What is that you got, Joyce?" Trudy asked.

"It's some incense we bought at the fair. It's Myrrh and Frankincense, they said it's the same thing that the people burned in churches when Jesus came. If they burned it for Jesus it sure should be fine for this odor in here." Joyce said.

Clifford sat down and looked at Trudy. Joyce lit several sticks of the incense and set them in the flower pots. Toni began to look for something that she could use to burn the clothing in the bag that Isiah's people had brought. Toni found a small metal pail that a mop was sitting in and removed the mop. Her search had drawn Trudy's attention to her. Clifford just sat and watched. He seemed to know that Trudy was watching Toni and was curious about what she was doing.

"I guess it'll take them folks about three hours or so to get back up that road where they live." Clifford said.

"Yeah, it's about that long, but they can take ninety-five most of the way." Trudy responded.

Toni took the plastic bag and headed for the backyard.

"Tonitia, what you about to do with that bag?" Trudy asked.

"I'm getting ready to burn everything in it." Toni snapped.

"Oh no, you ain't." Trudy responded. "My things are in there, all I got to do is put them in the wash and they good as brand new."

"No, mama, they won't be as good as brand new. I don't trust those people and something is telling me not to even open this bag, just to burn it."

"You done lost your mind, girl. Those things are good, give me my stuff." Trudy demanded.

"No! I'm burning this bag and everything that's in it, mama. Don't you smell that odor in the house? I might not know what is truly going on but I'm gonna follow my mind right now and burn this stuff. Those people are evil and I don't care what you say."

Toni could not get the plastic bag down into the metal bucket so she got newspaper and spread on the ground. She placed the plastic bag in the center of the paper. Joyce came out and stopped Toni and handed her a foot tub, which was a little larger than the mop pail. The foot tub had been used by Wilson to soak his feet, but Joyce said that they could always buy him another. Joyce had a small can in her hand, which she gave to Toni.

"This is some charcoal lighter fluid, it should get this fire started." Joyce told Toni.

"Okay, let this stuff burn. Close the backdoor and the kitchen window so the smoke won't get in the house." Toni told Joyce.

Clifford walked out of the house as the two sisters prepared to burn the contents of the bag. Clifford stood with his hands in his pockets and watched silently. Joyce closed the kitchen window and walked out of the backdoor closing it behind her. Toni rolled back the top of the plastic bag exposing the contents and squirted the fluid from the can into it. Clifford struck the match and dropped it on the bag. The fire began to rise as the uncle and his two nieces stood back and watched. As they watched the fire burn the flames grew taller and taller. Toni watched in awe, as did Joyce and Clifford. The flames were red, yellow, then blue appeared in the midst. Toni thought that she was seeing things or that her imagination had taken control of her sight as she watched what appeared to be figures in the fire. It looked like there were human forms in the fire trying to escape but the flames would devour them as they tried to rise up.

Clifford now was watching the fire with great curiosity as the flames rose and fell. Clifford knew that there was something mysterious, if not totally evil about what they were watching. Inside the flames Clifford too, saw what appeared to be figures trying to get out. Clifford was watching the flames intently when he saw a figure rise up that was larger than any of the others that he had seen. There was no mistake, he thought, his eyes were not playing tricks on him and his imagination had not taken off on some wild goose chase. The large flaming figure seemed to stand straight up in the fire and take note of what was happening, but the flames seemed to have been a chain that kept it in fire. So astonishing was the figure to the trio as they watched that they all sounded shocked and simultaneously shouted, "Jesus Christ."

"Did y'all see that?" Joyce asked.

Toni, still somewhat in shock was slow to respond. Clifford clapped his hands and stamped his feet on the ground as though he was trying to dig a hole.

"Lord, have mercy. What, in the name of Jesus, did those people do? Did you see that, did you see that? I know my eyes ain't playing tricks on me, those people did something with those things. Whatever they did or tried to do, it's going back to them." Clifford said as he circled the small fire in the backyard.

"You see, that? Mama sitting up in there thinking that these people are her friends and they trying to hurt her and us. I don't know what else to do, but I just ask the Lord to take this away from us and give it back to the ones that brought this here." Toni said.

The three stood in silence for a moment just staring at the flames. Clifford looked around to see if he could find a stick or something that would allow him to stir up the remaining contents of the bag so they could all burn into ashes. After finding a small stick and stirring the contents, Clifford threw the stick into the flames as well. As they watched, Essie, the neighbor lady from across the street came past and spoke to them. She walked over to where they were standing and watching the fire, which was now dying down.

"How y'all doing, Cliff?" she asked.

"Doing good, girl, how about yourself?" Clifford responded.

"Blessed, blessed." Essie responded. "How Trudy doing? How is Henry, when he gonna get out? I seen when you and Toni brought her home today. I didn't want to just rush over to the house before y'all got things straightened out."

"She doing pretty good, a little weak, but that's to be expected. Henry is out, but he'll be with me." Clifford said.

"Praise God, I believe that's best for him, now. Well, God still in control, believe it or not. He'll work everything out to His satisfaction." Essie said. "What y'all burning there?" She asked.

"These were some things she had on when she went to the hospital Saturday morning. That boy's people brought them by here not too long ago." Clifford said.

"Oh, yes sir, yes sir, y'all doing the right thing, don't let those things be mixed with nothing else. I seen them folks pull up and I couldn't help but to pray when I seen them. I just knew it was Isiah's people when they drove up in his car. There ain't nothing but evil in them people, Clifford. I was shocked that they would even come here." Essie said.

"Well, they did. When me and Toni knew anything they were already on their way here. But my niece here just had this feeling to just burn the things in the bag. Trudy, she wanted to put them in the washer. But, Toni said uh, uh, these things gonna be burned. That's what we doing." Clifford said as Toni and Joyce watched and listened.

"Praise God, that child had the mind to do what she did, Clifford. I'm telling you there ain't nothing in my Holy Ghost that tells me that them peoples meant any good. Now, I'll tell you this, when all that is cooled down, get a shovel and pick up the ashes and put it in a bag and tie it up and put it in the garbage can to be carted away from here. Matter-of-fact, all of this should be thrown right into the river." Essie said.

"Okay, we'll sure do that." Clifford said.

While Essie was still standing there, Joyce said that she would get a large trash bag from the kitchen, but that she did not have a shovel. Essie said that she would bring one back. Essie returned with a shovel and used it to chomp through the charred remains to make sure that everything had been burned. As she sifted through the remains, there were several pieces of cloth that had not been burned. Essie asked for a piece of paper so that she could light it from the smoldering flames and get the other pieces lit so it could burn. Toni got several pieces of paper and squirted a little of the charcoal lighter fluid on them before handing them to Essie. Essie laid the pieces of paper over the unburned pieces of cloth.

"Clifford gimme your matches." She said.

Essie struck one match and dropped it on the paper. Within seconds of tossing the lit match on the paper, the cloth shot up in a furious and ferocious flame. The flame shot out like an explosion had taken place and seemed to be reaching out to grab any and everything within its reach.

Essie began speaking in a demanding tone but with a language that Toni knew to be tongues. She had heard it many times before and knew that Essie belonged to the Holiness Church. Everyone became silent while Essie walked around the fire praying in tongues. Essie finished her prayer in English, telling the invisible to, "go back to where you come from in the name of Jesus. The blood of Jesus stand against you devil, your assignment here is cancelled, and your work destroyed, in the name of Jesus."

Toni did not understand all of what Essie was doing or saying, but the words seemed to cling to her memory and she knew that they would not go away too soon. Deep down inside, Toni felt a chill that almost made her shiver, but the words that were spoken by the neighbor lady were more than comforting.

"I tell y'all right now, in the name of Jesus, them people had already done something to these here pieces of clothes before they got here. I thank the Lord that

Toni had something in her to hear what the Lord was saying and to put fire to this mess." Essie said.

"I know without a doubt in my heart, girl," Clifford said, "that something was devilish about them people. When they left up out the house, good God, they left a scent that you would not believe. I ain't talking about a scent cause they didn't bath, it was a strange odor, Essie. Joyce got some incense and lit it to get that odor out of there." Clifford said.

"Lord have mercy." Essie said as she faced their backdoor. "The devil won't have no victory here. Come on y'all, we gonna say a word of prayer right now, in the name of Jesus."

Toni and the others joined hands as Essie prayed. The prayer was so powerful that Toni felt herself rocking back and forth. Essie prayed in tongues and in English. Toni had not heard anyone pray like that before, the boldness of the neighbor's prayer gave Toni a measure of confidence that seemed to fill the very spot where she had felt the chill with a warmth that caused her to begin sweating. The neighbor blessed each of Toni's siblings, Toni, Trudy and Clifford. She also blessed everyone who would reach out to help them through their situations. Then she said something that seemed to cover Toni like a layer of skin, "Father, I cover Toni, with the blood of Jesus…"

When the prayer was over, Clifford was still thanking God. Toni still was unable to speak. Joyce was crying openly. Essie assured Joyce that everything was going to be alright and not to cry. As they were all standing around waiting for the flames to go completely out, Wilson walked up.

"How y'all doing? How you doing Miss Essie?" Wilson said to the neighbor.

"I'm blessed, Will, how about yourself?" She asked.

"I'm, I'm just like you, Miss Essie, I'm blessed, too." Wilson responded. "For a minute there I didn't know what to say, but something said be whatever Miss Essie is, so I'm blessed, too."

"Yes, you are Wilson, and don't you ever forget that either." Miss Essie said.

Wilson wanted to know whether Isiah's people had shown up. Joyce and Clifford told him what had happened and why they were all standing in the backyard. Wilson shook his head and asked where was Jeremiah. Wilson went in the house and returned a short time thereafter to tell them that he had covered Jeremiah up and that he was fast asleep. Joyce commented that Jeremiah seemed to be very tired that evening and not as inquisitive as he usually was. Wilson walked over and sat on the steps and watched as the others talked and used the shovel to sift through the ashes to make sure everything was burned and there were no flames before they put the ashes into a trash bag. There were still some hotspots, so Toni told them that she would wait until everything was cold and put it into the bag.

Clifford said that he was going to head for home so that Henry would not be alone. Toni told Joyce to go in and get ready for bed since she had to go to school the next day. Miss Essie raised her hand toward them and said goodnight as she blessed them one more time.

Toni walked inside the house to see what her mother was doing and to see whether she needed anything.

"Mama did you take your medicine?" she asked.

Half-asleep, by now, Trudy looked up and around. "Oh no, I dosed off looking at the television. Give me a glass of water, please mam."

Toni walked into the kitchen and washed her hands before getting the water for her mother. Walking back to the living room, Toni felt a lump in her throat and had to fight the sudden urge to just break down and cry. How she longed for her father. If he were still alive, she thought, none of this would be going on. But, her daddy was dead and there was nothing that she or anyone else could do to change that.

"Where your pills at, mama?" Toni asked as she looked over at the lamp table.

"I think they're upstairs. I don't believe I brought them down here. Joyce brought one to me before in her hand, so I think they're still up there."

Toni set the glass of water on the table and went upstairs to get the pills. There was Jeremiah, again, in his mother's bed. Toni walked into Jeremiah's room and pulled back the blue bedspread with the picture of the Corvette on it. As she situated the pillow for his head, she felt the cold, cold teardrop roll down her cheek. She walked back to her mother's bed and lifted Jeremiah and carried him to his own bed. At the same time, Wilson came out of his room.

"Toni, bring Jeremiah in here and let him sleep in Henry's bed so he won't be in there by himself."

As she turned and walked toward Wilson's bedroom, he could see the tears rolling down his big sister's cheek. Wilson moved toward Toni and took Jeremiah from her arms and carried him into the bedroom. Toni walked back to her mother's room and looked for the bottle of pills. After giving her mother a pill and asking whether she needed anything else, Toni walked back outside and sat on the back steps. Wilson came to the door and told Toni that Alma had called and said she was on her way there. Without turning to face Wilson, Toni acknowledged that she had heard him.

"Oh she is? Okay, I'll keep my eye open for her."

Toni sat on the step and cried the coldest tears into her own lap. The water coming from her eyes did not feel like it was coming from within because it did not have the slightest warmth to it. Toni felt like she was releasing buckets of ice water. As the tears soaked into the material of her pants it became even colder. Toni did not have any thoughts running through her mind as she had had before. The cold tears flowing from her eyes continued its output without ceasing. Toni opened her legs so that her pants would not become saturated with the cold water from her eyes. As the tears flowed, Toni began to feel a weight lift from not just her physical shoulders, but a weight and tightening from within began to be lifted as well.

Toni got up and took the shovel and sifted through the ashes to see whether there were sparks or hot spots left. As she sifted through the ashes a tear fell upon a hot spot. Toni heard the sound that results when water hits fire. Stopping briefly to try and capture what she had just heard, Toni stood still and stared down at the heap of ashes through blurry wet eyes. She could not see what had happened but was sure of what she had heard.

"Hey girl." Alma said, as she came around the house walking to meet her friend. "What you doing out here?"

"I'm burning the clothes that Isiah's people brought by here tonight to mama."

"Say what? You mean to tell me, Toni, that those people were bold enough to come here?

"Yes, they came by invitation, though."

"What you talking about? Did you invite them?"

"No! Mama invited them to come here. I was over at Uncle Clifford's house with Henry because I had just gotten him bailed out."

"Praise the Lord, he's out now. How Henry doing?"

"He doing okay, as far as I can see, Alma, but he said that he can't stay here in the same house with mama."

With her hands on her hips, Alma looked at Toni with love and pity.

"Toni, I don't know what it's like to have to deal with all of this, but I pray that Henry don't hate Miss Trudy. I can understand him not wanting to be here, but I sure hope he will still talk to his mama."

"I don't know Alma, but so much that I cannot see seems to be going on. These things that I'm burning were the clothes mama had on when Isiah shot her and she went to the hospital. I was at Uncle Clifford's house when Joyce called and said that mama had told Isiah's people to come by here before they leave town. So we shot back here to the house like bats out of hell."

"Didn't Miss Trudy think that those people might just be pretending to be Christian-like just to get inside and hurt somebody?"

"I don't know Alma whether mama even thinking in her right mind. All that I could think about when Joyce called is what if those people came and Wilson was here and they thought that he was Henry."

"That wouldn't have mattered to people with a depraved heart, girl. All those people would have wanted was an eye for eye and a tooth for a tooth, and even a son for a son. Shoot, even Christian people can get all revengeful. You just can't ever tell what's in the heart or even the minds of people like that."

"We got here before they did. I had a pistol sitting right there at the kitchen table. Uncle Clifford had his pistol in his belt. We had already discussed it that if anyone of those people tried anything we would have lit their behinds up right in that living room."

"Toni, something tell me that those people meant evil for y'all. It's a good thing you and Uncle Clifford was here. Was Wilson here?"

"No, he came in and found out that those people were coming and he left the house. But he was mad at mama. He's back home now."

"Miss Trudy said anything about Margaret, yet?"

"Alma, you know what? Mama ain't said one word about Margaret or even Henry's whereabouts. The truth is, mama ain't said anything about Henry since I told her that Henry shot and killed Isiah after he came to the house to try and kill Henry."

"Come on, Toni. Maybe she just don't know how to ask about Henry, maybe she just feeling a little ashamed about what happened to her and that she might have caused all the stuff that's happening."

"Maybe, just maybe, you're right, Alma. But she still hadn't asked about Margaret. I thought when she was told that Isiah had shot at Henry that she would, at least, ask whether Henry was okay, but all that she said was that she told all of us that if she had any problems with anybody, that she would take care of it."

"Toni, I'm telling you, girl, Isiah and his people put something on Miss Trudy. Your mama don't really know what she doing now. I'm telling you, I've seen what can happen to people who got roots on them."

"Alma, I don't know what it is, but I believe that Isiah did something to mama. It's just that mama can't see that something is wrong with her. I don't understand all of this mess, but Alma, when those people left this house, there was a strange odor that started to rise up in there. Joyce found some of Wilson's incense and lit them. Mama claimed that she didn't smell anything."

"Oh, no! Those dirty bastards. They came into this house dressed, as my uncle and them say. Whatever they had on them they had it so that it would stay when they left. I pray to God that whatever they brought with them go right back to them."

117

"Something in me said to burn everything in the bag that they brought. These were the clothes that mama had on the other night. Isiah had left them in his car and his people brought them here. Mama didn't want me to burn them, but I didn't pay her no mind, girl."

"All that I can say is that you did the right thing. Burn everything in there."

"Miss Essie came by as me, Joyce and Uncle Clifford were out here burning this stuff."

"You mean Miss Essie cross the street, there?"

"Uh huh."

"Did she pray, Toni?"

"Did she pray? That lady put down a piece of praying out here, Alma. I don't know what it is, but I got a feeling of confidence as Miss Essie was praying. It was almost as if she was speaking directly to the devil and telling him that he had better not come near us."

"Toni, I'm telling you, Miss Essie can pray. She is a woman who is truly anointed of the Lord."

Toni did not know exactly what the word anointed meant, but she felt that it meant something having power.

"Alma, while we were out here, you could see things in the flames that looked like spirits or something. They looked like they were trying to get out of the fire. Then after Miss Essie came by and started sifting through the ashes for hot spots and to make sure that everything was being burned, girl something weird happened."

Toni and Alma moved over to the steps and sat down. Alma was eager to hear what her friend was about to tell her. Alma grabbed her friend's hand and reassured her that Miss Essie had put the word of God on the situation and that nothing was going to happen as Isiah's people may have designed it.

"Alma, there were a couple of pieces of the clothes that had not burned thoroughly. So I sprinkled just a little bit of the charcoal lighter fluid on a few pieces of paper and laid them on the top of the material. Miss Essie struck a match and dropped it on the paper. Girl, about that quick," Toni said snapping her finger, "a flame jumped up and looked like it just tried to grab everybody standing around. But Miss Essie started praying in tongues and speaking some stuff I ain't never heard before."

Alma was excited and started to clap her hands.

"Oh glory to God. Thank you, Jesus for Miss Essie."

Toni stared at Alma as though it was the first time that she had seen her. Toni was surprised to see her friend respond in that manner, but she was also glad to know that Alma understood what Miss Essie had done and approved of it.

"Toni, I'm telling you, girl, the Lord sent Miss Essie by here. The Lord knew that those people had done something to themselves and to those clothes of Miss Trudy's. They probably thought that none of y'all was smart enough to take the stuff and burn it and not let your mama wear them. Girl, I bet you if they knew what all that happened here tonight, they would buy a dog just to kick it to death. But the Lord knew what they had planned. We can see up to the corner, but God can see around the corner. Miss Essie done put the word of the Lord on that junk."

"Why you out this time of night? Don't you have to work tomorrow?" Toni asked.

"You know I gotta work, but I'm working the second shift and don't have to be there until three o'clock."

"Oh, that's not bad at all. I should be thinking about getting myself back to Connecticut soon."

118

"I know, but I don't get to see you too much, girl. I hate having to see you under these conditions, but I'll take what I can get."

"Alma, come hell or high water, it wouldn't matter where we are, they've got some type of transportation to bring us to each other. I've got to make some decisions about school, too, girl."

"Toni, I don't care what it takes, you have to finish college, girl. You're the only one of us girls who ever even started, so you have to finish."

"It's never too late for you to start, either now."

"Girl, I know you for real on that. But you know what, Toni, I've seriously been thinking about getting my degree in nursing and going into the Navy or the Air Force as an officer."

"Alma, do it! Girl you would look sharp as a tack in a Navy uniform, girl. Don't think about it, just go on and do it. You can get your degree, put in twenty years, travel and still retire with a good pension before you're fifty."

"Come on, Toni, retire before I'm fifty?"

"Yes. It'll take you what, another two years to get your degree at Baptist College?"

"Uh huh."

"Then you'll be twenty five or twenty-six years old. Okay, you enlist and twenty years later you're forty-five, forty-six. Girl you can retire and get that pension for the rest of your life and go to work again at the hospital with one of those big titles because of your experience."

"Ooh, Toni, that sure sound like a good way to get a little bit of everything in life. I can take my son with me wherever I go and he can see other parts of the country as well."

"Now what is there to think about Alma? Get your hind parts in gear girl and get that degree. I heard that they have an officer program while you're in college and they commission you as soon as you graduate."

"Toni, thank you sweetie. I'm gonna do all of my little background work first. After I get the information I need about the officer program then I've got my goal and I can work toward that."

"Look, even if you change your mind about the military, don't change it about getting that degree, you can use that anywhere."

"Sure you right, girl. But seriously, Toni, I want to get out of here for a while and see what else is out there. I like the military and the idea of them having to salute me is worth a little something. Now that retirement before I'm fifty years old is right up my alley, girl."

"Shoot, go for it, Alma. I need to have a few more places to visit when I become Judge Tonitia Spann."

The two friends sat in the cool night breeze sharing their future plans and laughing. The fire had been dead and cold for quite sometime when they took the shovel and lifted the ashes into the garbage bag. Toni tied a knot in the top of the bag and she and Alma walked to the garbage can and dropped it in.

Alma had forgotten that she had brought a couple of cans of beer, but had left them in the back seat of her car. They walked to Alma's car and got the beer, then returned to the back steps where they sat talking and sipping the warm beer.

"You scared Toni?" Alma asked her friend.

Toni's eyes filled with tears immediately. She held the can with both hands staring straight ahead, but at nothing in particular. The tears began to flow and seemed endless. As the warm salty fluid streamed steadily down her face, into the crevices of her lips it seemed to softly pry open her mouth and settle on her tongue. Toni looked at Alma, whom she knew that she could be completely honest with.

"Alma, I'm afraid, but I don't know exactly of what. I'm afraid that mama won't see what is happening or even want to look at what it's been like since daddy died. I'm afraid that Henry hates mama. I don't even know where Aaron junior is. Joyce and Jeremiah and even Wilson need somebody there for them and I have dreams of my own. These people of Isiah's, only God knows what they're up to. I'm just afraid, I guess, of almost everything at this point."

"We've been through a few things girl and somehow we landed on our feet. Remember when I realized that I was pregnant?"

"Remember? Shoot, how can I ever forget? After you drank all of that turpentine I thought you would either vomit to death or start bleeding like a stuffed pig."

"Oh now don't forget those little pills that somebody else had told me about. What were they called?"

"I don't remember, but I do remember not being able to buy lunch that Friday so you could have enough money to get them. I sure did want that fish and macaroni that day, too."

"Yes, yes, yes, but after the initial shock and shame things were okay, weren't they?"

"Yeah, they were. But that was something different though, Alma."

"That's true, but it was like I had committed the unpardonable sin in mama's eye. My daddy couldn't even talk to me for weeks after that. When I started showing I thought daddy would just keel over and die."

"I remember that."

"I was so happy that Miss Trudy didn't act like those other ladies. Miss Trudy didn't stop us from being together and she let me come around here and sit on the porch or in the house. Miss Trudy was very kind to me and the only thing that she ever said to me was that everybody was allowed one mistake and not to make that a habit. Even my mama was grateful for that because she worried that I would be so isolated it would cause me to get sick."

"I know Alma, but look at you now, almost a Navy Nurse and world traveler. I understand, even though I really don't."

"Toni, whatever happens after this, I just got a feeling that God is going to use it for good. I heard the preacher on the radio today talking about how Job had to go through a lot of things but God allowed it, then gave him twice as much as he had before. I can't say that I fully understand what the preacher was talking about, but somehow it stuck in my spirit. You know what I mean?"

"I think I do. I heard Rev. Lampkin say a long time ago, that the weapon might be formed against us, but it wouldn't prosper. No matter what happens, girl, it's only to make us who we're supposed to be. This too, shall pass."

Toni and Alma sat on the back steps with their arms locked together strengthening each other for what was ahead of them. They sat in silence looking up at the sky and examining every star that they could see. When they began to talk again, Toni and Alma promised that they would always stay in touch and never allow anything to come between them.

Alma suggested that they go inside so she could sit with Trudy for a few minutes before going home. Toni left the shovel leaning against the house and they went inside.

"Miss Trudy, how you feeling?" Alma asked.

Trudy had been asleep and appeared groggy as she tried to focus her eyes. She grunted and groaned just a little as she tried to adjust her position on the sofa.

"Alma, that's you, baby?"

"Yes mam, it's me. How you doing?"

"I'm so-so, baby."

"You want me to give you a sponge bath while I'm here and massage your back and legs? You know a massage will help your muscles to relax so you can sleep better and heal faster?"

"No, not tonight, sweetie, but I sure do appreciate the offer. Maybe you can do that for me some other time, though."

"You just call me and let me know and I'll sure give you a good massage."

"Mama, I think it's time for you take some medicine, again." Toni said.

"You think so?" Her mother asked.

Toni went upstairs to get the pills and left Alma downstairs with Trudy. It was quiet upstairs; Joyce, Jeremiah and Wilson seemed to be sound asleep. Toni believed that they had been wearied by the events of that evening and the days prior to that and had probably fallen asleep before their heads hit the pillow. She got the pills and returned to the kitchen to get water for her mother. Toni stood by watching as her mother swallowed each pill then handing her the water glass after each. Alma sat and watched the television, which had been playing nearly all evening.

"Well Alma, how your mama doing?" Trudy asked.

"She doing fine, Miss Trudy."

"Mama don't you wanna go upstairs and get in your bed, now?" Toni asked.

"Yeah, this couch ain't the most comfortable piece of sleeping equipment."

Toni and Alma helped to get Trudy up and on her feet. Toni assisted her as she walked toward the stairs. There was a groan for every step that Trudy took as she made her way upstairs. Toni made sure that the sheets were pulled tight and fluffed the pillows. Trudy sat on the side of the bed and slid back so that she was nearly in the center of the bed. Toni then lifted her legs and helped to swing them over into the bed and covered her mother with a sheet, bedspread and a light blanket.

Toni began to walk out of the room when she heard Trudy's voice.

"Mama you said something?"

"Yeah, I said to make sure you get yourself a good night's sleep. I can see that you been going and going and ain't had too much rest."

"Yes mam."

As Toni walked away from the room, she thought to herself that something must have changed in her because she did not feel the same as she had before about doing something for her mother. Earlier Toni had felt anger toward her mother and lacked the desire to help her. But as she readied Trudy for bed and got her medication she had done so without a thought. Quietly, Toni thanked God for allowing her to help her mother without the anger or hostility.

Toni walked Alma out to her car and watched as she turned the corner. Although she was tired, Toni was not ready for sleep and decided to just sit on the porch in the dark. She watched the corner where the streetlight shined down. No one was there to bath in the light. The night air was sweet and the atmosphere had a special kind of quiet and comfort in it.

Toni thought that she would leave South Carolina on Saturday and return to Connecticut. She thought about Margaret and how she must have felt, the frustration that must have reached overflowing within her. Aaron Junior must have reached that point and beyond when he left. No one had heard from him in more than a year. She prayed as she sat there that God would protect Aaron Junior and help him to live with the situation without losing himself or his mind. Henry, the thought of what Henry would have to face now and for the rest of his life was so overwhelming that Toni began to cry.

The darkness of night was a good cover for her to silently vent and cleanse her soul through tears. She wondered whether her father had gone to heaven and whether he was observing the things that had happened. Her throat began to tighten up; a lump the size of an apple felt like it had suddenly seemed to appear in her throat. She allowed the tears to flow and continued to watch the corner where the streetlight shined.

She watched the corner through floods of tears as though she were expecting someone to step into the light. Gradually, Toni began to feel as though the light from the street lamp had walked up to the porch and was shining down on her. There was a flood of something other than the tears, a brilliant warmth that seemed to dry every tear within her.

Toni felt herself being bathed in the warmth of the distant street lamp, she knew without a shadow of a doubt that everything was going to be fine. She could not figure out how it was going to be done, but for that brief moment she knew that it would. It felt as though this truth was being burned into her spirit.

She sat in the dark and closed her eyes so that she would not have to watch the corner where the street lamp shined. As she closed her eyes the light shined even brighter in her mind. As the light grew brighter in her mind she began to rock back and forth like she was being hit by the waves of the ocean. She began to climb, in her mind, above the waves that rocked her back and forth and to see lights burst like little bombs.

As she clinched her eyes shut, Toni began to see colored lights and felt like there was no weight to her body. She raced through the colored lights chasing after them to touch them and feel them burst in her hands. As she began her mental pursuit of the colored lights and feel the carefreeness of her flight, Toni felt herself gasping for air. She was trying to touch as many of the little colored lights as she could, then her eyes were opened again.

For the first time Toni did not try to figure out what had just happened or why it had. She got up and walked into the house. She began to clean up and prepare the house for the next morning. Her mind ran on Kim and she said a prayer in her heart for her friend whom she knew was praying for her and her family back in Connecticut. Toni finished the dishes in the sink, swept the floor; damp mopped it, dusted the rest of the downstairs, cleaned the bathroom and turned off the lights.

16

"Hey, Toni, Toni, you better get up, we're leaving." Wilson said as he stood in the door of the bedroom.

Toni had slept while her siblings prepared for work and school. She had not heard them as they walked back and forth in the hallway. Her first thoughts were of Jeremiah, her little brother.

"Where's Jerry?" she asked.

"He's downstairs eating."

Toni jumped up from the bed and grabbed the robe that lay at the foot of it. She did not want Jerry going off to school without a hug or a sweet word. As she hurried down the steps she heard the telephone ringing. She did not know how long she had slept but knew that she had needed every minute that she had slept.

Joyce answered the telephone and as Toni stepped into the living room she could hear Joyce telling the caller to wait.

"It's for you, it's Kim, she wants to talk to you for a minute."

"Thanks." Toni said as she took the telephone from Joyce. "Good morning, how you doing girl?"

Kim told Toni that she was concerned because she hadn't heard from her and her heart would not rest.

"So much has been going on, Kim, but Henry is out of jail and I need to wrap up a few things before I head back there."

The two friends spoke for a couple of minutes and Toni focused her attention on Jeremiah. The love she had for her little brother was like that of a mother for a son. Jeremiah pinched her on the arm and smiled. His little eyes lit up whenever she was around.

"Hey sleepy head, your hair look like a curly mop, but you still look cute." Jeremiah said to his big sister.

"Flattery will get you everything, sweetie, thank you." She responded as she kissed Jeremiah on his forehead.

"You should just run your finger through your hair Toni and that's all. No kidding, it look cute."

"You think so, Jeremiah?"

"Yep, I wouldn't tell you no story."

"Okay, I'll try it just for you."

Toni sat down for a moment and just smiled at Jeremiah. He chatted away about things at school and how he wished a little girl would stop singing his name. Toni teased him about having a girlfriend but he steadfastly denied that the feeling was mutual. Toni asked whether he wanted her to fix him a lunch or did he want to buy lunch. Jeremiah jumped at the opportunity to buy lunch. Always trying to find a way to bring happiness into the life of her siblings, Toni gave Jeremiah a dollar and gave Joyce two.

After Joyce and Jeremiah had left for school, Toni went upstairs to check on her mother.

"Mama, you want me to run some water in the tub and help you take a bath?"

"Would you please. Don't make it too hot. If you can just help me get in the tub, I can bathe myself, but I'll need some help getting out."

"Okay."

Toni washed out the tub again, to make sure that it was clean for her mother. After placing the stopper in the drain she squirted a little bubble bath to make some bubbles. She placed a hand towel and bath cloth at the end of the tub so her mother would not have to reach far for them. Trudy placed her foot in the tub to test the temperature of the water.

"Yep, this is just right. Those sponge baths don't get all the spots, but they do help. A good bath just make you feel better." Trudy said as Toni helped lower her into the tub.

"I'll start some breakfast for you and come back and get you out."

"Okay. Don't rush cause I'm kind of slow here and I want make sure that I wash the possible and the impossible real good."

As Toni walked away from the door, she realized that her mother was trying to have a sense of humor. Then she wondered what this was leading up to. Toni tried to banish the thought that her mother's behavior was a ploy to soften the entrance of yet another scheme.

Toni went to the refrigerator and began to pull out the sausage when the telephone rang. It was Margaret; she had finally gotten enough strength to call. Toni had decided that she would leave her alone for a few days so that she could think clearly. But when Margaret told her what she had done, Toni was nearly speechless.

"Margaret, why couldn't you just tell me so that you could at least have family standing with you?" Toni asked.

Margaret and Lloyd had gotten married the night before. Toni thought it strange that Margaret, or even Lloyd would get married at a time like this. But Margaret had said that Lloyd did not believe in shacking and had to make it right, if they were going to live in the same house. Toni thought that this was pretty admirable of Lloyd, but also thought that they should have waited until some other time to get married. But, it was done and there was nothing that she could or even wanted to do to undo what they had done.

Toni went back upstairs to check on her mother in the tub. To her surprise, Trudy had gotten herself out of the tub without any assistance and was slowly drying her body.

"You need any help mama?"

"No, I think I just about got it. All I have to do is take my time and I can finish up here. You go on and finish what you doing."

"You sure, now?" Toni asked.

"Yes, mam. But I'll call you if I need some help."

As she walked down the stairs, Toni thought of how she would tell her mother that Margaret was now married to Lloyd. As she cooked the grits and stirred it, she tried to think of a way to break the news. Suddenly, Toni decided that it was not her responsibility to tell anyone. It was Margaret's business and if she wanted others to know then, Margaret could tell them herself. But, she thought, if anyone asked about Margaret, she would certainly mention the fact that she had gotten married.

Toni shook her head; it was hypocritical for her not to say anything yet become talkative when and if anyone should ask about Margaret. It was better she thought to not say anything at all and let Margaret be the one to tell about her marriage. But it still puzzled Toni why her sister would marry at a time like this. Surely, she had to consider the situation now facing the family. Toni was confused and believed that Margaret was looking for a safe shelter from everything that was happening. It wasn't because Lloyd was not a good person. It just didn't seem right, Toni thought, at this time.

Trudy was trying to do more for herself to diminish the guilt that she was feeling inside. She did not know what to say that would be acceptable to Toni or any of her children. As she tried to put on a pair of panties Trudy was weakened by a sudden wave of pain and loneliness. She sat on the trunk near the window and let the tears flow. The pain in her heart was so great that she thought that it was just better to lie on the floor and let death cover her. As the tears flowed, Trudy's heart began to separate into what seemed a million pieces. She felt like there was no one else on the face of the earth but her. The loneliness, the pain and the guilt of being responsible not only for the death of her lover, but the jailing of her son, as well. She cried because no one in the world understood her and her needs.

As she tried to dry the tears from her eyes, Trudy tried as best she could, to pray that Toni would stay downstairs long enough until this thing had passed over. No matter how much she tried the pain caused the tears to flow even more. The lump in her throat seemed to be growing bigger and bigger. Trudy thought that she would choke to death from the lump. How could she have been so silly? Why could she not see that a relationship with Isiah would lead to her demise? What were her children thinking? And Toni, poor Toni, she thought. So much had fallen on Toni's shoulders, she thought. Trudy thought that Toni was being quiet because she had had as much as any person could take from a delinquent parent.

"Lord, I know they say that still waters run deep. Don't let Toni hate me, God. God please, let her know that I appreciate everything that she has done. I don't even know how to tell her thank you, Lord." Trudy prayed.

"Why am I this way Lord?" Trudy asked.

As she tried again to put her feet into the legs of the panties the tears continued to flow. Trudy felt sorry for Isiah. She didn't know how to ask about Henry and did not know how Henry would react to her after this. She knew that she had done so much to make her children ashamed of her. She wondered what they would do now because she knew that she had gone beyond any limits that would allow her children to respect her. Now where were her so-called buddies? None had showed up at the hospital, nor had they called the house to find out how she was doing.

Trudy began to sob uncontrollably, as she thought about her situation. She admitted to herself that she loved Isiah, but did not know why. He had done things to her that she would never have allowed her deceased husband to get away with when he was alive. It was true, Trudy thought, she had chosen Isiah and a few others over her children. Each time that Toni had come to town to straighten out some little mess that she had caused, she could see the frustration in her face. Trudy had found herself fearing that Toni would hear about what she had done and she would try to concoct another story to explain away her own guilt. It was beginning to look like Toni was the mother and she was the wild child.

Trudy managed to get her panties on and walk back to the bathroom to get the washcloth and wipe her face. As she was wiping the tears from her face Toni came up the steps.

"You need any help? I've got breakfast ready." Toni said.

"Oh, everything ready? Let me put a little pep in my steps, sweetie."

"I can help you, if you need it."

"Oh, no. All I got to do is put on that little zip up duster you bought me. That little dress is just the right thing for me now. You go on and put the food on the table, I'll be right there."

Toni turned and walked down the steps. As she walked back to the kitchen she felt pity for her mother. She wanted to talk to her mother. Toni wanted to know what her mother was going to do different now than she had done in the past. There was a pain in Toni's heart as well. She now had to pay for Henry's defense and try somehow to keep up the spirits of her siblings, finish college and keep her own sanity, from Connecticut. The tears rolled down her face as she took the plates from cabinet.

As Trudy entered the kitchen, Toni began to spoon grits into the plate.

"Mama, is this enough for you?"

"Let me see. Put another little spoonful more on there for me, please mam. I feel real hungry this morning."

Toni thought that this was a good sign that her mother was getting better. Toni put more grits on her mother's plate and eggs beside it. She placed the small Pyrex dish containing sausage and bacon in front of her mother. Toni turned again to the stove and heaped grits onto her plate. Toni set her plate on the table in the place at the head of the table and went to the refrigerator to get the butter dish. As she set everything including the orange juice on the table within her mother's reach, Toni wondered how the two of them would get through breakfast. There was no one in the house but the two women, mother and daughter.

Trudy realized at or about the same time that she and Toni would be sitting together, alone at the table. They had not had a period like this for years. As Trudy took her fork to pick up meat from the Pyrex dish she wondered whether she should strike up a conversation with Toni, or just allow the silence to fill the kitchen. Trudy thought that if she began a conversation that she could also dominate the conversation. But, she thought, that would perhaps allow her fear and nervousness to show. Toni was no fool, she thought. Toni would see through this like glass. But, she thought, if she could steer the conversation in a path that would not allow for even Toni to slip something in that would give way to conversation about her, Toni might not realize it.

Trudy placed the sausage on her plate and reached for the butter. She looked over and smiled at Toni.

"Thank you for fixing breakfast for me." She said.

"You're welcome."

Toni felt a little uncomfortable and prayed for a distraction. She realized that her mother, too, was uncomfortable and she didn't want anything that she would say make her even more uncomfortable.

"Margaret and Lloyd got married last night." Toni blurted out, but with a calmness.

Trudy looked like she was changing colors for a moment. The announcement had come as a shock to her. As she looked straight at Toni, Trudy tried to compose herself so that she would respond in an appropriate fashion.

"What? Margaret got married?"

"Yes, mam. Last night she said that she and Lloyd got married. You know Lloyd is saved and he said that he was not going to live in the same house with her and not be married to her."

"Well, I guess that says something for him. Many men wouldn't even think that way about a young girl, today. Heck, it ain't too many old men who think that way."

Toni could see that the announcement had shocked her mother, but she had a real cool comeback, Toni thought.

"Well, I hope to God that this work out for the two of them. Margaret is grown and she certainly don't need nobody to sign for her." Trudy said.

"Yeah, I just wished that they had let somebody know so we could have done something for her, like a little reception or something like that."

"Oh that sure would be nice. You know, it ain't too late for something like that. I see on television many of them folks get married and later they have a big formal ceremony so their friends and everybody can come." Trudy responded.

"Yeah, I've seen that too in real life. I have to give that some thought." Toni said.

"Well, Lloyd is a good person. She could have done worse, but he's a good man. Jeremiah sure as heck love him. Jeremiah sometimes get to the point where you'd think Lloyd come here to see him rather than Margaret."

"Yeah, he sure do like himself some Lloyd. I guess Lloyd take up so much time with him, getting him involved with baseball, hockey and some of everything else." Toni responded.

"Lloyd is real good with those kids. A lot of them around here wouldn't have the opportunity to get involved with after school stuff if Lloyd hadn't taken charge. Yeah, Lloyd is a good man. Your daddy used to take time with Lloyd, too, after his daddy got killed down there at the mill."

"Oh yeah? I didn't know that." Toni said.

"Yeah, Aaron used to let him ride with him in the truck when he would go from place to place selling vegetables on the weekend. He would make sure that he had money in his pocket so he could get things like the other big boys. His mama wasn't making a lot of money working for them white folks, so Aaron took a shine to Lloyd and Lloyd ain't never forgot that."

"Daddy helped a lot of people in this town. I've met other people who said that daddy would give their mama and daddy a few pounds of fish and some of the vegetables and stuff he had on the truck. If it hadn't been for daddy, they say they wouldn't have had anything to eat."

"Yeah, Aaron helped more people round here than they want to admit. But when he got down there sick you couldn't see any of them. None of those people came by here to even say here is a dollar Aaron to help you, or even to see how he was doing, whether they could take him out for some fresh air or anything. You can be as good as you want to some people and they don't appreciate it."

Toni could see that her mother was hurting. She didn't know whether her mother's pain was from the memory of her father or what was now going on in within the family. But Toni decided that she would not say anymore. Trudy began to cry and the tears rolled into her plate. Toni went upstairs and got the facecloth for her mother and to dry her own tears away.

"Thank you." Trudy said, as Toni handed her the facecloth.

For a little while, the two women sat at the table in silence. Toni let her mother cry as much and as long as she had too. Something within Toni told her to let her mother cry and never to stop a person from crying. Toni did not understand what she was feeling but she, no less, obeyed the feeling.

Out of respect, for the tears, for her mother, Toni stared out of the window rather than watch her or ask silly questions like what's wrong. Hell, everything was wrong, Toni thought. Why ask a stupid question. Toni tried to put herself in her mother's place and feel what she might be feeling. It was hard for Toni to imagine what it felt like to be responsible for the death of a person and your son being the person who did the killing.

Something in Toni began to correct a portion of her thoughts. Isiah was responsible for his own death. He had not foreseen his death because he had been hell bent on killing Henry. The one responsible for Isiah's death was dead. Toni thanked God that her brother was alive and with God's help and forgiveness, she thought, Henry would live a full life.

"Mama, you're not responsible for Isiah's death." Toni heard herself saying.

The statement made Trudy jerk her head up from her chest where she seemed to have laid her chin.

"Say what, baby?"

"I said that you're not responsible for Isiah's death. Isiah caused his own death, not you. He came here hell bent on killing Henry, but he failed to include God in the equation. I only regret that Henry will be called a murderer and he got to go trial, maybe. But I'd rather pay for a trial than a funeral." Toni responded.

Trudy did not know how to respond, but felt relieved that Toni had said what she did. It was an intense moment for the mother and daughter, and even Toni could not believe that she had been so bold in her statements.

"Mama, I believe that the devil was fishing for a soul that night but he forgot that the Lord work the night shift, too. The devil got what he wanted, God just made sure that he didn't get who he wanted. I just don't believe that it was ever in Isiah to be a good person, so he just went to who he served. I just pray that the rest of his people lay down all that voodoo and whodoo they've been using all of their lives and turn to the Lord. They still got time."

Trudy was still sitting at the table that was in the kitchen but her mind seemed to have taken her on a long journey without suitcases. Toni could see that her mother's body was still there but wondered where her mind had gone. Had she said too much, Toni thought, and it had had a devastating impact.

Toni looked out the window and allowed the silence to penetrate the moment. Trudy picked up her fork and finished her breakfast. Toni thanked God, silently, that the conversation had not effected her mother's appetite.

Toni stood up and walked to the sink and began running water to wash the breakfast dishes. The room seemed to be filled with some kind of invisible cloud that was increasing and taking up all of the air in it. Toni felt as though she was suffocating and needed more air than she was getting.

"Mama, I'm going to open this backdoor a little bit and let some fresh morning air in here. You gonna be okay over there?"

"Yeah, I'll be okay. I was just feeling like it was stuffy in here. Go on and crack that door. Sometime breathing the old air can make you feel bad, too."

Toni opened the door just a little and a rush of sweet smelling air rushed into the room. Within a few seconds it seemed like the room had returned to its normal size. The kitchen seemed to have been swelling and the space could not contain that which was filling it. But when Toni opened the backdoor it was like sticking a pin or needle into a balloon.

The rising sun poked its head into the door and made its way across the floor where the open door allowed its presence. Soon the crisp morning air had filled the kitchen and at the same time opened a passage for the invisible cloud that had filled the room to flow out. The breeze flowed through the house now and the air became lighter. Toni thought that she had smelled a faint odor of perfume, but she did not recognize the scent.

"That breeze feel good." Trudy said. "Seem like it was so stuffy in here for a minute my head started to spin."

Toni smiled, knowing nothing else to say or do. But she knew now that she was not alone in her feelings of being closed in by the invisible cloud. Toni went upstairs and got her mother's medication. Trudy shifted her body in the chair so that she could look at the houses behind hers through the window. Her thoughts were of her life when she was Toni's age, what a difference she thought. Toni was not married and did not depend on anyone, it seemed, to take care of her. She didn't have a boyfriend, Trudy thought and she didn't live with anyone. A brave young woman, Trudy thought. Her daughter was taking care of business and cleaning up messes caused by her and others, mostly by her. The depression came over Trudy like a blanket. She silently envied the woman that she had given birth to.

Toni made sure that her mother took the medication and began washing the dishes and cleaning up the kitchen. Trudy situated herself on the sofa in the living room and turned on the television. She was not particularly interested in what was on but needed a distraction more than anything else. Thoughts began to flood Trudy's mind and she tried to turn them off. The television did not serve as the distraction that she so needed. As Toni went about her chores, Trudy wondered what was going through her mind. Surely, Trudy thought, her daughter must be thinking that she was crazy.

Trudy found herself thinking about Isiah and the times that she had spent with him. She wondered whether she could continue life without him. It did not dawn on her that she had buried a husband and still lived through that experience. Trudy could not believe her own thoughts. She was lying on a sofa with a bullet wound through her chest because Isiah had shot her. She had not given much thought to the reason why she was taking medication and the wound in her lung. But now the thoughts seemed to be dominating her mind. Aaron had not shot her or even beaten her like Isiah had done, but why had she hated Aaron. She could now admit it, she had hated Aaron, but thought that she loved Isiah. Aaron had cheated on her and she had caught him red handed, right in the act. Isiah on the other hand had beaten her and tried to dominate her life, then he shot her just to prove that he was in control.

In her mind, Trudy replayed the night that Isiah had shot her, over and over. She remembered sitting at the table with Clara and several other women who should have been home at that hour of the night with their children. She and Clara had been drinking and having themselves a good time. Isiah walked in and saw her there. He had told her before that he did not want her with Clara, because Clara was "no good and a bad influence."

Trudy remembered the cold distant look in Isiah's eyes as he walked over to the table where she, Clara and the other women were sitting and talking. Isiah walked around to where she had been sitting, pulled the chair back and had told her to go home. At first she was shock because his boldness had taken on a new dimension. At first she had resisted his order for her to get up and go home. One of the women at the table had told Isiah to go on because they were just talking and not bothering anybody. But Trudy remembered that Isiah had turned to the woman and made such a sarcastic remark to her that even she had felt bad.

"Bitch, I ain't fucking you. I'm fucking that bitch right there, so you just keep your mouth shut." Isiah had said.

Even now Trudy felt a flash of heat that left her as embarrassed now as she had felt that night. She was embarrassed because Isiah had not respected her enough to refer to her by her name, but had called her a bitch. But she had heard it before. Then, Trudy thought, for as many times as she had heard Isiah refer to other women as bitches, she had kept silent. It was just a matter of time before he would begin to attack her the same way. How could she have been so stupid, she thought?

At first, Trudy thought, it was kind of cute to see Isiah act like he was jealous when anyone would look at her. The attention had made her feel like she was someone special. Other women who frequented the same drinking places would almost disappear, as she and Isiah would enter. But the isolation was beginning to take a toll on her. When she was not with Isiah people would talk to her but their eyes would be searching the immediate vicinity for the appearance of Isiah. They had never done that with Aaron. Many of the people that she had been acquainted with when Aaron was alive no longer spoke to her. At first, she had chalked it up as them showing their "true color." Now, as she sat with a hole in her chest she knew that they were only concerned about her wellbeing.

When she and Clara got up to leave the club, her only intent had been to get away from Isiah and go home. But as she and Clara had gotten to her car, Isiah was right behind them calling her. She remembered Clara saying to her that there was something strange about Isiah and that she did not feel good about it inside.

Isiah was calling her to him like she was a child. She had tried to ignore him so she and Clara could leave. But she remembered hearing Isiah telling her something about he would blow her "ass away," if she didn't stop. She stopped and turned to face Isiah so that she could tell him to leave her alone so she could go home. But as she looked into his eyes, all that she remembered seeing were two dark glassy pools of distance and evil.

Trudy remembered that although she had never looked into the eyes of a snake, she felt like she was about to be bitten by one. She remembered backing away from Isiah but the two glassy pools seemed to follow her and fix its scope on her. She was frightened. The liquor that she and Clara had consumed earlier seemed to have been sucked right out of her. She had very little courage and seemed to be trapped in an invisible snare. She no longer felt special and realized for the first time that she had been tricked.

Isiah had ordered her to come to him. But Clara had told her not to, just get in the car and go home. But she had hoped to calm Isiah down enough so that he would not become violent and try to hurt her again. She had remembered the time that he had slapped her so hard in front of a crowd of people that she fell in the dirt. Isiah had snatched her up by one arm and nearly dragged her to his car then slammed her against the trunk. She had felt so embarrassed by this because one of Aaron Junior's friends had witnessed this and demanded that Isiah keep his hands of off "Mrs. Spann." The young man had shown more respect for her than she had deserved. But why, Trudy asked herself, had she not stopped seeing Isiah, then?

As she walked toward Isiah that night, she heard Clara saying, "oh Lord, please help us, Jesus." Trudy tried hard to remember what Isiah had said to her as she began to walk toward him in an attempt to calm him down. No matter how hard she tried, she could not remember. It was as though she had been in a trance of sorts.

But, she remembered, as she stood in front of Isiah, his breath had a strange and pungent odor. So strong was the odor of Isiah's breath that she turned then walked back to her car. She had only walked a few feet away from Isiah when she felt a sharp pain rip through her back. At first it felt like someone had run up from behind and hit her in the back. The pain came quickly and the realization that she had been shot came just as quickly. As she leaned against the car and saw the front of her blouse begin to change colors because of the blood, she had hoped that no one would see her. Clara began to scream like she too, had been shot or was about to be shot. How could she, a mother of seven children be near death outside of a nightclub. This is something that only happened to young foolish people, she was neither, or was she? Trudy did not know. She truly was not young, although very foolish.

Clara's screams had drawn the attention of several people who were leaving the club because they had heard the gunshot. The shock of having been shot in the parking lot of a nightclub had made her ashamed. Pride had rushed in quickly, very quickly. She had not thought about dying, even though she knew she had been shot. Going to the hospital was not even one of her first thoughts. She had seen the fear in Clara's eyes and the pistol in Isiah's hand, but dying was not one of her thoughts. Pride had told her that she needed to get away from the scene before anyone realized what had happened to her.

Everything that folks had warned her of became a beacon light in her mind. Everyone would be laughing at her now because she had not heeded their advice about Iisah. Surely there would be an abundance of "I told you so."

A flood of heat and excruciating pain had come over her entire body and weakened her so much that she slumped to the ground. Clara ran from the passenger side of the car screaming and to help her up. It was only now that she began to realize that Clara's life, too, had been in jeopardy. Isiah had never liked Clara and on many occasions had told her that he did not want her to be around or with Clara. But, it was Clara who had helped her from the ground and assisted her to get into the car. She wondered why Clara had not come back to the hospital or to the house yet to see her. Maybe, she thought, Clara had finally realized that it was Trudy who was a "bad influence."

Isiah had stood by and watched as Clara helped her from the ground into the back seat of the car. Then he had walked over to where she sat and looked at her. It was then that she realized that Isiah was not an ordinary man, but that he was the epitome of evil. A cold chill ran through her body and caused her to shiver as she thought about that Saturday morning in the parking lot.

Trudy thought that she must have been in shock or something because she did not remember saying anything at all to Isiah after he had shot her. Maybe it was best that she had kept silent, her life was spared.

By the time the ambulance arrived, a number of people had gathered in the parking lot trying to comfort her. But she did not remember seeing Isiah after the people started to gather. When she was placed in the ambulance, it was Clara who held her hand talked to her during the ride. Trudy wanted to cry because she had been a foolish woman. She had done things her way and all that it had done was bring misery and heartache. She stared at the ceiling in the ambulance and tried to avoid even Clara's eyes. The medical technician had started an IV and her left arm was immobile. She could feel the pain in her chest and back and every part of her body in between. But her thoughts were about what people would say when the news that she had been shot by Isiah began to circulate.

Trudy replayed certain scenes in her mind over and over. Before the ambulance had come and before people started to gather, Isiah had stood over Trudy and the pools of blackness that replaced his eyes had seemed to dance and bob from side to side. She had not seen a human being standing before her. Isiah did not appear as a man to her, but a serpent. She became more frightened then because she thought that Isiah would shoot her again to make sure that he had killed her.

Trudy shuddered as her mind replayed the events of that night. Isiah calmly, but in a voice so different than what she had heard before told her, "bitch, let this be a warning to you. I could have killed you, if I had wanted to."

Trudy tried to stop the pictures in her mind so that she could focus on Isiah's eyes. There was something about his eyes that she could not forget and even now caused fear in her. She remembered that Isiah had often referred to himself as the Cobra and had a brass cobra sitting on the dashboard of his car. She thought that what she had seen in the parking lot that Saturday morning was a man changing his form to suit and reveal his true nature. But how could that be? Trudy asked in her mind. She should have hated Isiah with every fiber of her being, but Trudy could not explain why she did not. What was wrong with her?

Now she thought about Henry. Why had Isiah hated Henry so much that he would come to the house and try to kill him after shooting her? Had Henry seen anything like what she had seen in the parking lot? Trudy's mind was filled with questions. She did not want anyone to see her and knew that people would whisper whenever they did. It probably would have been better if she had died in the parking lot that morning, she thought. Then she would not have to endure what she knew was to come.

There was not another woman around who had been shot by a boyfriend. If she had not made herself such a fool about Isiah, she thought, maybe, just maybe, people would now be sympathetic. But she had insulted many and stopped speaking to them because of Isiah. Even her own children had walked out of her life because of this.

Trudy looked around to see where Toni was. She watched as Toni cleaned the kitchen. What was going through her eldest daughter's mind about her, she thought. She had not been much of a mother to Toni, she thought. She had taken care of her as a baby because she couldn't do anything for herself, but as soon as Toni had been able to do for herself she become a free spirit. Trudy could not remember a one on one conversation ever, with her daughter. They had never shared. Matter-of-fact, Trudy thought, she had never had any of that with any of her children. Her pregnancy with Jeremiah was one of the most unwanted things in her life. Sure, she thought, she had loved him, but a baby at her age then was not something that she had looked forward to. Then Aaron died while Jeremiah was still in diapers. The older children had actually raised him.

Trudy lay on the sofa and allowed the thoughts to consume her. As she lay there feelings of loneliness began to overtake her. She thought about what she would do now that Isiah was dead. Her life had ended up like garbage on the side of the road. Yet she was in love with someone, she thought, that had been the worst enemy of her soul. What was she thinking? She asked herself. All she wanted was to be loved, was that asking too much, she thought? She didn't have the answers and had long ago seemed to have lost contact with anyone who might.

What did her children think of her, Trudy asked herself? She quickly shrugged it off and thought that people were just jealous of her and wanted to run her life. In the middle of the thought there was something that stopped it and brought to her attention that even those whom she did not care for had spoken the truth. The truth was that all that had been said about Isiah had come to pass. Trudy dropped her head in shame as the thought penetrated her mind. She thought about Aaron Junior and wondered where he was and how he must have felt when he left. The decision, she thought, must have been hard for him. She questioned almost everything about herself and her life. There was so much work that needed to be done in order to get herself together.

Toni swept the floor in the kitchen keeping her eyes on the floor. There was very little on the floor in terms of trash, but she gently went back and forth. Carefully she ran the straw broom under cabinets and chairs and drew them forward into an invisible pile. Again, Toni placed the broom in the same places as though she were making a clean sweep of anything that might have been missed. As she continued to sweep she thought of the situation facing the family and getting back to Connecticut. She needed to be away from it all so that she could think and come up with a plan. So much had happened in the last five days that she had had little time to really put together a plan.

As she continued to sweep the floor, Toni thought that most of her short life had spent taking care of people. Everybody could count on Toni, but she did not want to be the one that everyone could count on. In many ways, she thought, she was like the broom that she was using. She was always cleaning up the messes that had been made by others. Out of nowhere Toni heard herself speak out, "I'm the cleanup woman."

"You said something to me, Toni?" Trudy asked.

Toni jumped. Her thoughts had spoken out without her permission.

"No, mam. I didn't say anything. I must have been talking to myself."

Trudy tried to laugh. "Sometimes that's the only way you can get the right answers."

"I guess so. But I'd better be careful because people will say that I'm crazy."

Trudy smiled and looked back at the television. She was glad that something had broken her thoughts. The thoughts had been too much for her to try and analyze. But Toni, she thought, was too young to be talking to herself.

For the first time she had thought of her daughter as too young. Toni had always seemed to be an old woman and Trudy realized that she had placed responsibilities on Toni that were beyond her age. Somehow, she thought, Toni had managed to carry out those responsibilities without problems. Was that the reason Toni had left and traveled so far to make a new home? Would the rest of her children leave as well? Trudy began to realize that there was the possibility of all of her children leaving home and she would be left alone. But more than the idea of their leaving, it was the reality that they would leave because of her. Aaron Junior had left and she was the reason, why wouldn't the others?

The ringing telephone broke Trudy's train of thought. Toni picked up the telephone in the kitchen. Trudy raised herself up on the sofa in an attempt to hear what she could of the conversation.

"Yes, you've reached the Spann residence, what is your name, please."

Trudy was even more curious now than before because it sounded like Toni did not know the caller. She listened even more intently now, hoping to get more information.

"Yes sir, Mrs. Spann is here, please hold for just a moment." Toni said.

Trudy quickly tried to settle herself and look like she had not been listening. Toni told her that a man claiming to be an undertaker wanted to speak to her because it was urgent. Trudy, at first thought that it might be something about her father. Toni helped her to walk into the kitchen where she could sit at the table and talk to the man.

"Hello?"

Toni stood at the kitchen sink and watched her mother as she listened to what was being said. The conversation was actually one way, with Trudy listening and the man on the other end speaking. Trudy's whole physical appearance seemed to have changed as she listened. All that Toni could hear was an "uh huh, yes" from her mother. Toni's curiosity was more than peaked as she watched her mother's reaction. Toni wanted to run upstairs and pick the phone so that she could hear what was being said on the other end. Finally she heard Trudy say "thank you for caring, sir, God bless you, too." Trudy handed the telephone to Toni to hang up.

"Mama who was that?"

"It was the undertaker up that road where Isiah people had the body taken."

"Well how did he get our telephone number, it's unlisted?" Toni asked.

"He said that he called the operator and told them he was a undertaker and needed to be in touch with me because it was an emergency."

"What did he say, mama?"

"He said that Isiah's people had come to him this morning and asked him to let them stay the night in the funeral parlor cause they wanted to do something with the body."

"Say what?"

"Yeah, that's what he said. They wanted to stay the night in the funeral parlor to do something with the body before they buried it."

"So what did he tell them?"

"He said he told them no. He said they came in there smelling strange and he just knew they were trying to do evil, but he wasn't gonna be part of anything like that."

Toni had to sit down, now. She shook her head in disbelief and looked at her mother as though she were looking through a clear piece of glass. Toni began to feel lightheaded and for a moment the room started to spin. Toni leaned forward in the chair and tried to catch her breath.

"Jesus, Jesus, Jesus, help us, Jesus, let no hurt, harm or danger come unto us Jesus." Toni said.

Trudy looked at her daughter in amazement. She was now at a loss for words and could not muster up a word to speak. Toni asked whether she wanted to go back to the sofa and lie down, but Trudy just wanted to sit at the table. Trudy did not know exactly what all of this meant, but deep inside she could sense that it was not good. She wondered what Isiah's people wanted to do with his body? It must have been something evil, like the undertaker said, otherwise he would not have gone to the trouble to contact her.

Trudy's thoughts were flooded with the word, "warning." It was a warning, she thought to herself. She stood up for a moment and positioned the chair so that she could stretch her legs out where the sun came in. The warmth on her feet felt good. But the thought of what the undertaker had said would not go away.

Toni was now standing on the front porch. She looked up and down the street allowing her eyes to rest on each house. The neighbors had gone to work and there was no one walking the streets. Every now and then a car would pass the corner, but no human could be seen. Toni walked down and sat on the edge of the porch and stretched her legs down the steps. She had been so caught up in thought that she had not noticed Miss Essie, her neighbor from across the street, approach her.

"Oh, Miss Essie, I didn't even see you coming. How you doing this morning?"

"I be just fine Missie, how you doing?" Essie asked.

"I don't know Miss Essie. The undertaker for Isiah's people managed to get our unlisted telephone number and called mama just a while ago to warn her about something Isiah's people wanted to do."

"Oh, Jesus, stay the hand of the devil." Miss Essie said. "What they trying to do, baby?"

134

"Mama said the undertaker told her that they showed up at his funeral parlor smelling strange and asked him to let them spend the night in the funeral home with the body."

"They up to no good, Toni. Bless that undertaker for warning your mama. Oh they gonna try something hellish, but it gonna backfire on them, you hear me, it'll backfire on them."

Toni and Essie sat on the steps for a few minutes in silence. Toni could tell that there was no silence on the inside of Essie, she was praying and Toni could see her lips moving.

"Let me go inside here and see your mama for a minute."

Toni shook her head as Essie got up from the step and walked up onto the porch. Knocking at the door first and calling out for Trudy, Essie prayed as she walked in.

"Bless this house Jesus. I bind any and everything that is of the devil that is here and cast it down, in Jesus name. I release peace here, in Jesus name. Holy Ghost take control and rest, rule and abide in this house. Thank you, Jesus. Trudy, how you doing, girl?"

Toni got up from the steps and walked to the edge of the house and looked over where Isiah's lifeless body had lain just a few days earlier. She looked as though she were trying to replay the moment. She noticed Helen Baker's house, her godmother, and was tempted to walk there, but remembered that she worked during the day. Toni decided that she would go and visit her godmother before she went back to Connecticut. As she turned and walked back to her mother's house, Toni saw her Uncle Clifford's car turn the corner. She felt a relief inside.

"Hey babe, how you doing this morning?" Clifford asked.

"I was doing okay until we got a call this morning from the undertaker handling Isiah's funeral."

"What he calling here for, we ain't paying for the funeral and we sure as hell won't be going." Clifford stated angrily.

"Well he got the operator to call here saying it was an emergency. He told mama that Isiah's people had asked him to leave them in the funeral parlor all night with the body. The undertaker said they walked in there smelling strange, but he told them no."

"What the hell these people trying to do?" Clifford asked as he leaned against the hood of his car.

"Uncle Clifford, I don't know. But we both know that these people believe in roots and all that kind of devilish mess. I just told Miss Essie about it. She went inside to talk to mama."

"Oh, Essie in there now?"

"Yes sir."

Clifford and Toni turned and walked into the house. Toni went upstairs to bath and change clothes. She thought about Henry as she washed her face and prayed that God would protect him. As the warm water ran down the front of her Toni began to scrub her body as though trying to remove some invisible coating. She began to tremble as the tears flowed from her eyes. She knew, somehow, that Isiah's people were planning something horrible. Toni started speaking in a whisper, "God, I don't know what to do. My mother is out of control, my brother has killed a man and now that man's family is using roots and witchcraft to bring harm to my family. I don't know how to pray like I should, but I am asking you to stop what these people are trying to do. Save my family, God. Please save my family."

The tears began to flow as rapidly from her eyes as it did from the shower. Toni's body shook violently as the beads of water hit her body and flowed down into the drain. Toni started to get out of the shower but could not bring herself to turn off the water. Something inside made her stand under the water. Toni stood under the running water until she could feel that the time for her to turn off the water and step out of the shower was right. Soon the shaking stopped and Toni could grasp the faucet and turn off the water. As she dried her body, Toni knew that something strange had happened in the shower but could not articulate what it was.

As she began to put the Vaseline on her feet, Toni felt a tightness on her left side. She grabbed the lotion and smoothed it on her left arm and down the side of her body and leg. The tightness was still there. Toni, for a moment thought that she had had a stroke or something while in the shower. She had learned that strokes did not always cause the person to become unconscious but it did have a paralyzing affect on some part of the body. At first, there was a moment of fear, but the fear seemed to be quickly swept away.

After dressing, Toni walked downstairs where Trudy, Clifford and Essie were still sitting around the kitchen table. Clifford had perked a fresh pot of coffee and the trio did not pay any attention to Toni as she walked into the living room and began watching television. Toni did not particularly care for soap operas, but did not have the strength to walk across the floor and change the channel. As she sat watching the pictures on the television screen, her eyes became heavy, so heavy that she just allowed the sleep to overtake her.

Toni fell into a deep sleep and began to dream. Toni dreamed that she was sleeping and could not wake up. In the dream she saw herself on the sofa and trying to get up but was so sleepy that she did not have the strength to get up. She tried to roll over to cast herself on the floor, but was unable to do so. She lay with her head on the back of the sofa having the desire to get up and the knowledge that she wanted to get up but the sleep was more like a spirit that was trying to overtake her. Toni struggled inwardly to wake up. She turned her head to the left and the sleep seemed to block her path. She tried to turn her head to the right and raise her body up but the sleep blocked her and she fell back on the sofa.

In the dream Toni fell into a sleep but was suddenly awakened, again. This time she had a little more strength than she had had before the sleep had completely overtaken her. However, the sleep was not about to release Toni from its clutches. She tried to sit straight up in the dream and the sleep hit her so hard that she fell back on the sofa and to the side. After some struggle, in the dream, Toni was finally able get up.

At first, Toni opened her eyes and looked at the ceilings. Why had the dream seemed so real? She asked herself. It was like nothing that she had experienced before. Her struggle to awake from the sleep seemed so real. Toni felt the warm perspiration running down into her face from her forehead and down her neck into her bosom. In spite of the warm perspiration upon her body, Toni felt a chill. She sat forward trying to figure out what had happened. Trudy, Essie and Clifford were still seated at the kitchen table. Toni wondered how long she had been asleep, or whether she had been asleep at all. The whole thing had been so very strange. Toni shook her head and sighed, "Jesus, Jesus, Jesus."

Toni walked out to the front porch and sat on the steps. She had not been able to bring herself to sit in either of the chairs on the porch since Isiah had tried to drag Henry from one of them. She watched the corner as though she was expecting someone. Essie finally came out of the house and touched Toni on the shoulder.

"Hang right on in there, girl, don't let it get the best of you." Essie said, as she walked down the steps.

"No mam, Miss Essie, I'll fight to the finish."

"Toni, you just remember the name of Jesus. At the name of Jesus every knee shall bow, that's human knees, devil knees and anything else with knees. Just don't you forget the name of Jesus, call that name and send demons packing. You hear me child? The name of Jesus, don't ever forget that." Essie said.

Toni nodded her head in response to Essie's statement. The words had already been etched in Toni's mind. She had heard the entire statement before, although Essie had only stated a part of it. But hearing it today seemed to have meaning for Toni. She watched as Essie walked across the street and up the flight of steps leading to her front porch.

She had not seen Henry in a couple of days and needed to see him. Toni wondered how he was feeling since Saturday night and being released from jail. She had not had much time to talk to him after he was released because her mother had invited Isiah's people to the house. She had to spend some time with Henry and thought, maybe she should just spend the night at Clifford's house. But there was no one to stay with Trudy and the children. For a moment Toni became angry with her older brother and Margaret, they had taken the easy way out, she thought and left her to take care of everything else.

The anger passed after a while and Toni drew her knees to her chest and laid her chin on them. The tears began to well up in Toni's eyes, but another anger began to rise, as well. She was tired of crying and feeling helpless, enough was enough, she thought. She did not know what else to do, but more than anything else, she thought, there was nothing that she could do until it was time to do something.

She thought about what Clifford and her mother may have been talking about inside. She hoped that Clifford would be able to talk to her mother about the way she had been living her life. She also thought about Alma's idea of finishing her degree in nursing and going into the military as an officer. That, she thought, was a grand idea. Toni then felt a bit of sadness for her friend Kim, back in Connecticut. She was saddened because she had caused Kim to relive a very traumatic time in her life as a child. That was unfair, she thought, but Kim was her friend and she was faced with a situation that she could only share with a friend.

Toni stretched her legs out on the steps and stared up at the clouds. The gentle breeze felt like continuous hugs. Then the soft smell of honeysuckle made its way to her nostrils. Toni took one hand and removed the bobby pins from her hair so it could blow in the gentle sweet breeze. For a while Toni did not have a thought to cross her mind. Other than her breathing, and an intermittent chirp of a bird, there were no sounds to disturb the peace that enveloped her.

The billowy white clouds against the blue background of the spring sky, was the closest, Toni thought that she could get to paradise. Everything that had happened and every unresolved situation confronting her disappeared. Every breath she took seemed to flood her insides with peace and strength.

Toni enjoyed her time in her temporary paradise. It was as though time had stood still for her and she was the only person in her world. The gentle sweetness of the breeze seemed to be soap and water that washed, rinsed, and then dried her. The moisture in the cool breeze felt like lotion scented by the fragrance of the honeysuckle lavished its richness over the long brown body on the steps. The joy suddenly burst inside of Toni like several sticks of spiritual TNT. As she inhaled, Toni's spirit soared like an eagle in flight. The experience was so exhilarating that Toni felt like she was gently being lifted upward toward the billowy white clouds so that she could grasp a handful of the fluffiness. Every part of Toni's being seemed to be in a process of renewal that used unexplainable peace as the primary building block and unspeakable joy as the glue.

17

 Toni learned from her uncle that Henry had gone to work that day. Still, Trudy could not bring herself to even speak Henry's name. Not a question had been asked by Trudy about any of her children and their whereabouts, or even how they might be doing. Toni decided that she would not say anything either. She did not think it wise to force a subject upon her mother.

 Trudy wanted to sit on the sofa and watch the soap operas, so with a little help from Clifford, she walked to the sofa and sat down. Clifford had his favorite soap opera as well and the two sat in almost silence with their eyes glued to the television set. Toni decided to check the refrigerator to see whether she should prepare something extra for dinner that evening. While checking the refrigerator, Toni remembered that she had bought several boxes of Jello. Jeremiah deserved a treat, she thought, so she began fixing a fruit Jello for him.

 Clifford was curious about what she was doing in the kitchen. Toni told him that she was fixing Jello for Jeremiah. Clifford asked her to make one big enough for more than just Jeremiah because he liked Jello, too.

 "Hey, Toni, fix me a little lunch plate while you in there. I'm feeling a little lunchy." Clifford said.

 "You want anything in particular, Uncle Clifford?"

 "No, you know how to fix me up, a little bit of this and that in a lunch portion."

 "Okay. Mama, you want a lunch portion, too?" Toni asked.

 "Yeah, but make it a little smaller, like a child portion. I feel like eating a little something but not too much. You know how to do it." Trudy said.

 Toni went about getting smaller pans to warm up portions for her mother and uncle. She thought how everybody relied on her. They just trusted that she knew everything about them including their desires and likes. Toni prepared two beautiful plates for her mother and uncle and pulled out two of the television trays and set them up before them. As she placed the silver and glass of Kool-Aid on the tray before Clifford and Trudy, Clifford got up and went to the bathroom to wash his hands. Toni went upstairs and got a wet soapy face cloth for her mother to wipe her hands before eating.

 Toni piddled in the kitchen as her mother and uncle watched television. She began to assess the dinner menu again. Now she was going about the task without the pressures that she had had before. The least that her brothers and sisters would have is a good meal so long as she was there. But she was grateful that there seemed to be peace between her mother and uncle. Little did Toni know that her mother and uncle had talked about the situation before them while she had sat on the steps in the breeze. There was no tension in the air and it looked like old times between the in-laws. She would prepare enough food for Uncle Clifford and Henry so that they would have a good dinner today as well, Toni determined.

 Toni wanted to talk to her friends, Kim and Alma, but they both were at work. She tried to busy herself in the kitchen hoping that either one or even both would eventually call her, when time permitted. She wanted to talk to Margaret, as well, but even Margaret was at work now. After starting everything that she planned to cook, Toni resigned herself to sit in the living room with her mother and uncle and watch the stories.

Toni heard the school bus stop at the corner. Soon Jeremiah was walking through the door with his school bag thrown over his shoulder. That was a bright spot for Toni; she loved the little boy so much and wanted so much more for him. She began to think about taking him back to Connecticut with her so that she could be sure that he would get all that she thought and believed that he should have as a little boy.

"Good evening, everybody." Jeremiah said.

"Hey boss man, how was school today?" Clifford asked.

"Okay."

"Just okay?"

"Yes sir. Those girls got on my nerve today."

"Oh yeah? What they did today to get on your nerve?"

"We started practicing today for the school closing play and they just giggled so much that I couldn't hear the teacher."

Trudy raised up a little on the sofa and smiled at Jeremiah as he tried to tell his uncle about his day. She watched Jeremiah as he began searching his book bag for something. Toni smiled at him and stretched out her arms.

"I don't get a little hug, today?"

"Oh yeah, I got a kiss I saved just for you, too." Jeremiah said as he dropped the book bag and went to Toni's outstretched arms.

"What you cooking Toni?" Jeremiah asked.

"I'm fixing you some dinner."

"It sure smell good in here. When we gonna eat?"

"In a little while."

"Mama, you feeling alright?" Jeremiah asked.

"Yeah sweetheart, I'm feeling okay. Why?" Trudy asked.

"I just asked, that's all. I don't want you to be hurting."

"Thank you baby, but mama doing alright. You don't have to worry about that."

"When they gonna bury Mr. Isiah?" Jeremiah asked.

The entire room went into deafening silence. Trudy appeared to squirm a little bit and Clifford looked at the floor. Toni just looked at Jeremiah. He deserved an answer, a truthful answer and Toni spoke up.

"We don't know, Jeremiah. Maybe his family will bury him this week some time." Toni responded.

"Mama you going to his funeral?" Jeremiah asked.

Quickly Trudy answered his son. "No, baby, I am not. Why you ask?"

"Cause he was your boyfriend."

Before anymore could be said Toni told Jeremiah to go upstairs and change his clothes so she could fix him a sandwich until dinner. Jeremiah picked up his school bag and ran up the stairs. Toni got up and went into the kitchen to check the pots. As she went to the pantry, Toni could see Clifford and Trudy staring at each other as though they were sending silent messages. When she returned to the living room and sat down she could see that her mother's face had taken on a different look. The sadness upon her face seemed to have triggered something within and it was still on her mind. One day, Toni thought, all of this would be behind them and no one would have to shrink back in fear.

Alma and her son came over just as Toni was preparing the table for her family. Alma and her son had dinner with the family and her son played for a while upstairs with Jeremiah. The noise generated by the two little boys at play was unbelievable. But the adults pretended not to hear and allowed them to roughhouse as they saw fit to.

Toni and Alma were almost in shock when Margaret and Lloyd showed up. Toni was glad because she could at least have one more conversation with Margaret before she left for Connecticut. Jeremiah was so glad to see Lloyd that he jumped into his arms and Lloyd carried him about as though Jeremiah was a baby.

"Oh, how you doing Mr. Troy Pierre?" Lloyd said when saw the little boy coming down the steps.

"I'm fine, how you doing?" Troy Pierre said as he stood watching Lloyd.

"I understand that you're going to sue me, sir, so I don't know whether I should be talking to you too much." Lloyd said with a little smile on his face.

Alma turned her head and laughed to herself. Troy Pierre dropped his head for a moment and did not have a ready answer for Lloyd.

"Should I have my attorney get in touch with your attorney, Troy Pierre?"

"Well, no sir, I didn't have the money to pay the lawyer and mama wouldn't lend me none." He responded.

Alma and Toni stood in the kitchen and laughed as Troy Pierre tried to squirm out of the conversation with Lloyd about suing him. Lloyd continued to talk to Troy Pierre anyway.

"So how your grades in school this term, Troy Pierre?"

"My grades?" Troy Pierre asked.

"Yeah, your grades. How are they?"

"I think they okay, you have to ask my mama."

"Tell Lloyd about your grades, Troy, you know what they are, so stop acting like you never looked at your report card."

Troy Pierre stood looking up at Lloyd as though he wished Lloyd would go away or forget what he asked him.

"Which one of my grades you want to know about?" Troy Pierre finally asked Lloyd.

"Let's start with the grade you got in conduct. What's that like?"

"Well, I don't think the teacher really like me, so she gave me a C." He responded.

"Now if you don't bring your conduct grade up to a B this term you'll have to sit out the first part of the summer league. You understand that?"

Troy got a spark in his eyes then and answered immediately.

"You don't have to worry about that, I'm gonna play the whole summer, Mr. Lloyd. Can I play shortstop this time?"

"I'll see how you grab and throw in practice, okay?"

Troy seemed to be glad to hear that he would be given an opportunity to play the position he most wanted to play. But Lloyd was not finished with him yet.

"By the way, Mister, if your mama tell me that you've been cutting up at home and not doing what you're supposed to do, I'll have to bench you. You've got to be fully disciplined in order to play and learn."

"I'm gonna be good, Mr. Lloyd, my mama gonna tell you that."

Trudy sat up on the sofa and smiled as the conversation between Lloyd and Troy wound down. Margaret was sitting next to her mother with a stern look on her face. The look was not hostile, just stern.

"How you feeling Miss Trudy?" Lloyd asked.

"I'm doing better, Lloyd. Congratulations to you and Margaret. I should be mad cause y'all didn't tell anybody so we could at least be there, but thank God y'all did the right thing." Trudy said.

"Thank you, mam. Right is right Miss Trudy and God don't accept anything less than what He says." Lloyd said.

"Jeremiah, why Lloyd got to carry you around like you some little arm baby?" Trudy asked.

"I don't know."

"Well, why don't you go and finish playing with Troy Pierre?"

Lloyd put Jeremiah on the floor and he went back upstairs to his room with Troy Pierre. Margaret talked with her mother while Toni and Alma sat in the kitchen. Wilson and Clifford had walked out to the backyard before Lloyd and Margaret's arrival. As Wilson walked into the kitchen he saw Lloyd and started congratulating him. Margaret got up and spoke to her uncle as he made his way through the kitchen to the living room.

"Hey babe, you all married now, congratulations."

"Thank you sir." Margaret responded.

Joyce was at the sink washing dishes with Toni's help. Joyce yelled out to Margaret that if she wanted to eat that she should do so immediately so that she could wash the dishes before the water got cold.

"If you cooked I better not eat." Margaret said as she pinched Alma on the shoulder.

"Shoot, if I did the cooking for you and your husband you might stay married for a long time." Joyce snidely remarked.

"Ooh, y'all sure hitting below the belt today." Alma said as she laughed. But Margaret was not to be outdone with Joyce's remark or attempt to play the dozens.

"Girl ain't nobody studying Joyce. Who in the world started that lie anyway that a woman supposed to do all the cooking? All of the so-called great chefs are men, so men can learn to cook for their wives." Margaret said as she washed her hands in the dishwater.

"Well you and Lloyd had better get a charge account at Burger King or Kentucky Fried Chicken, if you don't come over here everyday for dinner." Joyce said.

Alma and Toni were laughing and getting a kick out of Margaret and Joyce's back and forth bantering about cooking.

"Who needs food when they in love." Margaret shot back.

"Love can help you make some sweet music, but it can't make you have a bowel movement." Joyce retorted.

Toni and Alma got a good laugh. Margaret had to laugh at the statement.

"Then why don't you move aside so I can fix myself a plate? Lloyd, you want me to fix you a plate, too?" Margaret asked.

"Yeah, a little bit of everything." Lloyd replied.

Jeremiah came downstairs and asked for some Jello for himself and Troy. Alma got up to fix the Jello for the little boys. No one had eaten any Jello, yet and the large bowl of Strawberry Jello with fruit cocktail looked beautiful as Alma took down the bowls. Toni had also bought some cream whip and allowed the boys to put as much as they wanted on their Jello. After Jeremiah had gotten as much Jello as he wanted in his bowl, he told everybody else that they could have some.

Toni, for a short while forgot the problems that were facing the family. She had hoped that Henry and Aaron Junior could have been there. But she had prepared food for Henry for Clifford to take with him when he left for home. By nine o'clock that night everybody had left and Toni made sure that Jeremiah bathed and prepared for bed. By ten o'clock even Joyce was tired and in her room for the night. Wilson, who had left the house earlier, had finally returned.

"Hey, where you been boy?" Toni asked Wilson.

"I just went by a friend of mine's house. He just signed up for the Marine Corps and going to take his physical tomorrow." Wilson replied.

"Those Marines sure look good in their uniforms, don't they?" Toni said.

"Yeah, they do. My friend was just telling me that the Marine's uniforms are custom tailored before they get their final set. The other branches don't do that."

"Sound like you might be getting a weakness in your knees for the military."

"No, not me. I don't mind going in the military but I want a college degree first. I want to be an officer, if I go in. Let them jokers have to say 'yes sir' to me."

"Now that's how you do boy, go for the gold or silver or whatever color the officers wear."

Wilson, Toni and Trudy engaged in small talk for a few more minutes. Trudy began to nod and close her eyes as they talked. Toni could see that her mother was tired and should perhaps go upstairs to bed. Wilson went upstairs and took a shower while the two woman sat downstairs watching the television.

Toni went to the kitchen to make sure that all of the food was put away and finish the dishes after Alma left. As she damp mopped the kitchen floor, Toni felt a strange breeze and looked in the living room. Seeing nothing she continued to mopped the floor. Something inside told Toni to walk into the living room. Following her instinct, Toni walked into the living room and found the door open. Thinking maybe Wilson or Joyce had come downstairs and walked out to the porch, she leaned the mop against the wall and walked toward the door. The latch on the screen door was off but there was no one on the porch. Toni walked out onto the front porch and looked around expecting to see one of her siblings. There was no one there.

Toni turned around and went back into the house. She was confused, but knew that there was an explanation for this. She went upstairs calling Wilson and Joyce's name, but there was no answer. She opened the door and looked inside Wilson's room, he was there, asleep. She checked Joyce's and Jeremiah's rooms and they were asleep, as well. Toni panicked and began to search the upstairs wondering if there had been someone in the house that had left without her knowing. But how could anyone have gotten inside was the question she could not answer.

Toni decided to get closer to each of her siblings to make sure that someone had not killed them as they slept. Leaning over each one of her siblings, Toni could see that they were breathing and there were no bloodstains on the bedding. Something was not right, she thought as she went back downstairs. Trudy had fallen asleep while Toni was sweeping the kitchen floor and damp mopping it.

A strange hush or quiet had fallen upon the house like a thick blanket, without notice. The quiet was almost deafening. Taking the mop, again, she finished the kitchen floor and went to the back door to throw out the water. Toni stood up and took note of the change in the atmosphere. As she looked over at her mother in the lamplight her breathing had changed from heavy to almost shallow. She walked up the steps and looked in on each of her siblings, again. Everyone seemed to be sound asleep, very sound.

As Toni walked back down the steps a familiar smell met her. As she inhaled the smell was stronger. The scent was so strong that it stopped Toni in her tracks. It was the smell of Old English after-shave that her father used. Toni turned quickly and went back up the stairs. She searched the medicine cabinet and underneath the sink to see whether Wilson used Old Spice. All that Toni could find was an Avon brand of after-shave lotion, but she was certain of what she had smelled.

Making her way back downstairs to check on her mother, Toni felt a chill that seemed to penetrate her body. So cold was the chill that it seemed to reduce the temperature of her blood and caused every hair on her body to stand up. Something had drastically changed in the house. The room felt like it was so full that it was closing in on her, but she could not see anything. It was not just a matter of the air not circulating in the house but it felt filled with invisible bodies.

Toni walked into the kitchen and turned the small light on above the stove. As she turned to walk back into the living room she felt another chill. Suddenly she was filled with fear and realized that the chill she had felt within was a deposit, an evil deposit. The fear began to build quickly, so quickly that her body began to shake and tremble violently.

"Jesus, what is this thing?" Toni heard herself say.

She could not see what it was that was making her so fearful. The fear was so overwhelming that Toni was unable to put one foot in front of the other. She seemed to be frozen in the spot where she stood.

"Sweet Jesus, what's going on here? Something is not right, Lord and I don't know what it is." Toni whispered. She walked into the dining room and ran her hand across the long mahogany table.

"He prepared a table before me in the presence of mine enemies." She said. Standing now in front of the china cabinet and staring at the dishes and crystal glasses inside, Toni shook her head in wonder. Again, she touched the table as though caressing each grain in the wood. She touched the back of each chair as she walked around the table. Having circled the dining table and touched every chair, Toni stood for a moment at the head of the table and looked down the length of it. Not really knowing why, she circled the table several more times saying the "Our Father" prayer, before she was able to stop or stand still.

Tears were pouring down her cheeks. She lifted her hand and wiped her face with the back of it. There was a large crystal goblet on the middle shelf of the china cabinet. Toni stared at it through her tears and wondered had she cried enough in the last few days to fill the goblet. Why was she crying now? The fear, yes the fear. That's what had caused her to cry.

Toni's attention was drawn back to the living room when she thought that she had heard her mother speak.

"Mama, you said something?" Toni asked as she walked back to the living room.

Trudy appeared to be sound asleep and the only noise that could be heard now was from the television. Thinking that maybe, just maybe, she was letting her mind run wild, Toni sat down in the recliner and tried to watch television. Then, Trudy began to speak, again. This time Toni did not say anything, instead, she tried to listen to what her mother was saying. The words Toni could not understand so she moved over to the sofa and asked her mother whether she was feeling okay. Trudy's speech was slurred and she appeared to be incoherent. Within in a matter of hours, it seemed that her mother's condition had deteriorated. Toni was very concerned and thought that she should call her uncle to take her mother to the hospital. Maybe the doctors had failed to see something wrong that had been caused by the bullet, she thought.

Toni walked into the kitchen intending to call her uncle so that she could take Trudy to the hospital. Then she thought about Trudy's car that had been brought home and parked in the garage. No one had wanted to drive the car because it had been driven by Isiah.

As she reached for the telephone there came a strong smell of pipe tobacco. The smell was so strong that it took Toni's mind off of what she had come into the kitchen to do. There were only two people that Toni knew that smoked a pipe, her great grandmother on her father's side and her grandfather, Trudy's father. But why was this pipe tobacco so strong in the kitchen? Toni asked herself.

Trudy's mumbling drew Toni's attention back to the living room. Something was going on, Toni thought, and she did not know what it was. Toni went over to the sofa and leaned over her mother.

"Mama, do you want to go to the hospital?"

Trudy was so weak that she could not sit up. Trudy's eyes were so white that they looked like pools of shimmering milk and set back in their sockets. Her tongue also seemed to be falling out of her mouth. Toni was more than a little shocked at what she was seeing and experiencing. The fear, which had died down, or disappeared earlier, started to build again.

"No, just let me sit up a little bit." Trudy whispered. "Give me some cool water, please." Trudy asked.

Toni turned quickly on her heels and went to the refrigerator to get some ice to put into a glass of water. She continued to look back in the living room at her mother. As she walked back toward her mother Toni could see that she was gagging. Toni rushed over to try and help her mother sit up a little more so that she would not choke. Trudy was having a difficult time breathing and seemed unable to throw up whatever was choking her.

The room seemed to be spinning. Trudy was trying harder and harder to breath and throw up. Toni helped her to sit all the way up and patted her on the back so that whatever was lodged in her throat could come up. Toni took one foot and pushed the coffee table further away from the sofa. Now that Trudy was sitting up, Toni ran to the kitchen and got the small trashcan out of the pantry and removed the plastic bag from it. Just as she was about to return to the living room something said to put another plastic bag into the garbage can. Toni replaced the old plastic bag with two new ones. She quickly, but carefully, placed one bag in the trashcan then another bag inside of it, and placed the trashcan in front of her mother, just in case she threw up.

Trudy's breathing began to get better. Toni situated the pillows under her mother so that she would not choke in her sleep, or while lying almost flat. Toni watched her mother as she drifted off to sleep - a sleep that seemed to be more of a coma. The tension in the air felt like the ire of a million angry men. The smell of the pipe smoke and her father's after-shave cologne were just as noticeable as the tension. In spite of the unseen tension in the room, the pipe tobacco and after-shave were strangely comforting.

Toni thought that she was losing her mind. There was intense activity in the room; the feel of so much going on. She sensed a flurry of invisible movement in the room. Toni stood still, not even breathing, listening for a sound. But there was no sound to be heard. There was activity in the room, lots of activity, but nothing to be heard. Toni felt strange as she tilted her head from side to side, trying to hear something coming from the activity that she could only feel.

Toni sat down in the chair and watched her mother's breathing. As she watched her mother, she was struck by a peculiar darkness looming over her. Toni was shocked by what she was seeing. There was light in the room, a lamp sitting on an end table in the corner. Toni stared at the peculiarity as though she was microscopically analyzing it. The light cast by the lamp went up and down from the shade then outward. But the small cloud of darkness seemed to loom somewhere in the middle just above Trudy's head and chest. Fearing that she would miss something, Toni would not blink an eye. She stared as though the darkness would disappear if she looked at it long enough.

Something had happened while she was staring at the dark cloud. Toni felt like she was half-asleep and tried to get up from the chair. It seemed like a dream because she was paralyzed and too weak and helpless to move. Even in the dreamlike state she could see the dark cloud just above her mother. Toni felt like she was drugged and could not make absolute sense of what was happening. She struggled and struggled, but could not move. Not even a sound would come out of her mouth. Toni realized that she was not dreaming; but that something or someone that she could not see had pinned her to the chair. She could see her mother thrashing about on the sofa and choking. But no matter how she tried, Toni was not able to get up, or move a muscle. She could think and heard her own thoughts as though a microphone was attached to her thoughts. But she could not free herself.

"Oh God help me, please. For the love of Jesus, God help me." Toni thought.

Toni began to recite the Twenty-third Psalm over and over as she watched her mother choking. It looked as though this invisible force had, also pinned down Trudy, now. She was no longer thrashing about, but choking. Toni thought that her mother was dying at the hands of the invisible force and there was nothing that she could do.

"Father, in the name of Jesus, help me, please." Toni thought.

She thought about her siblings who were asleep and wondered what might be happening to them.

Suddenly Toni felt something stirring from deep within her. The stirring felt like a small twister or tornado and seemed to be coming from someplace far deeper than her stomach. As the stirring moved up to her throat Toni could open her mouth. Out of her mouth came words that made no sense to her. As the words came out of her mouth the paralyses left and she was able to get up.

Toni dashed over to the sofa and sat her mother up. She grabbed the trashcan and set it in front of her mother and began patting her in the middle of her back. Trudy gagged and choked as she gasped for breath. Toni patted her even harder in the back to try and dislodge whatever was choking her. Trudy began to throw up but there was very little fluid in the mass that began hitting the bottom of the plastic liner inside the trashcan. It looked like Trudy had just thrown up a mass of flies. Fear struck Toni, again, and she almost let go of Trudy, but the strange words began to flow from her mouth.

Trudy was trying harder now to empty her stomach. But Toni could only hold the trashcan up to her and watch in horror as the mass fell into it.

"Help me, Jesus." Trudy whispered, as she gasped for breath.

The strange language and words continued to flow from Toni's mouth uncontrollably. Trudy gagged again and began coughing like she was choking. Toni hit her in the back so hard that she thought that she might have injured her mother. She could now see a large black piece of something coming out of her mother's mouth. The black object fell into the trashcan and Trudy was able to breathe normally.

"Thank You, Jesus, thank You, Jesus." Trudy began to say. "Please give me a glass of water." She asked Toni.

Toni reached over and took the glass of water she had prepared earlier and held it to her mother's lips. Trudy drank the water as though she had not had a drink of water for days. The glass was empty when she brought it down from her lips.

"Thank you," Trudy said to Toni, "let me get some sleep now."

Toni fluffed the pillows and helped her mother get comfortable. She pulled the cover up to her mother's chest and smoothed it out. Trudy was fast asleep before Toni had finished smoothing the covers.

Toni went upstairs to check on Wilson, Jeremiah and Joyce. As she opened each door and walked into the room, a soft sweet smell came from each of her siblings. When she walked into Wilson's room he was curled up like a baby in a crib. Then Toni noticed the sweet smell, it was not overpowering as some perfumes were, but she had never smelled anything like it before. The smell had not been obvious when she walked into the rooms. She had not thought much about it even as she went to Joyce's room and Jeremiah's room where the same smell seemed to rise from them as she stood over them making sure that they were still alive and well.

Toni went to the bathroom and sat on the toilet waiting for the pee to come down. As she sat on the toilet her eyes roamed about the bathroom and rested on the crumpled soap paper on the top of the laundry hamper. She reached over and smelled the inside of the paper but it did not smell like the perfume she had smelled coming from her siblings. While the pee was still coming down, Toni pulled back the shower curtain and grabbed the wet bar of soap to make sure that she had not missed anything. The wet soap smelled nothing like what she had smelled coming from her siblings.

The room began to spin as Toni tried to seat herself again on the toilet and finish what she had come in to do. She rolled the toilet paper from the spool and dried her private area and pulled up her panties. She then dried the floor where she had dripped trying to grab the bar of soap and flushed the toilet. She hurried down the hall and back into each one of the bedrooms, sniffing her siblings; the smell was no longer there. But it had been there earlier, she thought, and she was sure of what she had smelled.

As she walked down the stairs trying to figure out what to do with the contents of the trashcan, the scent that had been on her siblings met her at the bottom of the stairs. Toni stopped in her tracks, momentarily frozen. She inhaled deeply, trying to fill her lungs with the sweet and strange smell. She did not want to just smell the scent, she wanted to taste it in her mouth and in the back of her throat. Somehow, she had to get enough of the smell on the inside of her to savor it, although she did not know what it was.

Toni sniffed around but the smell was gone. For several minutes, Toni stood still waiting for the smell to rise again. But it had left and she could no longer smell it. Fearing that a sudden or quick move would cause the scent to flee, she slowly placed one foot in front of the other and entered the living room. There was a peace now on her mother's face. Toni was the only person awake in the house and she had a mess to deal with.

18

The trashcan was setting where she had left it. The contents, she was not really sure of. She knew what she thought she had seen, as it was coming out of her mother's mouth, flies and a black frog. "But how in the hell could flies and frogs be inside of someone?" She asked herself

Toni stood in the middle of the floor and stared at the trashcan. What should she do with the trashcan was one of the questions running through her mind, the other was how did those wicked people do something like that to her mother?

Lost for an answer to her questions, Toni sat down and stared at the trashcan, she was afraid to touch it but also afraid to let it just sit there in the middle of the floor. The strange language started to come out of her mouth again. She placed her hands over her mouth but the language seemed to be uncontrollable. She tried to keep her lips closed but it was to no avail. She stood up and began to pace the floor between the kitchen and the living room, but the strange language became more intense. Something in Toni's stomach roared and raced from side to side, up then down like the waves of the Atlantic Ocean as they splashed against the pilings at Folly Beach. Finally, there was silence. The strange language stopped. Toni stood in the kitchen and looked around, she felt different and the house felt different. The air seemed lighter, no tension could be felt. But the trashcan was still where she had left it.

Finally, it dawned on Toni that she had been speaking in tongues, just like Miss Essie and the people at the Holiness Church. She was almost in shock and did not know what she should do with this new language. Toni became fearful because she did not know when it would start again and she did not seem to have any control over it. Toni walked to the door and peeped across the street at Miss Essie's house. She saw a light on and without thinking about the hour of the night closed the front door behind her and ran to Essie's house.

She knocked on the door and Essie opened it almost immediately.

"Daughter, how you doing?" Essie asked, as she looked Toni in the eyes.

"Miss Essie, I don't know how I'm doing right now. But I got to ask you something."

"Child, you look like you done had a visitation. I knew the Lord kept me up for something. Go on, honey, ask me."

"Something was going on Miss Essie that I can't even talk about right now. But I know it was evil, Miss Essie, I just know it and I think it's got to do with Isiah's people. But I was sitting in the chair and at first I thought I was dreaming that something was holding me down. I felt paralyzed, but Miss Essie, I wasn't sleeping or dreaming, it was real."

"Uh, huh, they sent a evil spirit to your mama and y'all. Jesus, Jesus, Jesus."

"Anyway, I could only think in my mind and asked the Lord in the name of Jesus to help me because I could see mama choking but neither one of us could move. Miss Essie, I felt something like a whirlwind or a hurricane start rising up on the inside of me. It felt like a twister coming from way down deep in my stomach, then it got up to my throat."

Essie's eyes had turned to small little slants as she listened and hung onto every word that Toni spoke. Essie did not appear to be surprised at what she was hearing from Toni, but angry it seemed by what had happened.

"When this thing got to my throat, Miss Essie, words started coming out of my mouth that I didn't understand."

"Glory be to God, thank You Jesus for sending the Holy Ghost." Essie shouted.

Toni appeared to be in shock now as Essie began to praise God and speak in tongues. As Essie began to speak in tongues, the new language began to pour out of Toni's mouth, again. Essie pushed Toni into her living room and the words continued to flow. As Toni spoke in tongues, Essie paced the floor with her hands held up to the ceiling repeating "thank You, Jesus." When Toni had finished speaking in tongues Essie told her that she had received power from God and she was now filled with the Holy Ghost with the evidence of speaking in tongues. Essie further assured her that she could control it.

"Now daughter don't be afraid of this gift. When you pray from now on or you feel the need to pray directly to the Father, just pray in your new prayer language. Nobody, including the devil and those he use know what you telling the Father."

Toni stared at Essie in unbelief and tried to make sense of this gift as she called it.

Toni decided that she should tell Essie about what her mother had vomited and find out what she should do with it.

"Miss Essie, all I could do is just look at the trashcan sitting there in the floor."

"We gonna get rid it right now. You go and tie the bag up, you know, make a knot in the top of the bag, not a tight knot, cause you gonna have to unloose it again. We gonna drive down to the river and cast that thing in deep running water."

Toni walked out of Essie's house feeling just a little bit better about what she was experiencing. As she crossed the street, she decided to test what Essie had said about being able to speak in tongues when she wanted to. Toni opened her mouth and the prayer language came out. Then she spoke a Bible verse in English. Then quickly decided to speak in tongues. Toni marveled at her new language, a prayer language. She thought that it was wonderful that God would give her a language to speak privately with Him.

The trashcan was still where she had left it. For some unknown reason, she had thought that it would be gone by the time she got back in the house. Thinking clearer, now Toni thought that if the trashcan had not been there when got back she probably would have had a heart attack. Toni loosely tied the top of the plastic bags, then looked around the room to make sure that everything was still in place. The clock on the stove said that it was twelve eighteen. She turned around, picked up the trashcan and headed for the front door. Essie had already cranked up her car and was sitting in front of her house with the motor running.

As Toni opened the car door on the passenger side, she asked Essie whether she should just hold the trashcan between her feet on the floor. Essie assured her that it was okay to do so. As they turned the corner Toni did not know what river they were going to and it really didn't matter. She was grateful that Essie had helped her to understand what she had experienced. For a few minutes the two women drove in virtual silence until Essie turned on the radio.

"Ain't much to listen to this time of night, daughter."

"Miss Essie, you know what else?"

"Uh huh, tell me baby."

"I went upstairs and everybody was sleeping, they seemed to be in a coma or something. I went to each of their rooms and there was this sweet smell that came up from them. I couldn't smell anything when I walked in the door. As I stood over Wilson, Joyce and Jeremiah, I could smell it. It wasn't like anything I had ever smelled before. At first I didn't pay much attention to it. I thought it might have been the soap they used to bath with, until I saw the soap wrapper in the bathroom. I smelled the wrapper and the cake of soap and it didn't smell anything like the scent around Wilson and them. Then I was going back down stairs to check on mama when that sweet smell met me at the bottom of the stairs. I tried to sniff around to catch another whiff of it but I couldn't, it was gone."

"Bless God, baby, that was the Holy Spirit. The old saints, when I was first saved and filled with the Holy Ghost, used to talk about that strange perfume announcing the presence of the Holy Spirit, Himself. Now, the Holy Spirit, He's always there, but that's one of the ways He let us know that He is there. Then I smelled it for myself one day. Daughter, I was just a step or two from losing my mind. It was right after my husband Jake got killed, remember that?"

"Yes mam, right up there on I-26, that Friday morning."

"Well, I made it through burying him and found out that my house was about to be taken from me. People was calling for money that I didn't even have. On top of that my Robin tell me she pregnant for that Hilton boy. Robin had just turned fifteen.

I was sitting in the kitchen that evening and I started crying for no reason. I started feeling like I was being separated from myself. I couldn't even recognize where I was, honey. My mind was racing back and forth, some of everything was coming up in my mind. I got mad with Jake cause he didn't take care of things the way he should have. Only the Lord knows what he did with the money. But my mind just got to moving so fast that I started seeing things crawling around me and on me. Somehow I knew that I was loosing my mind. There wasn't much that I could do, something in my head said give up and you don't have to worry about this anymore. But way down inside, something else was saying don't give up. I could see myself just rocking back and forth and mumbling to myself.

Daughter, wasn't nobody home that evening but me. There I was swatting butterflies and shooing some other things away from me. All of sudden I felt this breeze stirring around me. This here breeze felt like it was cool and warm at the same time, you know what I mean? Anyhow, this breeze felt like it was wrapping me up in a cocoon or something. Then I smelled the perfume. Everything stopped moving. I tried to sniff, just like you did, I got my nostrils filled with the scent and jumped up from the table. I started speaking in my prayer language and went throughout my house for a while just praying. When I got through, honey, I repented to God for not talking to Him in the midst of all that mess. I was filled with the Holy Ghost then with evidence, but for some reason my troubles got so bad that I forgot to use it."

Toni sat quietly listening to Essie and waiting for more. Without having paid attention to where they were going Toni could now see the river. Essie parked the car in a spot off the side of the road.

"Get the bucket baby, let's go get this over with. Don't forget to untie the top of the bag."

"Yes mam."

The two walked a little distance and down a steep path.

"Be careful where you put your foot, honey. Sometime them snakes crawl out of the water and lay on the dirt."

"Oh don't say that Miss Essie, I hate to leave you and this bucket here."

The two women laughed and continued to walk toward the water. There was no one out that hour of the night on the river. Essie led the way down then they walked a little distance and came upon a small bridge. Essie began to pray in tongues, Toni began to pray the same way.

"Cast that whole thing over in that water, daughter."

Toni threw the trashcan and everything in it into the water. The two stood on the bridge praying and watching as the water carried the trashcan away. They watched until the can was out of sight.

"Father in the name of Jesus, wash this evil away and neutralize every power of the enemy. No weapon of the enemy formed against us or any member of our family shall prosper, and what so ever the enemy tries will fall upon his own head. Thank You Jesus for all that You've done and all that You will do." Essie said.

Toni watched, but she could no longer see the trashcan bobbing up and down in the water. The little anxiety that she had felt on the ride to the river had disappeared, but fatigue was setting in. She was tired.

"Come on child, it's over now. Them folks didn't know that God had anointed you for this. They thought that they would just send their evil spirits to the house and take charge. Oh but God had a whipping waiting for they tails. I bet you, and I ain't no gambling woman, them folks is wondering what happened cause them spirits they sent to y'all came back to them."

"Miss Essie, how do people do things like that? You know sending spirits like you said and doing stuff like what they did to mama?"

"I can't really say, daughter cause I ain't never dealt in that kind of stuff. But I been bothered by it because people tried to do the same thing to me and my family. People just let the devil take over and dictate to their soul. Just like me and you worship God in heaven, these people worship the devil. They act like they god on this earth. But the Bible speaks to all of that including witchcraft."

"Miss Essie, thank you for helping me and mama and them."

"Daughter, the Lord always got a ram in the bush. That's what we supposed to do. Your mama is backslidden, but God anointed you to cover your family, and now He has given you power to stand against everything the enemy throw out there. You got a great gift now daughter and God expect to get some mileage out of that. You got an assignment now Toni, you can't let nothing or nobody take you away from that. You hear me, child? Keep your hand in God's hand. The enemy gonna do some things, baby, to try and scare you and cause you to be of no affect for the kingdom, but remember, go to Father for instructions, you got a secret language that only He understands."

"Miss Essie, that sounds real scary."

"That's why you received that power, daughter. Open your mouth in those times, honey and let it roll, the enemy have to flee. God knew it would get ugly, that's why He gave you what you got now. But don't fear this gift Toni, it's your spiritual sword. Use that sword to cut down everything the enemy try to plant."

The words seemed to stick in Toni's mind, spiritual sword. The two women drove back home talking about the Bible and how God reveals Himself to His children. Before Toni got out of the car Miss Essie told her not to say anything to her family about this night and to get back to Connecticut as quickly as she could.

Toni walked into the house to quiet, a peaceful quiet. She stood at the door for a moment and allowed her eyes to sweep through the rooms. Trudy was still sleeping.

There was no sign of the invisible struggle that had been present earlier. The clock on the stove showed that it was nearly five o'clock. She was tired now but there was no time to sleep because she had a lot to do before she left to go back to Connecticut. She had to talk to Henry again and say goodbye to Alma.

The thought of leaving now weighed heavily on her. Margaret had gotten married and left home at a time when she was needed there. Jeremiah needed a mother and so did Joyce. Wilson was not able to allow his feelings to show and only God knew where Aaron Junior was.

Everybody needed to know and see that Trudy cared for her family. Henry needed the support of everyone and especially Trudy, but she had not been able to even ask how he was doing.

As Toni pondered the present and the future of her family a peace seemed to cover her like a warm soft blanket. Inside and in her mind a great security that all would be well filled her. She walked into the living room and sat in the chair where she had sat before. There was no fear and she desired sleep now. Once again, her eyes swept the room as though she was marking it visually with armed guards to protect as she slept. Sleep came upon Toni quickly.

19

The ringing telephone jarred Toni awake. She jumped up to find that Joyce had gotten up and started breakfast.

"Toni, it's your friend, Kim." Joyce said.

Still a little under the influence of sleep, Toni walked into the kitchen and took the phone from Joyce's hand.

"Hey girl, how you doing?" she asked.

"Sister, I don't know what's happening down there in big foot country, but I couldn't sleep last night. I prayed and prayed and asked the Lord to just keep His hand on you and your family. When do you think you'll be coming back this way?" Kim asked.

"Today, girl. I got something to tell you, Kim, that'll knock the elastic out of your pantyhose."

"I'll be here, when you get back. What time should I pick up from the airport?"

"I don't know, but I'll call you at work and let you know."

"Okay, I'll be listening for your call. Love you sister and my prayers are still with y'all."

"Thanks, girl, I appreciate you."

Joyce had stopped everything and was watching her big sister. She had come to the realization that Toni would have to return to Connecticut and she would not have the protection and comfort of her sister.

"How you doing, baby girl?" Toni asked.

"Fine. How you doing?" Joyce responded.

"I didn't hear you in here stirring around. Can I help you with something?"

"No, I'm finished, now. I thought that you were tired and knew for sure when I dropped a pan on the floor and you didn't even flinch. You need some rest Toni, I don't want you to get sick."

"I'll be okay, Joyce, really. I do need to get back to Connecticut and go to work because that lawyer won't take excuses or honesty for payment."

"Toni, I'm praying for when all of this stuff will be over and we can just have a good time as a family."

"Keep praying Joyce, we sure need as much of that as we can get. No matter how bad it looks, things won't stay the same. I don't know how it's going to turn out, but like the old saying goes, the best is yet to come."

"You ever wonder where Junior is?" Joyce asked.

"Yeah, and I pray that the Lord is protecting him. He'll show up one day, Joyce. You know boys don't take things the same way girls do."

Silence fell upon the kitchen. Toni stood at the kitchen window with her hands on her hips and stared out at the sunlit morning. She had no idea about what to do. She just wanted it all to be over and quickly. Jeremiah came up behind her and put his little arms around her waist.

"How you doing sweetie? Did you sleep well last night?" she asked.

"Yeah. I was tired, Toni. I think I snored." Jeremiah responded.

"I thought I heard a hog up there last night. All that grunting and groaning, now I know who it was." Toni teased her baby brother.

"That must have been Wilson, cause I store cute, don't I, Joyce?"

153

"Well, they got cute little hogs, so I guess cute little hogs snore cute. You're a cute little hog, too, Jeremiah."

"I'm not a hog, I'm a lamb." Jeremiah shot back.

"You're a cute little hog that look like a lamb." Joyce responded.

The siblings laughed together. Jeremiah looked confident and safe with his older sisters even though he was the object of their teasing. His innocent laughter filled the kitchen. Toni looked at the little boy and almost wished that he would never grow up and have to face all of the challenges that the future would bring. She felt a strong urge to take him back to Connecticut with her, but she knew in her heart that it was not possible for her little brother to grow up without having the experience of living.

The thought came to Toni's mind that God had sent an angel to protect Jeremiah, her job was to love him and pray for him. She bent over and hugged the little boy so tight that he had to tell her that she was squeezing him too tight. Releasing her grip on his little body she could feel love being transferred to him. Jeremiah tiptoed and kissed her on the cheek.

"Oh, I know, I didn't give you your hug yesterday, huh, Toni." Jeremiah said.

"That's right, little boy. See what happens when you cheat me out of my loving from you?

"Okay, then I won't forget when I come home today."

"You'd better not or I'll squeeze you until your eyes bug."

Big sister and baby brother threw their heads back and laughed. Jeremiah pinched his big sister on the arm.

"What was that for, Jerry?"

"You didn't ask me whether I wanted to buy lunch today."

"Oh, I'm sorry, do you want to buy lunch today, Master Spann?" she asked.

"I think I do, Miss Spann, but I don't got any money."

Jeremiah pretended to have a different accent as he played with Toni.

"Can I buy that lunch for you, Master Spann?" Toni mocked.

"I'd like that Miss Spann, if it's not too much, mam."

"Sit down here, Jeremiah and eat your breakfast before the bus comes." Joyce said. "You already got your mind on lunch and haven't had breakfast yet."

"You cooked, Joyce?" Jeremiah asked.

"Uh huh."

"You cook good Joyce."

"Well thank you, sir, for that compliment, Jerry, but I'm not the one that's going to give you two dollars today."

"No, for true, Joyce, you cook real good. I like it when you cook. I don't like it when Margaret cook, except for spaghetti."

"You got a point there. I'm glad Lloyd can cook cause Margaret needs help. She'll get the hang of cooking now though, she got a husband."

Toni laughed as she went for her purse to give Jeremiah lunch money. Trudy was awake now and was trying to sit up on the sofa.

"You hungry?" Toni asked.

"Yes, I am. I heard my stomach growling in my sleep. I think that's what woke me up. What y'all done cooked in there? Give me some of it."

Toni was delighted to hear that her mother was eager to eat a meal. She went upstairs and got the medication so that it would be close when Trudy was finished eating.

When Toni returned to the living room, Joyce was bringing a plate with grits, eggs and sausage to her mother. Jeremiah brought his plate and knelt at the coffee table to eat with his mother.

"Mama you feeling alright now?" he asked.

"Yeah, baby, mama feeling better. How you doing this morning?"

"I'm doing fine. Toni tried to squeeze me up like toothpaste but it didn't hurt."

"She was trying to squeeze all the sugar out you?"

"I think so cause I forgot to give her a hug yesterday."

"Oh, so you forgot to give her some sugar and she was trying to squeeze out a little bit just in case you forgot again."

"I won't forget, but if I do, she can just remind me."

"Alright, Master Spann, here is your lunch money, you even got an extra dollar, better save it and not spend it all in one day." Toni said as she handed Jeremiah the three-dollar bills.

"Thank you, Toni. Toni, you going back home today?"

"I think so Jerry. Why?"

"I don't want you to go before I come home, please."

"Okay, I'll wait until you get home before I leave."

"Toni."

"Yes, Jerry."

"Please cook for me and Joyce before you go."

"Is there anything in particular you want?"

"Yeah. I want some roast and candied sweet potatoes, and some macaroni and cheese."

"You don't ask for much do you, mister?"

The little boy smiled at up at his big sister and finished his breakfast. Joyce sat at the kitchen table and stared off into space. Toni could see the pain in the face of her sister and wished that she could somehow just speak a word and bring some happiness into her life. There were no promises that even a big sister could make that would bring happiness into the situation that Toni was about to leave her siblings in. But now she too, had been worn to a near frazzle and there was a strong desire within her to leave and get back to her quiet apartment. She wanted to stay longer, but with a debt to the attorney for Henry's defense, she had to go back to work, not even the government had the kind of patience that would allow her the freedom to stay as long as she needed to in South Carolina.

Toni stared out of the kitchen window, again. She looked at the clock on the stove and realized that she had been asleep for less than two hours.

"I made some coffee, Toni." Joyce said.

"Oh you did, thank the Lord, I sure can use some this morning."

"Toni, what's on your mind?" Joyce asked.

Toni was surprised that she was now the one being asked what was on her mind. She poured the coffee and sat at the table with Joyce while Jeremiah entertained Trudy.

"Girl, I have so much on my mind, Joyce, that I get tired if I even think about it too much. I need to get back to Connecticut so I can get a little rest and try to figure out what the hell is going on."

"Toni, I know you worrying about all of us. I want you to stay but I know you gotta go back. We'll be alright until you come back. I don't know how, but I know, it's just a feeling I got way down inside that someway, somehow, it's gonna be alright."

"I've got the same feeling, too, Joyce. This is something that only the Lord can fix and I pray that He does it soon."

"Well, let me ask you this, can me and Jerry come and spend the summer with you?"

"Yeah, I'll send for both of you. You guys need a little vacation. I got a two-bedroom apartment and it's really nice, too. I don't have anything in the other bedroom, yet except a television and a chair. I think I'll get a couple of single beds and put in there for you and Jerry. It's a nice size room so it can hold two single beds."

"I don't care if I have to sleep on the floor, Toni, I just want to get away from here the very day school is out. Can you send for us then?"

"Yeah, you can plan to leave here the day school is out, okay?"

Joyce was so happy that she was going to spend the summer in Connecticut with her big sister. The promise had put a spark in Joyce's eyes. Toni could now see the joy rising in her sister. That would mean that her mother and Wilson would be the only ones in the house during the summer. Maybe, just maybe, she thought, her mother needed time alone. Trudy would be strong enough by then to take care of herself without help. School would be out in less than a month and that did not give Toni a lot of time to do all that was necessary to accommodate her brother and sister and purchase the tickets.

"Don't forget to cook, Toni." Jeremiah said as he went upstairs to get his schoolbag.

Toni walked out to the front porch and waited for Jeremiah to come out. She took him by the hand and walked him to the corner to wait for the bus. Several children had already gathered on the corner to wait for the bus. A few of the children sheepishly waved at Jeremiah as he and Toni approached the corner. Toni looked down at the little boy and smiled as they stood waiting. He held her hand unashamedly, then leaned against her as though she was his wall of protection. As she stood at the corner holding Jeremiah's hand and letting him lean against her, Toni could feel the hunger for love and attention inside of him.

It almost broke Toni's heart causing tears to well in her eyes because Jeremiah had had to grow up too quickly. The little boy, she realized, had gotten good at hiding his feelings. He had seen his brother almost killed, then witnessed his brother killing the person who tried to kill him. A child should never have to experience these kinds of things, she thought.

The other children chattered and played as they waited for the bus. Toni watched them and smiled. It was like watching innocence at play. But Jeremiah was content to just lean on his big sister and hold her hand. Finally the big yellow bus turned the corner and headed for where the children were waiting. Toni stooped down and straightened Jeremiah's pants and belt.

"You got your money sweetie?" she asked.

"Yeah, it's in my pocket, but I only brought a dollar." Jeremiah responded.

The little boy hugged her neck before walking to the bus. She kissed him on the forehead and told him to have a good day. A little girl said something to Jeremiah as he was getting on the bus but he only shrugged his shoulder. Toni stood at the corner and watched until the bus was out of sight. Slowly she turned and began walking back to the house. Essie was standing on the porch with her blue uniform dress on.

"How you this morning, daughter?" she said.

"I'm fine, Miss Essie, how you doing this morning?"

"Believe it or not honey, I feel like I can leap over walls and run through troops. It's like the Lord has restored me girl."

Toni walked over to Essie's house and stood on the walkway in front of the steps leading up to the porch.

"Miss Essie, you know we haven't had much sleep?"

"God got a way of keeping us awake until the right time for us to sleep. We'll be okay today. I can't give no guarantee on later this evening, but we'll probably start snoring in front of everybody." She laughed.

"I'm gonna call the airlines and see what time I can get a flight out of here. I need your telephone number, too, Miss Essie."

The two women exchanged telephone numbers. Essie hugged Toni and blessed her. Toni walked back across the street and walked into the house. Trudy had gotten up from the sofa and the covers had been removed. Joyce was still in the kitchen. Toni had almost forgotten that Joyce had never come out of the house to catch her bus for school.

"You're not going to school today, Joyce."

"No, I wanted to stay with you, today, that's alright isn't it?"

"Yeah, I guess I haven't spent much time with you baby girl."

"Oh, Alma called while you were out there with Jerry. She said don't you leave the state before she get off from work today."

"She sure is bossy, ain't she?"

"I like Alma, though, she's real people and she ain't phony. She may not give the time of day to everybody, but she's real." Joyce responded.

Joyce told Toni that their mother had gone upstairs on her own to take a bath, after folding up the covers.

So badly Toni wanted to ask Joyce questions about the night before and whether she had heard anything but decided that she should not. It didn't make sense to add more confusion to the situation.

Toni told Joyce that just as soon as their mother was finished in the bathroom that she would bath and they would go to the grocery store and pick up a few things so that she could cook before Jeremiah came home.

Wilson finally came down stairs and sat at the table with his sisters.

"Jerry went to school already?" he asked.

"Yeah, I walked him out to the corner and waited until he got on the bus." Toni said.

"I slept so long, this morning. I meant to give him some money for lunch."

"I gave him some." Toni replied.

"Thanks. You like those pants and the belt I bought for him?"

"Yeah, he looked like a big boy. That leather belt was real nice."

"I saw that pants last week and thought that might look good on him. Man you should have seen him when I gave him the bag." Wilson laughed.

"Sometimes it looks like Wilson trying to make Jerry a little Wilson. Toni, you should see that little leather jacket Wilson bought him for Christmas. Girl, Jerry thought he was grown when he put that little jacket on." Joyce said.

"You gotta give it to him now, Jerry was sharp wasn't he?" Wilson chuckled.

"Jerry must be the sharpest little boy in the school." Toni remarked.

"Yeah, he and Alma's little boy. You know Alma and her mama keep his little spike head behind sharp." Wilson said.

"Wilson, you want me to fix you something to eat before you leave?" Joyce asked.

"Yeah, just give me anything you got over there. Toni, when you leaving?"

"I'm thinking about later tonight, if I can get a red eye with Eastern. I promised Jerry that I would cook for him before I leave."

157

"Well, if you cooking, I'll save my appetite until I get home."

"Oh no, please eat before you come home, Wilson, so we can have something left over." Joyce said.

Everybody had a good laugh because Wilson had a very good appetite.

"You not going to school today, Joyce?" Wilson asked.

"No, I'll go tomorrow."

"Okay, remember if you gonna be a teacher, you have to start practicing now to be there everyday."

"Yeah, but I got college before the real deal, brother." Joyce responded as she tapped Wilson on the head. "In a few weeks me and Jerry going to Connecticut for the summer, too."

"That's good. That'll be a good vacation for y'all. Toni, you want me to help with the tickets?" Wilson asked.

"That would be good, Wilson. If you can pay their way there, I'll pay their way back. They want to be on the way the day school close so make sure you get the tickets by then."

"How they gonna get there, plane or train?"

"Train." Joyce said quickly.

"It's done. I'll check this week to see how much it cost and take care of that. Joyce you have to let me know exactly what day school close for you and Jerry."

"Okay, but I think it's May 30. I'll check and make sure tomorrow."

Toni was glad that Wilson had made the offer to help with the transportation for Joyce and Jerry. Now she could concentrate on getting the beds for them. Already she was thinking about where she would go to get the beds. It was important to her that the children be comfortable while visiting her. She knew that her apartment would accommodate the three of them. It was not a huge apartment but she had been fortunate to get such a unique one. The apartment had two bedrooms, a nice size kitchen and a real nice sized dining area that had a window. The living room was spacious and had an alcove that she had not done anything with. The alcove was large enough to be a den and could be a good place for Jerry to play when it rained. As she thought about it, with the right pieces it could also be the family gathering place for them.

Wilson left for work and it was just the two sisters left in the kitchen.

"I can't wait for school to close, Toni. You don't know how excited I'm getting. Did you tell mama that we spending the summer with you?"

"No, I'll tell her before I leave, though."

Shortly thereafter Trudy came downstairs wearing the housedress that Toni had purchased days earlier. There was a glow on Trudy and she walked a lot better than she had just the day before.

"Mama, the day school closes Joyce and Jeremiah will be coming to Connecticut to really spend the summer with me. Joyce will make sure that their bags are packed and Wilson will see that they get on the train. They'll really have a vacation this year."

"That's a long time ain't it for them to be gone?" Trudy asked.

"No, it's not long at all, mama. Summer rolls around so fast, it's gone before you know it. Besides, mama, they need to get away for a while. You and Wilson will have the house to yourselves, just send me a couple hundred dollars a month of their Social Security check."

"Now how I'm supposed to do that?" Trudy snapped back.

Cautious now, Toni took her time in responding.

"Mama, you just get a money order and send it to me, that's all."

"That's a whole lot of trouble for nothing to me. If they was here I wouldn't have to do all of that."

"Mama, how is that a lot of trouble? It's money that daddy left for them and besides, I ain't asking you to send all that they should get."

"Well you don't have to get all huffy about it. I ain't said whether they could go yet." Trudy snapped.

Immediately a flash of heat rose up in Toni and her tone changed.

"I didn't ask you whether they could come, mama, I told you that they would be coming. The day school closes, they had better be on the train headed for Connecticut. There ain't a reason why they should have to stay here in South Carolina for the summer. With everything that has happened here, I should be taking them back with me now. If it's such a bother for you to send them a little bit of the money that their daddy left for them, then you keep it and do whatever you choose to do with it. I can take care of them without it. That little bit of money I asked you to send wouldn't make a difference in anything anyhow."

Trudy's eyes were like round saucers. She had not expected her daughter to be so stern in her speech. But it was very clear that Toni was not about to be threatened or have her siblings held as pawn in a vindictive game by her mother.

"I didn't say that they couldn't come, so why you getting angry and huffy?"

"It's the same thing, mama, you said that you hadn't said that they could come to Connecticut. You were threatening and I ain't the one to be played with. I heard what you said and knew what you meant by it. These kids need something that they hadn't been getting and you can't give it to them now. You need to take the time while they're in Connecticut and get your life together so you can give them what they need when they get back here."

The tension in the air could now be cut with a knife. Trudy's attempt to control the situation had been met head on by Toni and she knew that she would lose this battle. Joyce sat at the table with her head down. She was glad that she had not had to say anything and that she had an advocate for her and Jeremiah.

"And by the way, mama, when I leave, I don't want these kids to have to suffer because of what I just said. They don't need anymore hell in their lives."

"What hell have they had that you blaming me for?"

"Now you really have lost your mind. Do you understand what's going on here and now? None of us was sleeping with that Isiah or running up and down the streets with him."

"Oh so that's what this is all about. I was waiting to see how long it would take you to bring that up."

"Well you don't have to wait anymore. There it is, now you deal with it and take this time to get yourself together. This ain't no time for you to be doing crazy things, mama. We have a serious situation here and I just gave up every dollar that I have in the world to protect my brother."

"I ain't the one that made him do what he did. I told every one of them that if somebody did anything to me I would take care of it. So don't come blaming me."

"You don't see where you're responsible for anything here?"

"Hell no! Henry pulled that trigger, not me."

"Oh you pulled the trigger long before the bullet came out. But if you choose to claim innocence, that's fine. I'll take care of my brother, your son. I pray to God that He will help you. You have shown more interest in Isiah and his family than you have for the children you birthed and we're here trying to nurse you back to health. Not once have you asked how Henry was doing. But you got on the telephone and searched the state to catch up to those evil people of Isiah's and invite them and more evil up in here. You put everyone of us in harms way."

Trudy was silent. The tears began running down her face. But Toni's compassion for her had vanished.

"I'm sorry that what I said had to come out like it did, mama. But mama, I meant what I said. I pray that you let God help you because you have a problem whether you want to admit it or not. Everybody else can see it, you should be able to do so as well. Mama, I'm not saying this because I want to hurt you anymore than you've already been hurt. But far be it for you to even try and claim innocence. I don't know how any of this is going to end, I just pray to God that nobody else is hurt and somehow peace can be found."

"You had it in you all the time to say what you said, Toni. You always been a hankty ass heifer. Ain't too many people measure up to your standard, so you don't have to apologize for nothing. You always thought that you was better than me and everybody else. You can go on back to Connecticut and forget me, cause I don't need you or anybody else. I been taking care of myself and these kids and will continue to do so. If I say they go to Connecticut, then they'll go, but if I say that they stay right here, regardless of what you say, they'll be right here."

For a moment Toni stood at the arch between the living room and the kitchen and stared into space as though looking into another world. The words spoken by her mother seemed to take a while to sink in. After she had repeated the words spoken by her mother in her mind an anger rose up in her that seemed to have no end. For a few seconds she considered not saying another word, but before she could reach a conclusion she was sitting at the table across from her mother. Joyce had turned from the back door and started walking away from the kitchen. Toni could see the tears in her eyes and the awful hurt and fear on face.

Toni looked at Trudy with eyes of steel. The look on her face was void of emotions. There was a strange composure in her body and voice. Joyce sat in the living room with her head hung down.

"Mama," Toni began slowly, "I don't want you to misunderstand one word that I'm about say. I have been silent almost all of my life about a whole lot of things. But right now, I'm in no way about to be dictated to by anybody but God. You don't even know what I've had to experience the last few days, right here in this house. Some things, mama, that many people would not believe and would probably call me crazy if I were to tell them about it. I have a lot more that I must do before this is all over with. If Joyce and Jeremiah are not on a train headed to Connecticut the day school is closed, I guarantee you that you'll have to deal with the woman in me that you have never seen before. I have said that they need a real summer vacation and they will get one. You need time to sort through your mess and decide the type of life you want to continue living so you had best take advantage of it. By the way, mama, if you have to deal with the woman in me, I will get legal custody of those kids and their Social Security check will never be a part of any money you get. By the way, if I think, dream, or even get paranoid that you have put your hand in the face of any of these kids, believe you me, you'll wish that you had died when Isiah shot you. I am not a suicidal woman, mama, I am very homicidal."

As she began to get up from the table, Trudy's eyes followed her. It looked like for once, Trudy was beginning to see her daughter as a woman with purpose and not a daughter who was getting older. Trudy's eyes were lifted up and the tears had stopped.

The tone of Toni's voice and her deliberate words seemed to have killed any vindictiveness inside Trudy.

"Mama, I love you, but right now, I love my brothers and sisters more, they don't have anyone to protect them. You, on the other hand, can steer your own ship. I don't regret anything that I have ever done to help in any form or fashion, but this is a very, very serious situation that's before us. Have I made myself very clear to you about the kids?"

There was stark silence in the room. It seemed like everyone had stopped breathing. Toni's eyes stared at Trudy like piercing brown flames formed from refining fire. Trudy tried to return the stare, but dropped her head and looked away.

Toni decided that she would not say another word and walked upstairs to take a bath and dress. When she returned to the living room, Trudy was lying on the sofa and Joyce was sitting in the chair. There was no tension in the air, just a quiet that seemed to be an invisible dominator. If any tension had appeared in the room, the peace that blanketed the room would have quickly absorbed it.

Trudy had never had Toni to speak to her like she had today. The shock seemed to have taken any and all fight out of Trudy. Joyce sat quietly and stared into space. She had never heard her big sister speak to her mother like she had, but inside she was ecstatic that someone had made her mother back down from a crazy idea. Joyce quietly prayed that what Toni had said earlier would last and would have an impact on her mother's life. Inside, Joyce was hoping for a change, a positive change. She also feared that after Toni left her mother would retaliate against her. Many times she had been beaten and slapped in the mouth and face by her mother when she was angry or drinking. The thought of what might or could happen after Toni left made Joyce consider running away; but where could she go? So she cried.

Toni sensed what her little sister was feeling, but she also believed that it was up to her to also lay the foundation for peace and cut asunder any roots of retaliation that might have been planted. This was a delicate situation she realized, and Jeremiah and Joyce would be the ones to suffer after she left.

"Mama, why don't you get dressed and come go to the store with me and Joyce. I'll call a taxi and we can just take our time and shop for what I need to cook before Jeremiah get here from school."

Joyce's eyes bugged after hearing Toni's suggestion. Toni headed for the kitchen but she winked at Joyce as she passed.

"You want me to get you a pair of pants and a top mama?" Joyce asked.

"I really don't want to go, I can stay here until y'all get back." Trudy responded.

"You need to get out and get some fresh air, mama, it'll do you good." Joyce said.

"I promise to walk slow, mama, so you don't have to worry about moving too fast. That way you can pick out what you want from the store." Toni remarked. "Matter of fact, the three of us should go to Shoney's and have lunch. How about that?"

"That sure sound good, Toni, but I just don't want to go. I really appreciate that, maybe we can go another time. You and Joyce go and get what you need, just get me some ice cream."

"What kind of ice cream you want?" Toni asked.

"You know I like that Butter Pecan, girl, and get me a little piece of pound cake so I can put the ice cream on top of it."

"Oh so you want some cake ala mode?" Joyce teased.

"Cake something." Trudy laughed. "I just like some cake with my butter pecan ice cream. I've been having this craving for some ice cream."

"Alright now, don't let me have to take you for an examination after Toni leaves. Only pregnant people have cravings and you too old for that." Joyce teased her mother.

"You right about that, I better change my tune. I got a taste for some cake and ice cream, then. That sound better?" Trudy asked.

"Yes mam, that sound a whole lot better. I'm just teasing you mama, people have cravings all the time for things that they really like. I think I crave those hotdogs with chili from Edwards and the banana splits from Dairy Queen." Joyce responded.

"Oh girl, I don't know what it is about those chili dogs from Edwards. I remember buying six of them one time and eating every of them by myself." Toni said.

At almost the same time, Trudy and Joyce said, "six?"

"I was hungry." Toni responded.

"Hunger would have been two, no more than three, but six?" Trudy said.

"Yeah. I put that minced onion on every one of them, a little tad of mustard and I put that chili on every one of those hotdogs and sat down and ate them. I also crave those big juicy cheeseburgers from Dairy Queen and the strawberry milkshake."

"Toni, you just greedy, that's all. That's more than a craving." Joyce said.

"Oh, no, it's greedy if somebody else is paying for it. It's a craving when you can buy it yourself." Toni snapped with a smile.

Trudy laughed at what she said.

"Now that's the truth. Whatever you can afford is a craving, what you can't afford is something different if you take more than one serving." She said.

"I don't care what you and Toni call it, mama, six chili dogs is greedy."

"Come on girl before I make you watch us eat after I get through cooking."

"Yeah, right. I'll eat from everybody's plate until my belly is full before I just watch. I'd have my hand in mama plate, Jeremiah's plate and head for yours next."

"I didn't hear you say anything about Wilson's plate." Toni responded.

"You're right. With that appetite Wilson got, he could very easily mistake my hand for extra meat and I could lose a few fingers."

Trudy burst into laughter at Joyce's remark about Wilson. Trudy was tickled and laughed so hard that she started coughing.

"Mama come on and lock this door behind us. We shouldn't be gone too long." Toni said.

"Look, here come Uncle Clifford, maybe he'll let us borrow his car, Toni."

"Yeah, he'll let me use it."

They waited for Clifford to park and come inside the house. Toni took the keys and she and Joyce got into the car and left.

Toni and Joyce purchased everything that she thought that she would need to cook then stopped at the Burger King. The sisters sat inside the restaurant and ate their hamburgers. This is what Joyce had wanted, a moment away from the house with her sister.

"Toni, thanks for standing up for me and Jeremiah. Mama can get real ugly sometimes, but I think she got the message today that you ain't playing those crazy games she play."

"Joyce, I didn't want to get into a pissing contest with mama. But once we were there, I wasn't about to back down or hand over a victory to the devil. You and Jeremiah deserve to have a vacation and y'all gonna get one. I said what I meant, and I meant every word I said."

"I really don't want to stay with mama, Toni. After you and mama had that little squabble, I thought about running away cause mama might get spiteful. I don't think she will now, cause she know you wasn't just blowing smoke. I just get mad sometimes Toni when mama go out and get herself into all kinds of mess then it's us that have to take care of her. But she don't appreciate it. When you leave, it's gonna be me who have do all the cooking like I always do. I'm just sick of it, Toni."

"Joyce, I don't know what's going to happen, but I pray that something positive start happening."

"Yeah, we got to think about Henry now, too."

"You got that right."

"Toni, what you see yourself doing in ten years?"

"I hope practicing law, Joyce. I still got to finish undergraduate school, but I'm hoping to get into law school. Kim and I plan to open up our own firm."

"That sound good, real good. I bet the two of you can really do some good, too."

"How about you, Joyce?"

"I want to teach in an elementary school. Teaching fascinates me, you know, helping somebody else learn something."

"You'll make it, Joyce. When you graduate next year, we'll have you set up for college. Where you want to college at?"

"I've been looking at Morgan State in Baltimore."

"Well, Morgan State it will be. I think Wilson is thinking about college, too."

"For true?"

"Yeah. I listened to him last night talking about the Marine Corps and their uniform. He talked about an officer, though, and he needs a college degree for that."

"Sure you right, Toni. I remember that day when Miss Essie nephew, L.C. came to visit her and Wilson and them was outside and saw him in his Army uniform with the gold. Toni, it looked like Wilson was in a trance. He watched L.C. and got up and walked across the street and started talking to him. L.C. let Wilson put that Army hat on and Wilson looked like he had stepped into another world. From then on anytime something about the service would come on TV Wilson's eyes would be looking for the officers. Talk to him Toni about going to college, okay?"

"Okay. I will. I think he would make a fine officer. Wilson is a handsome dark skin fellow, now imagine him in an officer's uniform."

"Yes, Lord, I can see that, girl. Wouldn't it be nice Toni if all of us could go to college?"

"Yeah, that would be nice. We could then pool our money and make sure that everybody has a house, so nobody would be in the street."

"We can all do that anyway, Toni, if we wanted to."

The sisters sat at the restaurant and talked about their future. Joyce's confidence was increasing and she began to feel like she would be able to make it through the next year of school. In a few weeks she would be in Connecticut with Toni and would not have to return to South Carolina until the day before school would start. Joyce loved her big sister and looked forward to spending entire days with her.

By the time Jeremiah returned home from school that evening, Toni had almost finished the dinner. Clifford had fallen asleep in the chair watching television with Trudy. Everyone was waiting for dinner, especially Jeremiah. Toni found several pieces of Tupperware and set them aside so that she could take some food to Henry and see him again before leaving.

Toni called the airline and reserved a seat on the flight leaving at three fifteen the next morning. She would be there when Jeremiah went to sleep and gone when he awoke. The thought of leaving while he was asleep brought sadness to her heart. But in a few weeks he would be with her for the summer.

"Toni, how long before dinner ready?" Clifford asked.

"Not long, the bread soaking now. You hungry?"

"Both of us hungry." Trudy said.

"It'll be ready in just a few minutes. Joyce making Kool-Aid right now."

Toni called Alma to let her know that she was leaving the next morning. She asked Alma to come and pick her up so that she could go to Clifford's house and take something for Henry to eat. Alma suggested that Toni take enough food so that they could eat with Henry. Toni was glad that Alma had thought of that. Toni made sure that everyone was eating when Alma showed up. She had whispered to Joyce that she was going to Clifford's house to have dinner with Henry.

Alma didn't come inside the house, Toni met her outside and they drove off.

"Girl how you doing?" Alma asked as Toni opened the backdoor and put the bag of containers on the floor. She opened the front door and slid into the passenger seat.

"Alma, ain't nobody gonna believe what I have gone through. Sister, there are some evil people in this world." Toni responded.

"Ha, you ain't telling me anything that I don't know. But tell me what happened."

"Alma, I'm not crazy, and I don't deal in witchcraft or voodoo, but something was happening in that house last night and this morning that I know without seeing the devil's tail or pitchfork, came straight out of the pit of hell."

Alma drove along slowly as she listened to her friend. Alma's face showed no emotions as she glanced every now and then at Toni. Alma stared straight ahead and sighed. She reached over and turned the radio off.

"Toni I had to battle that same kind of evil a little while ago. I ain't scared of that kind of thing anymore, praise God. That's not to say that I am a fool and overlook what people are doing. But I went through that shit when I was seeing David. Remember him?"

"Yeah, did he try that mess on you, girl?"

"No, matter-of-fact, he was suffering from the mess, too."

"Girl, hold up a minute. What was going on?"

"You remember that big behind heifer that was a couple of years behind us in school that claimed that she had that baby for David?"

"Yeah, what her name is, Jeanie, Jeanie something or other."

"Uh, huh. That is one wicked woman, you hear me, she is a wicked woman."

"Didn't she marry one of the Simmons twins about a year or so ago?"

"Yeah, and he divorced her so quick it wasn't funny. They weren't together for six months, girl. He said that she had a black heart and was the devil's daughter."

Alma told Toni what had happened to you.

"My God, Alma." Toni responded.

"All I can say, Toni, is that the one child that I've given birth to is the only one that I will ever have. That's why David left here. He begged me to come and go with him to Maryland, but for some reason I just couldn't leave. You don't know how many times I wished that I had left with him. I want to get away from here for a while, Toni."

"You can always come to Connecticut girl and try life there. I'll help you get a place right in the building where I live. You can always get a job with your profession and even start working on your degree for your R.N. license."

"I'm thinking about that, girl, and I appreciate you for being my friend and my sister."

"Alma, we have been close since what, the seventh grade? We have shared some of the worse things and we're still sharing them. We are going to make it, Alma. I don't know how, but I know that we'll get through everything that has happened to us and everything that'll come down the pike."

"I know, Toni. Don't you ever forget this Toni, I love you so much."

"I love you, too, Alma, no matter what."

"Now we have to start praying for Henry's freedom." Alma said.

Tears were flowing from both the women's eyes as they pulled in front of Clifford's house. Lloyd's car was parked out front, so Alma pulled her car behind his and shut off the engine.

"Well I'm glad that Lloyd is here with Henry." Toni said.

"Has Miss Trudy said anything yet about Henry?"

"No, she hasn't. We had a few words this morning and I opened my mouth about that. I think that it shocked mama that I stood up to her and backed her down. She was about to play that crazy power game with me about she hadn't said that Joyce and Jeremiah could come and spend the whole summer with me."

"I bet that shocked her. So they're coming for the whole summer?"

"Yeah, I want them to come the very day that school closes. Joyce really don't want to hang around here for the summer."

"You let me know what day and I will make sure that they get to the airport or the train station, whichever one they'll be taking."

"Thanks, Alma, that's one less problem. I'll be leaving here on that three something flight in the morning. I need to get back."

"I think I'm gonna take a few days off in the next week or two and come spend a few days with you, before the kids come. Is that okay with you?"

"I would love that Alma."

"Okay, then it's a done deal. You, me and Kim can have us a shut in like they do at the Holiness Church and just pray all night, at least one of those nights."

"I'm looking forward to it."

Toni and Alma did not stay very long at Clifford's house. They allowed Henry and Lloyd to eat the food that she brought. She and Alma would go back to the house and eat.

Toni told Henry that she was leaving and that he could call her at home if he had any problems or wanted to talk. The four stood holding hands as Lloyd led them in prayer. He prayed the traveler's prayer for his sister-in-law and she and Alma departed.

20

The ride back to the house was full of talk about the future and better days. The friends made a pact that regardless of what the future might bring that they would continue to press forward and complete their education by the time they were thirty years old.

Clifford had left the house by the time Toni and Alma returned. Wilson was home and sitting in the den watching television. Trudy was sitting in the recliner, but there didn't appear to be any conversation between them.

"What's up Miss Gardenia?" Wilson asked.

"Good evening, how's everybody?" Alma asked. "Y'all didn't eat all of the food did you?"

"How you know some food was in here." Wilson asked.

"I know Miss Toni cooked some food in this house. My car still smell like the food she carried over to Henry. Now I'm here for the rest, that is if you left anything."

"Girl please, you know I don't eat that much. I eat like a bird."

Everybody, including Trudy started laughing at Wilson's remark.

"Yeah, I got your bird alright, must be a flying dinosaur." Alma responded.

Wilson laughed at the remark.

"How Henry doing, Toni?" Wilson asked.

"He's doing okay. Lloyd was there with him."

"Oh, okay, then, he need somebody like that with him."

"Wilson, didn't you want to go to South Carolina State College one time?" Toni asked.

"I still do. I'd go anywhere if I can get a scholarship or something like that."

"If I found you a scholarship, would you go in the fall?"

"Girl, if you found me some money, I'd go tomorrow. I can see myself in that Army uniform with them jokers saying yes sir, Lt. Spann, yes sir, Colonel Spann."

"Oh, you want the bird on your shoulder, huh?" Alma said.

"Girl, that's the only way to fly, officer candidate school."

"I like that idea, too, Wilson. I've been thinking about going back to school and getting my degree for my R.N. and go in myself. I like the idea of seeing the world and having those officer bars on my shoulder too." Alma said.

"For real? Alma you thinking about that too?"

"Yeah, I really think that's what I'm going to do Wilson. Look, let's see who get their officer bars first."

"Oh no, you would get yours first cause you don't have to go to school as long to get your degree, you already got your LPN. Let's see who takes the least amount of time to get Captain."

"Okay, what's the prize?"

"The one who takes the longest to get Captain pay the other one two hundred dollars."

Wilson and Alma stretched out their right arms and locked their little fingers and said, "bet."

Toni looked at them and started laughing.

"I'll hold the two hundred dollars until that time."

"Yeah, right, and she'll be at the shoe store with the money." Wilson said.

The food was again warmed. Toni and Alma sat in the kitchen eating with Wilson and Alma talking about college and the military. Trudy walked into the kitchen and got some peach cobbler in a small container and put it in the oven to get warm.

"Look like I ain't the only one in here that had seconds on the mind." Wilson said.

"Shoot, Toni put her foot in that peach cobbler." Trudy said. "I was laying in there thinking whether I should get another scoop. Then I just figure, just get some and stop thinking. Hand me that ice cream up there in the freezer."

Toni tucked Jeremiah in, then talked for a few minutes with Joyce. She and Alma sat on the front porch talking. Toni's bags had already been packed and she was ready to go. Alma called another nurse and asked her to work for her the next day because she had an emergency to come up. Wilson decided that he would ride with Alma so she would not have to drive home alone at that hour of the morning.

When Toni, Alma and Wilson arrived at the airport in Charleston it looked like a deserted place. Toni walked to the ticket counter and made sure that her name was in the system for the flight that morning. The woman at the ticket counter informed her that the plane would be arriving about forty minutes late, therefore her flight would be at least an hour late leaving Charleston.

Alma and Wilson were content just to spend a little more time with her. They walked outside and sat on the edge of a bench and smoked cigarettes and talked.

"Toni, seriously now, I will be in Connecticut in another week or so."

"I'm looking forward to it, girl. I just pray that everything stays calm here in Charleston."

"You going to Connecticut, Alma?" Wilson asked.

"Yeah, I really need to get away for a couple of days, Wilson."

"That's a good idea. I'm hoping to get out of here for a while myself. I think if I get out of here, though, I won't be coming back to live here, again."

"For real?" Alma asked.

"For real. I got so much in my mind that I want to do, girl."

"You got any idea when things are going to be over for Henry?" Wilson asked Toni.

"No, the lawyer is trying to make sure that a decision is made and there is no trial."

"I pray that he can get it done. The Lord be with him." Alma said.

For several minutes quiet ruled the morning. No cars or people moved about the airport property. Toni did not know what she could say to her friend or her brother. Alma did not know of anything that she could say either. Alma sensed that her friend was under tremendous pressure. She wanted to just take her friends hand and hold it; to tell her how much she loved her and that she would always be her friend and sister.

"Are you tired, Toni. I don't mean physically tired, because I know that you are. I mean are you tired mentally?"

"I think that I am Alma. I don't know where Aaron, Jr. is, Henry is worried about this situation and Wilson here needs a scholarship. I cannot begin to talk about Jerry and Joyce."

"I heard how you had to set mama straight today. Joyce said for a minute there she thought you was gonna grab mama by the throat and choke the doodoo out of her. She certainly had a different attitude when I got home this evening, too." Wilson stated.

"Yeah, mama tried to play that nutsiness with me when I told her that the kids were coming to me for the summer and I wanted her to send me a couple of hundred dollars each month while they were there."

"Oh, shoot! Talk about money and she act like all of that check belongs to her. She ain't too apt to play with you now." Wilson said.

"You know, I heard a preacher saying the other day that God sends angels to watch over us when we come to earth. He also said that the devil also assigns fallen angels to us and our families to make sure we never prosper. I believe, right now, that the angels that God assigned to watch us are watching Aaron, Jr., and all of us." Alma said.

"I believe that and pray that each angel takes good care of us." Wilson replied.

The time had come for Toni to board the plane and head back to Connecticut. The two friends embraced, kissed each other with tears in their eyes. Wilson kissed his sister then watched as she boarded the plane.

21

Toni slept on the flight back to Connecticut and had no time to think about the situation she was leaving behind in South Carolina. She hadn't bothered to call Kim or anyone else to pick her up at the airport.

Just after the sun had risen, the plane landed in Connecticut. Toni saw a taxi cab and asked the driver how much it would be to take her home. The driver looked at Toni and in a heavy West Indian accent, told her to give him seven dollars. She knew that what he was asking was far less than the ride would ordinarily cost. Grateful for such leniency in price Toni put her suitcase in the trunk as quickly as the driver had popped it.

"You okay, my sister?" the driver asked.

"Yes, thank you, I'm fine sir."

"I see, spirit in the dark, justice of the buzzard."

"Beg pardon, sir."

"God done forgive your brothers. The nurse, she be your sister."

"I don't understand what you're talking about."

"I know, but you learn real fast. Just use the gift right in your mouth, use it young lady."

Toni sat up in the back of the taxi and looked straight ahead at the driver. She thought this was another trick being played on her, but by whom? A calm surrounded her as she sought to hear what the man had to say.

"Keep your eye on the courthouse. But don't take up the issue again, let it be my sister."

Toni was in front of her building now and the driver was taking the suitcase out of the trunk. She handed him the ten-dollar bill and thanked him for his kindness.

"Young lady, the lost one, he on a big boat, he fine. Tell your mama, he fine."

"Thank you."

Toni stood on the sidewalk and watched as the cab pulled away and turned the corner. She searched her purse and found the door keys. She opened the front door and entered the lobby. Slowly, she walked to the elevator and pushed the button. The sound of the cabdriver's voice rang in her ear. If what the driver said was true, how did he know. But what did he mean by spirit in the dark? So many questions, she thought, and the so-called answers did not make any sense.

She stepped off of the elevator on her floor and became anxious at the thought of soon entering her apartment, her little piece of paradise on earth. As she unlocked the apartment door and steeped inside the foyer she felt confident, safe and secure. She closed the door and put the suitcase down. The kitchen was nice and clean as she had left it. The yellow dishtowels hung neatly on the wall near the kitchen sink. The yellow and white curtains at the small kitchen window with the neatly tied bows made for almost a magazine entry. The dinette set under the window with the chairs neatly in place and the place mats lined up directly in front of each chair made Toni feel warm inside.

As she moved through the apartment and stopped to look in the small dining room, she could see that the dust had settled on the brightly polished wood floors in front of the curio cabinet. She smiled thinking how she had arrived at the decision of buying the curio instead of a china cabinet. The dining room was not large enough to accommodate a china cabinet with the dining table and chairs. Besides, she thought, at the time she did not have any china to put in the cabinet, anyway, but needed something cute to complete the look.

"Looks good, darn good," Kim had said. "So good, I'm gonna do the very same thing." Then she bought a curio almost like Toni's. It had been fun for her and Kim, decorating their apartments, trying as they claimed, to get the sophistication of a couple of sisters who had already made it.

The second bedroom had to be taken care of before Joyce and Jerry came for the summer. As she walked through the apartment she decided that it was large enough for the three of them for the summer.

She called Kim at work to let her know that she was home.

"Hey, I'm home, girl."

"How come you didn't call me and let me know?"

"I don't know, I guess I just wasn't thinking. But I had a strange encounter, I guess you could say."

"What was it?"

"I'll tell you when I see you. But this West Indian man did say this, 'spirit in the dark, justice of the buzzard.'"

"What did he mean by that?"

"Kim, I don't know. Let's talk about this when I see you, okay?"

"I'll come by after work, I'll just skip my history class tonight."

"Oh, did you pick up my assignments?"

"Yeah, I've got them, and your Professor Anderson, sent you something, too. I think that guy is kind of sweet on you, girl."

"Well, he is single and what, thirty something?"

"Girl, you just ought to stop. See you after work."

Alma came as she promised and spent four days with Toni. Kim was glad to be able to spend some time with someone else who loved Toni as much as she did. The three friends forged a bond over the four days that could never be broken. They fasted two of the days and spent the time praying for every member of their families and themselves. They laid their plans and dreams for life on the altar and asked God to take them and guide them.

Kim was able to release a lot of anger that she had held inside since she was a little girl. It was obvious at the end of the four days that the three friends had begun a path of change that they would not be easily moved off of.

Alma had already applied to Baptist College to complete her education to become a Registered Nurse and enter the Navy. Kim and Toni were still on their path to undergraduate degrees and then law school. They blessed and prayed special prayers for each other.

Joyce and Jeremiah arrived afterwards. Joyce was so happy when she stepped off the train and saw her big sister and Kim waiting for her and Jeremiah. Toni was able to purchase two three-quarter beds for the second bedroom so that her siblings would be able to sleep comfortably. Within a few days of their arrival, Kim told Joyce that her agency had a new summer program called 'Stay-In-School' and she had signed Joyce up, if she wanted to earn some real money. Joyce was ecstatic, the thought of buying anything that she wanted was too much for her.

Jeremiah wanted to know what he would do if everybody was working? Toni was able to get Jeremiah into several day camps. Jeremiah was so excited when he went to the basketball camp where one of the New York Knicks was teaching. The ball player had taken a shine to Jeremiah and he wanted to bring him home for dinner so that Toni and Joyce could meet him. Jeremiah took pictures with the ballplayer who also signed them calling Jeremiah his 'Best Little Friend and Little Brother.'

The summer was a good one for Joyce and Jeremiah. Joyce used her money to layaway school clothes for herself and Jeremiah. She asked Toni to hold some money for her high school graduation ring and pictures, so that she would not have to ask her mother. She thanked Kim so much for getting the summer job for her. Kim beamed because the young girl's heart had been filled with joy and pride. Unbeknownst to Joyce Kim and Toni were also buying some cute outfits for her to take back when the summer was over. Kim's intent was that Joyce would be the best dressed senior in South Carolina. Toni promised that she would buy her the 'baddest' gown to wear to the prom with matching dyed pumps.

The summer evenings were spent as a family, except the two evenings that Toni went to class. Toni had decided that she would take a course in both of the four week summer classes which were fairly fast paced courses, so that she could speed up her graduation date. She had managed to earn six additional credits in eight weeks and still enjoy her siblings.

Toni had even taken Jeremiah and Joyce to class with her. Several times Joyce had gone to class with Kim and said that she was learning things.

She and Kim had wearied of taking the number of classes that the curriculum schedule said that they should. They were ready to have a degree and get on with their future plans.

Alma and Wilson had put the metal to the pedal and spent the summer trying to get into college for the fall. It had come down to now or never for them. Alma was even helping Wilson complete late applications for college and sharing any information she got with him. Alma got into Baptist College. Then Toni received a call in August from Wilson telling her that he had been admitted to a college in Louisiana to study engineering, if he could get there in nine days.

Alma was excited and so was Toni, but Wilson had not believed that the opportunity, with a scholarship would arrive on his doorstep so soon.

Toni told the good news to both Joyce and Jeremiah, who started cheering so loud in the background that Toni had to tell them to be quiet until she had finished talking to Wilson. Toni urged Wilson to pack up, get on a train and head for Louisiana. She encouraged him to forget about South Carolina and head for his dream to get a college degree.

"Captain Spann, I am ordering you to pack your bags, get on a train, and report for educational duties at that college in Louisiana. Do you understand me, Captain Spann?"

"Yes, mam, General Spann, I am on my way. General, thank you for leading the troops. I'll make you proud of me."

"You don't have to do anything more to make me proud of you. Please meet your destiny and don't look back. God speed, Captain."

Toni informed Joyce and Jeremiah that Wilson would not be at home when they returned because he would be in college. Kim was delighted to hear that Wilson had seized the opportunity and taken the courage to reach for his dream.

The day that Joyce and Jeremiah were to leave Connecticut was a sad day for everyone. Kim's aunt had gotten used to the kids being there and the times that she had babysat Jeremiah. She was not content to stay home while they went to the train station. Joyce cried and hugged Toni's neck so hard that she almost choked her. Toni prayed as she held her siblings.

Kim cried and hugged Jeremiah and Joyce and her aunt hugged them and blessed them. As the train pulled out of the station, Kim broke down and cried and began to bless them as though she had seen something awful in their future. But Kim had spent a lot of time with Joyce at work because Joyce worked as an assistant and clerk in Kim's department. They had eaten lunch together everyday and ridden to and from work together. Kim had grown to love Joyce as though she were her baby sister.

Toni had been putting money in a separate account for Henry's defense and hiding from her siblings what was actually going on back home. She had wanted them to have a very good summer, which they did. All of the new clothes had to be put in boxes and shipped back to South Carolina a few days before they left Connecticut so they would be there when they arrived. The judge had decided to try Henry for manslaughter and his trial would be in November.

Toni walked around the apartment staring at the room where her siblings had spent the summer in. She looked in the little alcove where Jeremiah laid and watched television when he was tired from all of the activities from camp. Jeremiah had been so full of joy that he talked incessantly in the evenings about what he had done. He had new ideas and dreams about what he was going to do when he grew up. His mind was so far removed from South Carolina that when he mentioned Wilson, Henry, or Lloyd, it was to say that he had better get something to take them so they wouldn't be jealous of him. That always made Joyce break out in laughter because Jeremiah was so serious when he said it.

Now the television was silent, there was no aroma floating through the apartment from either Toni or Joyce cooking. The baseball glove that Toni had bought for Jeremiah was folded over on the shelf of the bookcase. He had left it there for 'next year' so he wouldn't have to look for it. Toni's heart was broken and she could not hold back the pain she felt inside when she thought that Jeremiah and Joyce would not always be in the same house with her to protect.

Calls from Margaret about their mother having left the city for a day or two without telling them and returning with a picture of Isiah in the coffin made Toni question her mother's sanity. Margaret said that she had gone to her mother's house and seen the picture on the top of the chest of drawers in her bedroom. According to Margaret, she had felt strange in the house but couldn't put her finger on what was making her feel strange. But, when she went upstairs in search of something for Trudy her eyes were drawn immediately to the picture. Margaret said that she went over to the chest of drawers and turned the picture down. She was so angry with her mother, she wanted to slap her for bringing that 'shit' into her father's house. There were no pictures of their father in her bedroom, but she had the picture of a 'dead devil' up there.

Toni had been careful not to say much when the children were there with her. She had not wanted to disturb the children's peace and joy, and prayed daily that God would keep them safe when they got back to South Carolina.

When Toni would speak to Trudy during the summer, Trudy made it sound like she was happy that the kids were having a good time. When Toni told her that Joyce had a summer job with the government and would be buying her own school clothes, Trudy truly sounded happy saying that the job would look good on Joyce's resume and teach her how to conduct herself in the work place.

Jeremiah burned Trudy's ear about his many adventures and even said that he was going to stay in Connecticut and go to school. It really shocked Trudy when Jeremiah told her to pack up and move there with them.

The house was quiet now. Toni took her cigarettes and sat in the alcove looking across the street where a tree seemed to have merged with the blue sky and white clouds forming a natural picture. She sat in the chair until the sun started to go down. It was as though she had run out of steam and could not go any further, so she sat and stared. Only the urge of having to pee prompted Toni to get up. As she sat on the commode it became a great struggle for her to muster up the strength to get up and pull up her panties. The ringing telephone forced her to get up.

"Hey college boy, how you doing?" Toni asked.

Wilson called to make sure that Joyce and Jeremiah were on their way home.

"Girl, you wouldn't believe all of the things you have to do when you go to college."

"Oh, I wouldn't?"

"What am I talking about, you've been in college for what two years now?"

"That's right, Captain."

"Well I'm in the dorm. But check this out. I'm in a room by myself, girl. See, they decided that the room was too small for two people and I think they tried to use it for something else. Then when me and a group of other guys got here it looks like they just converted it to a dorm room for one person. Girl I'm down with that."

"That's good, Wilson, you don't have to share a room with anybody. Does it have a lock on it?"

"Yeah. It ain't fancy or anything like that, Toni, but I'm sure 'nough happy with it. I was praying on the train that the Lord would bless me with a roommate studying to be a preacher or something, so I wouldn't have to be tied down with a fool."

"See, the Lord heard your prayer."

"The Lord did one better. I got a bed, a table, a little bookshelf, chair, a chest of drawers and a few things that I need. I don't have a stereo or anything like that, but Toni, I'm comfortable. I just wish that Henry could be here with me. I got a little homesick the other day but I met this black professor who's in the Reserves and he is a real Captain. Anyway we talked and he told me to come to him if I have questions, need advice, or just want to talk. I told him about Henry and he said this too shall pass. I believe that, too, Toni, and I don't want you to stop school to pay for all of this, okay?"

"Don't worry about me, Wilson, we'll all get through this with the Lord's help. You just put your nose to the grindstone and keep your grades up."

"Hey I gotta do that. In order to keep this scholarship I have to maintain a two point five grade point average. Oh, yeah, the brother got me a little work-study so I can have a few dollars in my pocket. Look, what fraternity you think I should pledge?"

"I don't know. I haven't even pledged. Just take your time and check them out first. Remember, you're there to get an education first."

"Yeah, I know that. It's a whole lot of brothers here from almost every state. You know there're a few brothers here who talk worst than those people from Wadmalaw Island."

The brother and sister went into a fit of laughter before they recovered sufficiently to finish their conversation.

"They're either West Indians, or one of their relatives. Have some fun Wilson, enjoy college while getting your education."

"Thanks, Toni. Have you heard from Miss Magnolia?"

"Yeah, she's working part time and going to school."

"Tell her I said, thank you, again, okay? This school is some of the information she gave me. I might have to marry Miss Magnolia."

"Boy you're crazy. Alma would cuss you out if she heard that."

"Oh, Margaret expecting a baby. I know she hadn't told you, but her little stomach just as round as it can be."

"Say what? That little heifer didn't tell me anything and I was talking to her all along."

"Well she had just started to show a little bit when I left, but yeah, we gonna be aunts and uncles. Jeremiah probably will think the baby is his when it comes. I hope it's a boy."

"I hope that it's healthy."

"That, too."

By the time she got off of the telephone with Wilson, Toni was glad and sad. She was glad that Wilson had gone to Louisiana and sad that Margaret had started having children so quickly. She had wanted her siblings to get an education and be able to stand alone, if they had to. She wanted them to have something to bring into any relationship and not become dependent or so needy that it would chip away at their relationships. She knew they all had dreams that they wanted to see come true, but her heart was uneasy because Margaret had allowed the family situation to dictate her decisions.

Her heart seemed to swell with anxiety as she thought about Aaron Jr., and Henry. Then she remembered what the cabdriver had said, he was on a boat, but he was alright. How she wanted so badly to take comfort in that but there was no way for her to really know.

As she walked back to the living room and to the alcove it was completely dark outside. Then she remembered that she now had a prayer language, or did she? She had not tried to use it since she returned from South Carolina. So there in the darkness she determined that she wanted to pray in her prayer language and the words that she could not understand flowed like water from her lips. Toni prayed for quite some time in her prayer language. She cried and prayed and it seemed that there was no end to praying in sight. The more she prayed in her prayer language, the more the need to continue to do so grew. She felt pain and hurt rise and disappear, confusion appeared and disappeared. It felt like she was being washed, then rinsed, and washed again as she prayed. Finally a peace started to rise from deep within her and flood her entire being.

Toni had fallen asleep in the chair in the alcove. She had to strain her memory to remember what day it was. She had taken Friday off from work to take Joyce and Jeremiah to the train station so they could go home. It was now Saturday. She got up and went to the kitchen to see what time it was. It was not yet five thirty. She had slept in her clothes all night. She took the coffee can from the refrigerator and grabbed the filters so that she could have her liquid wake up. Her siblings should be pulling into the train station soon in Charleston. She was pleased that they had had a great summer.

It was too early to call Kim. But she wondered why Kim had not called her after they had put Joyce and Jeremiah on the train. They all had been sad that they had to return home. But come Tuesday they would be back in their classrooms. Joyce certainly would be the best-dressed senior at Bonds-Wilson High School and she could thank herself for that.

Jeremiah couldn't wait to start wearing many of the new outfits that he had gotten. His little eyes had danced like little brown torches every time that a new outfit had been purchased for him. He had summed it all up by saying that even the little shorts and shirts that Toni had bought for him to wear to camp were pieces that he would wear to school. According to him, no one at his school had seen him in it before. He was glad that the four outfits that Toni had bought for Troy Pierre were different than any of the many he had gotten.

Toni and Kim had time to decide what courses they would take in the fall and to just rest before starting their routine of work and school. Many of the church members inquired of Joyce and Jeremiah and vowed that they would continue to pray for them as well as Henry. Toni had decided that regardless of what she could not see, she would just believe that Aaron, Jr. was well and daily she prayed for his well being.

Toni tried to relax and allow herself to enjoy life, a little. Relaxing came hard. No matter how hard she tried, Toni felt guilty if it looked like she was enjoying herself. Kim was beginning to observe her friend and wonder whether the upcoming trial was having an effect on her mentally. Nearly every hour of the day was accounted for and it didn't include anything that looked liked fun. Kim tried almost everything she knew to get Toni to relax.

"Hey girl, you wanna go to the movies? They've got a few of those black movies playing this weekend at the theater on Grand. Every now and then they put on some of the old movies and draw a crowd. I wanna see Miss Cleopatra Jones. I always thought that you and that sister look a like. I can see you now with that law degree, your Jaguar convertible and tipping into the courtrooms for another big trial, that you'll win, of course. The brothers out there will be trying to get to the tall sister with the hair blowing in the wind."

"Yes mam, that sounds like the sister. I know I look good behind the wheel of a Jag. Anyway, I'm fatter than Miss Cleopatra Jones, you see how skinny her legs are? Now look at mine. Girl I would make a mini-skirt proud to rest on these thighs. I think I just might go with you, Kim. I'd like to see Superfly, too, if it's playing."

"Yeah, Superfly playing. That man so fine he would make a bow legged woman knock kneed by being in the same room, even if the room is Madison Square Garden."

"You mean he would do that to you, right?"

"Oh don't act like the man don't move your pulse, Toni."

"I didn't say that. I asked whether that's what he did to you."

Kim was glad that for a while she had managed to take Toni's mind away from her family situation. She knew that no matter what she did that it would not last but for a short while.

Henry was growing anxious and began to doubt whether he would be able to get a fair trial. So Toni was doing double duty, praying and encouraging Henry. Henry's attorney called and requested more money and told Toni that she would have to testify at the trial in November, something that she was not looking forward to. She did not trust the criminal justice system in South Carolina. She had even gotten angry that the state even wanted to try her brother.

Henry was finally able to go the house with Lloyd and spend some time with his mother. No one, not even Margaret, knew what happened there. Lloyd had never said anything other than Trudy had cooked and they ate and watched television.

Margaret was a person who required a blow-by-blow account of everything and if she didn't get that she considered what she was given as nothing. But Margaret also had her ideas of what had happened so if the account did not follow the script that she had written, she would then tell it the way it should have happened.

Wilson was adjusting to college life. He had to maintain a certain grade point average so he was resigned to studying hard in school. Wilson told Toni that he didn't understand it, but that he seemed to have a fondness for foreign languages. He had met a number of other black men who were bi-lingual. The thought that blacks were able to speak two or more languages fluently was overwhelming and had made him take a foreign language. When Toni asked him what language he had taken she was surprised to hear that it was Russian. Wilson told her that he could be a very valuable soldier, a black James Bond, because no one expected blacks to speak the language. He was proud to be learning new things in and out of the classroom.

School was taking a lot of everybody's time. Classes had begun for Toni and Kim and they were keeping a strict routine. But Toni was growing apprehensive daily. She and Kim had sought out different scholarships and grants and had managed to come up with enough money to pay for their tuition and books for the entire school year. So it wasn't money that was making her apprehensive, but the feeling would not go away.

Toni was being very conservative in her spending to be sure that she could help Henry pay the lawyer. She and Kim had found themselves a second hand store where they could buy some very nice pieces of clothing when they needed it. She had even managed to send enough money to Wilson to buy a tape recorder and a small stereo. As the days grew closer to November Toni became more and more unsettled. The unsettling feeling was not outward, it was an inner feeling of shakiness that caused her to lie awake at night. There had been nights she had laid awake turning things over in her mind. She would get up the next day and feel tired, yet she had to work and go to school until ten thirty at night.

Then the scariest of all thoughts came to her mind one day, Henry was convicted of manslaughter and sentenced to prison. The thought so unnerved Toni that she leaped from her desk and went to the bathroom and began praying in her prayer language. As she sat in the stall, she asked God to have mercy on Henry. Toni had never shared with Kim or Alma that she now had this new language to pray with. Even she wondered why she had never said anything to either of her friends about this language. She had listened to every sermon or lesson regarding tongues. She had made it almost a ritual everyday to get up, sit quietly and read the Bible before she got ready for work.

Two weeks before the trial, Toni's growing apprehension had almost isolated everyone including Kim. Kim had watched the change in Toni's behavior for nearly three months. Kim's concern for Toni's mental state had also grown. She feared that her friend's mental state might not hold up to support Henry or her family through the trial.

Toni was concerned about her mother's mental health and what it might do to Joyce and Jeremiah. Toni loved Jeremiah so much that Kim believed that Toni would turn on her mother if anything were to happen to the little boy. Toni was being pulled in too many directions, Kim had thought, yet she went to work everyday and classes at night. There was nothing Kim knew to do that would give her best friend what she really needed, except to pray for her.

Most of Toni's salary was being spent to help pay for Henry's defense. Toni had gotten her promotion to the next grade level in the government, which was a fairly good increase. She had been wise, though, not to use the increase for any reason. After receiving the first paycheck with her new salary, Toni made an allotment diverting the increase into a new savings account, which she had opened for emergencies only. Kim was still worried about Toni and tried all that she knew to keep her mind off of the trial.

Kim encouraged Toni that the trial would be over quickly and Henry could put everything behind him. She had told Toni that no one in his right mind would convict a young man who had done what Henry had done in the same situation. She assured Toni that Henry had not gone out looking for Isiah and shot him down. Isiah had come to where Henry lived and tried to kill him after trying to kill his mother.

Kim was not sure that she had helped her friend's confidence. Kim had not wanted to even entertain the idea of Henry being convicted and going to prison. She knew that Toni had been strong in the past, but was not sure that she would survive Henry's being convicted. So she prayed for Toni's strength to increase regardless of what happened during the trial.

Finally, the trial was just a week away and Toni was very, very anxious. She had made arrangements for the time off from work and for her lessons in class. Kim had witnessed a change, physically and spiritually in her best friend. It had happened before her eyes, yet she could not articulate exactly what she had witnessed developing.

Kim offered to take time off and fly to South Carolina to be with Toni during the trial. But Toni would not hear of it. She just asked Kim to stand in the gap for her and Henry while she was in South Carolina.

It had been weeks of anxiety for Toni. Before she left for South Carolina, the pastor had asked the church to stand in the gap for Toni and her family. Two of the church mothers said that they would be fasting from sun up to sun down for her, Henry and the rest of her family. She thanked them for their concern. Toni was struck by something Mother Manigault said to her that day.

"Come here, daughter, lemme whisper in your ear." Mother Manigault said.

"Yes mam." Toni said as she walked down the steps of the church and to the side with Mother Manigault holding onto her arm. Kim moved away.

"The Lord wants you to trust Him, don't question Him cause He is the One that sits high and looks low. Don't let what you see persuade you that He ain't there with you. The Lord say he got a plan for your life and He is the One Who gonna take you where you suppose to be."

Toni did not understand what Mother Manigault was saying. She heard every word that she had spoken. Toni listened carefully, anyway.

"The Lord wants you to hold onto your faith, daughter, even if you don't understand what He doing. Don't forget, daughter, no matter what, God won't forsake you, some things must be."

Toni thanked Mother Manigault and walked away feeling light-headed and dizzy. She felt like her world was crumbling around her but could not explain what was causing her to feel that way. She had told herself that she was prepared for the trial and had come to accept the fact that a trial would take place. Of course she did not like the fact that Henry had to stand trial, but determined that if this was another step that had to be taken so that this whole matter could be put to rest then she would accept that.

Kim walked up to Toni and put her hand on her shoulder. Toni's head was spinning so much that Kim's hand on her shoulder caused her to jump.

"Toni, you need to calm down."

"I'm okay, Kim. I just didn't see you."

"Oh, no, sister, it's more than that. You coming unglued girl. We need to pray together before you leave out of here."

Toni scratched her head. Kim was right, she was coming unglued. Wilson had wanted to come to South Carolina for the trial but the lawyer had said that he didn't have to be there since he was sleeping when the shooting took place. Toni told Wilson that she would call and let him know how things were going. She didn't want him to jeopardize his scholarship.

On Tuesday, Henry's trial would start. Toni had tried to hold onto the words of a sermon from a Sunday about how Esther had been raised up by God for a specific purpose, to save the Jews. But Mother Manigault's words would come to mind as well. Still, Toni did not have a clear understanding of what she had meant. She had one class that Friday. All she had to do was sit through an hour and twenty minutes of lecture and she could go home.

She had already begun packing her suitcase to make sure that she would not forget anything. A couple of suits, shoes to match, underwear and nylons were already in the suitcase. Toni's appearance was always important. Since she had been in elementary school she had made sure that her clothing for the entire week were clean and ironed by late Saturday evening. Many had spoken of how neat she was, everything regarding her clothing and life had to be organized. Her apartment was so neat and clean that Kim had not had a second thought about picking up any thing dropped on the floor and eating it. Toni hated clutter and her friends and family knew it, she detested clutter of any type. Her statement was always, 'keep it simple.'

Henry's lawyer had asked Toni to get to South Carolina at least a day before the trial, so that he could talk to her and let her know what to expect. He had said that the trial shouldn't last anymore than two or three days.

Toni wondered how long she would last, but even more, she wondered how long Henry would last. Surely he must have been going through hell with the trial coming up, she thought. How she wished that she could carry the burden for him, not wanting her siblings to suffer.

When she arrived at her class that Friday evening there was a note on the classroom door stating that the professor had had an emergency and his class had been cancelled. Toni breathed a "thank You, Jesus." She was glad to be able to go home and check her suitcase for all that she would need. She had gone to the credit union during her lunch period to withdraw enough cash for her trip. As she walked down the corridor she saw Kim rushing to her class.

"You're headed in the wrong direction, ain't you?" Kim asked.

"No, my class was cancelled, so I'm going home and finish packing."

"Oh, man, I wish that I didn't have class, we could hang out a little bit."

"We can do that after you get out of class. You drove didn't you?"

"Yeah. Wait a minute, let me talk to my professor, I haven't had a miss yet. I'll just let her know that I need to go home and see if she's going to give out any assignments for the weekend."

Toni told Kim that she would wait for her in the student lounge on the first floor and walked away. After she had walked away she regretted that she had encouraged Kim to skip class because she really wanted to be alone for a little while.

Shortly thereafter Kim walked through the door of the student lounge.

"Come on girl, let's stop by the Chinese restaurant and grab some take out."

"Okay. You know what Kim? Now don't laugh at me and call me crazy, but I sure would like to have a cold beer or champale."

"I'm not laughing at you, after all that I've been through this week, I thank the Lord that I never acquired a taste for anything stronger than that. Come on, we're twenty-one, lets get us one of those six packs of pink champale."

"I seen those wine coolers, have you ever tried one of them?"

"No. But that sounds good, too."

So they went to their cars with Kim leading. They stopped first to get the wine coolers then stopped and picked up the food. When Toni and Kim walked into the house the telephone rang, it was Joyce.

"Yeah I'm still here, I just got in from school. I'll be leaving here in the morning. Oh Joyce, call Alma and tell her to pick me up at the airport at ten thirty."

"Joyce trying to keep tabs on you, huh?"

"Kim, you know Joyce just want to make sure that I didn't forget to bring her those last two outfits that she wanted."

"Oh, that reminds me, I got that little pink sweater for her the other day. I'll bring it in the morning."

"What little pink sweater?"

"Now see how you minding me and Joyce's business. I know that Joyce's birthday is November 16, so I thought that like any high school senior she would want something that the other girls can't find down there. This sweater is so cute I had to get one for myself. So I hope you bought her a shirt or something that she can wear with the sweater."

"Oh, now I'm responsible for having something to match what you bought?"

Kim laughed at her suggestion.

"I got a sweater for Jerry, too, so he won't feel left out although it's not his birthday."

"Oh I'm sure he wouldn't feel left out."

"I didn't take any chances. Besides the little sweater was so cute that I couldn't leave it. My aunt was the one who saw it. I think my aunt wanted a few sons, but she never had any kids but me and my brother. But anyway, the sweater has this leather across the front and back. He'll think he's one of the big boys when he wears it. It's navy blue with red and yellow on the sleeve."

"Girl, you gonna spoil that boy."

"Like I'm doing something you haven't already done."

"Girl, Jerry and that Troy Pierre are like two little old men."

"That's Alma's little boy, right?"

"Yeah. That's the one that said he was going to sue Lloyd."

Kim started laughing.

"Yeah, he wanted to sue until his mama wouldn't give him that twenty dollars. Girl where do they get these ideas? At that age we didn't know anything about suing somebody. But homeboy had the right idea, huh, take it to court."

"Speaking of court, girl I've been feeling kind of strange Kim. I can't explain it, but this feeling of anxiety or something would come upon me so strong sometimes that I couldn't even sleep at night."

"Yeah, I noticed something about you that wasn't right. But I just prayed and asked my aunt to remember you in prayer, too."

"Kim, suppose the jury don't see things the way that it happened?"

"Oh, no, Missy. We ain't going there. Henry ain't going nowhere but back to work and hopefully to school in time to study electronics like you said he wanted to do. I'm just not going there with you, Toni. God ain't gonna let nothing else happen."

Toni could see that Kim was not going to allow any negative talk this night. Even though she wanted to talk about what she felt, she accepted Kim's belief that God would not allow anything else to happen. She even thought about telling Kim that she had a new language to pray in but something would not allow it. They turned on the television and watched the Friday night shows that they usually missed because they were in school.

For a few hours Toni's mind was taken off of the trial and she was even relaxed for a while.

"Toni, what kind of law are you going to specialize in when we go to law school?"

"I like constitutional law, so maybe in that area."

"I met a law student the other day in my building at work. He's in his last year and was there as part of some kind of law clinic from his school." Kim said.

"Really, is he white or black?"

"He's black. He said he was from D.C., graduated from Howard but couldn't get into Howard's law school, so he jumped on the first boat he said that came along. He wasn't taking any chances about education, so he got in his little putt-putt and it brought him every mile of the way to Connecticut. Homeboy said he had never prayed that long in his life as he did driving here from D.C."

"Was the car that bad?"

"I didn't see it, but that's what he said. He came from the projects he said in Southeast D.C."

"Another one like us, the first in the family to go to college?"

"Yeah, but at least after this we'll be able to help the rest of the family girl."

"Right now, Kim, you and I might be burning the candle at both ends with all those classes we're taking each semester."

"Yeah, but it cost the same thing if we take twelve credits or nineteen, cause it's all fulltime, so we might as well get as much mileage as we can out of this grant that we got blessed with. At least we didn't have to spend a penny out of our paycheck this semester, praise the Lord."

"You got that right. I still don't know how we got that much money in such a short time."

"Girl, you know how we got that money, the Lord. The Lord knew what you had to do with your paycheck and he knew I needed to pay my car notes and pay for that furniture that we had to have."

"Yeah, girl. Our little places look good, too. Kim we have to give ourselves some credit, now. We didn't do bad at all, everything that we have in our apartment is paid for and we're not in debt except for those car notes we have."

"Yeah that's because my aunt kept harping on that mess about having a car that wouldn't nickel and dime us like those old numbers we bought before from the used car lot."

"They say the ones we got now will last until the cows come home."

"I hope they make steaks out of them cows so they won't find their way home until Jesus make the worms spit them up, these Hondas have to last until we're out of law school.

Toni rolled onto the floor laughing at Kim's statement. Kim started laughing, too.

"I think they'll last that long, Kim."

"The Lord sure did bless us, though, Toni. Think about it, we got government jobs by working with that little summer program. Your cousin let you stay with her and we met. Your cousin moved down to New York, and you got your own place and that made me get up out of my aunt's house. Then look at my aunt, she got the job at the post office, got her a nice two bedroom place and a new Honda. God blessed us all the way around. I guess if somebody had to lead the way, it might as well be us. Toni, do you sometimes get scared?"

Toni thought about the question for a while before she answered.

"Truthfully, Kim, I'm scared most of the time."

The tears rolled down her face. She had not known that she had been that afraid, but now that the question had been put to her, truth burst forth without notice.

"I've been so scared sometimes, Toni, that I didn't want to get out of the bed. I had this dream one of those times about my mother. I saw my mama bloody and beaten, you know, like when her boyfriend had beaten her up. My mama was chasing me around this street and yelling for me to come and let her hug me. But I kept running because even though I knew she was my mama, I was scared of her."

"I think I've done just everything this far in my life because I was afraid of what would happen if I didn't do anything. Like now, I go to school because I don't want to have to depend on anybody, especially a husband or man to take care of me. At the same time, I want to be able to help my brothers and sisters so they won't have to depend on anyone."

"It ain't easy being afraid all of the time, Toni. I don't know about you, but many times I have to psyche myself up and go. Then I feel bad because I'm being phony, it's a façade."

"The whole time I was down south when my mama got shot, I was so scared, Kim. I even got mad with my daddy for dying. I blamed his death for what was going on. Then I thought about Aaron Jr., I got mad with him for taking the easy way out."

"No, he didn't take the easy way out, Toni, he took the only way out right then. Ain't no telling what else would have happened if he hadn't left. It takes courage I think to go when the situation demands you to stay."

"I guess you're right. It's kind of like suicide. It's harder to decide to hang around and play the hand you've been dealt. Shit, Kim, life is hard, too dam hard sometimes."

"Girl, I know what you mean. Every time I think about my mama and how she lived and died, I get scared again. If my daddy had kept his promise like he said, my mama would be alive. She did everything that she could to get over being betrayed, but it wasn't the right thing. I know it was hard for her to forget, too, because my brother look more like our daddy than the baby he had with the woman he married."

"Have you heard anymore from your daddy since your half sister died?"

"No. The Lord has told me so many times to forgive him and I think I have but I believe the Lord want me to tell him that I forgive him."

"Kim what do you think your daddy feels every time he hears his name announced on television when Georgetown plays and he see this young man that looks like him?"

"I don't know, Tee, but if he feels like anything, it's like a fool, because his only son, if not the only son, his first born son, has never talked to him. I guess that's the price you pay for breaking promises, huh?"

"I guess so. But that's a high price to pay, isn't it?"

"Yeah, but the Bible does say, 'let your yeas be yea, and your nays be nay.' God has a reason for telling us all of those things, Tee. We think that God speaks cause He ain't got nothing else to do."

"I wish that I could understand what God was doing sometimes."

"Shoot, if we did understand what difference would it make? We probably would try to change the outcome and screw up something so bad that the Lord would have to kill us to get things right again."

"I try to look down the road, five maybe ten years from now and see what I would be doing."

"And what did you see Sister Spann?"

"I couldn't even see next year, Kim. For some reason, I can't even see six months from now."

"I know what you mean, Tee. I mean I got plans and all that, and the way that we're moving we can graduate in another semester. But I can't see anything either."

"Well, I guess we just have to be thankful that we at least got plans. Not everybody got plans. Here we are almost twenty-four and twenty-five, we ain't got no kids, no husbands, no boyfriend, just plans and working on them, in addition to my family problems."

"I sure would like to have a boyfriend, though, Toni."

"Oh please, girlfriend, you had one and all you did was find fault in the poor thing. Then you had the nerve to get mad with him when he stopped calling your ass. Then when you saw him talking to that bow legged girl you got mad."

Kim started laughing at the way Toni was talking about her.

"Come on, Tee. I was testing him to see whether it was me that he really wanted, or some tunsie."

"Well, did he pass the test? Did you find out what he really wanted?"

"Hell no, boyfriend gave me my pink slip. I just said goodbye."

"Well, the next time you out sashaying your big behind around like you ain't never been saved, remember that you, too, are being tested."

"Yes mam, Miss Spann. But I still say that I want me a boyfriend."

"Well pray and ask the Lord to send a nice Christian brother for you. How about the brother from D.C., you met? How does he look?"

"Oh, the brother, to me, was fine. He was my kind of man. I mean, if you looked in the Kimberly Sanders Dictionary under fine, you would see the brother's face."

"Hush your mouth, girl. He's that fine, huh? Go on and give me the full description of this here man, please mam."

"Well he's about six foot tall, dark with medium brown eyes. You know he's really a Sidney Poitier type."

"Oh, yeah, my kind of man, too."

"Hush girl, so I can finish."

"I'm sorry, Missy. Please continue."

"His lips look like somebody placed a mold on them. He's got just a little, teeny tiny gap between his front teeth. His moustache is kind of thin; it looks almost like the angels drew the moustache on his upper lip with a thin heavenly pencil. When he looks at you, it's like he's looking down and up at you."

"Kimberly, it sounds like you already seen the man you want for a boyfriend. I don't think that you telling me the truth, the whole truth, and nothing but the truth about this man. You were running late when I saw you at school this evening. You want to confess about this now?"

"See, he had been coming to my building for about a little more than a month. I would say hello, but we hadn't really talked much before. Then today I was leaving the same time that he was and I said that I was going to get some ice cream and asked if he wanted to go. He was honest and said that he would like to but he didn't think that he had enough money. I told him to come on, it was my treat. He seemed shamed cause he didn't have the money. So I figured what's fifty cents?"

"Well, God will bless you for buying the brother some ice cream."

"Anyway, I invited him to go to church with me on Sunday and he said yes."

"What? He accepted your invitation? Girl, you really been swiveling them hips."

"No, I haven't. I just put on my Toni look everyday, just in case he came in."

"What do you mean, your Toni look?"

They began laughing like they were being tickled by an invisible being. Life seemed like it had been pumped back into Toni. For a while she was free of the worries of the trial.

"I just made sure that I had on my smoke gray pantyhose, my shoes polished and my outfits pressed with magic sizing and matching to the nines. Come on Toni, you know you can wear out a can of magic sizing and strut like you trying to make the hem of your skirt snap its fingers."

"We ain't talking about me, we're talking about your little flippy behind. Now tell me what are you going to wear to church on Sunday?"

"I don't know. He got my telephone number and said that he would call me on tomorrow for directions to the church."

"Kim, you have to break out the pots and pans and cook a little Sunday dinner now. Run the vacuum cleaner and get some fresh cut flowers for the table and invite the brother home after church."

"Toni, all that I'm doing is going to church, why I got to cook?"

"From what I can see, I think you like the joker. Anyway, what's his name?"

"Malcolm."

"Do it right, girl. You know, just think of him as another hungry soldier. Now, you know that black dress you bought last year at Ginger's, wear that with one of those nice scarves and black pumps. Don't forget your smoke gray pantyhose, but get the mesh, not the plain. Wear a light weight coat, the one that you and I have just alike."

"Miss Spann, you got the whole thing planned for me. Thank you. You know your sister needed a little help, so that she could impress the brother."

"You don't want to impress him, you want to effect him, my sister."

"Listen at you, Toni. I'm so sorry that you won't be here to meet him. But I hope that things work to a level where you can meet Malcolm when you get back. I love you girl, don't you ever forget that or doubt it."

Toni and Kim sat in silence for a while as tears streamed down their faces. Kim told Toni what time she would be there the next morning to take her to the airport and to pray before she left. When Toni closed the door behind Kim she felt so alone. As she removed the containers that the food had been in she could not shake the feeling of absolute aloneness. She wanted to talk to someone and wished that Kim had stayed longer or even spent the night. She heard the door across the hall open and she looked through the peephole. The woman across the hall was leaving, Toni looked for a bag or something so she could pretend to go to the trash shoot and have a conversation with her neighbor. The feeling of aloneness was almost unbearable for a moment, but she talked herself out of being foolish and tidied up her kitchen and alcove.

Toni went to the second bedroom where she had laid the suitcase on one of the beds and checked it to make sure that she had everything in it that she intended to take. She added a couple more pairs of underpants and pantyhose. Remembering her hair curlers, she walked quickly to the bathroom and placed the plastic bag in the suitcase. She lit a cigarette and sat on the bed next to the suitcase, not having the energy or the enthusiasm to go to her bedroom and get in the bed.

Toni was puzzled as to why she seemed to lack energy or joy. She felt as though a sadness was trying to set up shop within. The clock showed that it was eleven thirty but she almost dreaded going to sleep that night. The ringing telephone nearly scared her, she had not expected anyone to call her again that night.

"Hello?"

It was Alma calling.

"Hey girl, what you doing?" Alma asked.

"I was just sitting here on the bed trying to make sure that I packed everything. What are you still doing up?"

"I worked almost a double today. I went in at seven this morning and worked until eight thirty, so I made a few more dollars."

"How's school coming along?"

"School is good, girl. I'm working on my plan on how to get this piece of paper in two years flat. I'll let the military pay for my master's degree and a specialty."

"Now that's good thinking girl."

"Girl, I was laying here and you just kept coming to mind so I just said I'd call you. I know you'll be here tomorrow, but I had to call you."

"I'm glad you did. I've been feeling kind of strange lately, Alma. I don't know, I just keep getting this feeling of sadness."

"That ain't nothing but the devil trying to bring on some depression. On the other hand, Toni, you've been through a helluva lot the last few months. You haven't had any time off where you could just rest and forget about things and here the trial is right up in your face."

"I don't know, Alma, something is not right. I've been praying and I know Kim and her aunt's been praying, too. But something is not right within me."

"I don't know, Toni, I've been praying, too. But God won't allow us to suffer beyond what we can bear. You just gotta trust the Lord. I remember when I got pregnant with Troy, I was so scared and you know how my daddy took it. Then it was everybody around here looking at me like I had committed the unpardonable sin. I thought long and hard about suicide. Everybody kept saying that I would end up being nothing, but Mother Blake, God bless the dead told me to trust the Lord. I didn't know about trusting the Lord, but I kept saying the little prayers that I knew and you and I would pray and look what the Lord did. Now I'm going to school for my degree and making plans for my career. Look at you, almost ready for law school, despite the stuff you've had to go through."

"I know, Alma. But the truth is I'm almost afraid, hell no I am afraid, Alma. I just don't know exactly what all I'm afraid of."

"God loves us even when we're afraid. We're gonna get through all of this Toni. I don't know when, or even how, but I know for sure that it will be God to bring us through. Just trust Him."

"I'm kind of like you now, I don't how to trust Him. Sometimes I think that I'm trusting Him but then there are the other times when I don't know whether I am trusting Him."

"Don't stop praying, girl. I'll pick you up in the morning and we'll talk more when you get here."

Toni hung up the telephone and took a shower. She had hoped that the shower would make her feel better, but all that it had accomplished was to make her feel cleaner.

22

The flight to South Carolina had seemed short. Toni had not had much time to think or even enjoy watching the sunrise through the clouds when she took the early morning flight. She had not really slept the night before, just laid in the dark in a trance of sorts. There was an unspoken fear that if she closed her eyes something awful would happen. Toni subconsciously fought sleep, but the airplane ride had brought the sleep like the tooth fairy brought the money and left it under the pillow.

As she brought the seat back into its upright position she longed to see Henry and hold him. She wanted to see Jeremiah and Joyce, as well as Margaret who was now well into her pregnancy, but she did not want to see them as much as she needed to see Henry. She did not just want to see Henry. It seemed imperative that she see him. She hoped that Alma had the time to drive her to her uncle's house where Henry was still living.

The thought to rent a car came to Toni. She had never rented a car before. She grabbed her purse to see whether she still had the credit card that she had been given by the bank when she opened the account there to keep her emergency money. The woman had said that it would come in handy if she traveled and needed a hotel room or to rent a car. According to the letter that had come with the credit card, her limit was two thousand dollars, might as well make use of it, she thought. If she could rent a car with the card she decided that she would pay it off the next payday.

Alma was standing near the counter when she walked into the terminal.

"Hey sweetheart, how was your flight?" Alma asked as she hugged and kissed her friend.

"Alma, I don't know what happened. I got on the plane and just went out like a light."

"You got a lot on your plate right now Toni, but you need to get still in your spirit, sweetie."

"I thought about renting a car while I'm here, Alma. That way I can get around without having to tie up your time and to take mama and them to and from the court."

"Well there's a couple of those places out near the baggage claim place. We can check that out when we get the bags."

"Thank you, Alma, for always being here when I fly in and out. I truly appreciate that girl, you are truly a friend."

"We're sisters. We may not have the same parents, Toni, but we got the same Father, God."

The statement brought tears to Toni's eyes. Her heart had been so pierced by the statement that she was overwhelmed. Tears began to flow like a dam had burst inside of her. Alma began to cry as well, it was as though she could feel what her sister was experiencing.

"Go on and cry, I prayed to God to keep you intact. I was afraid that something like this would happen. But you got a right to cry my sister, just cry until it's all out of you. When you can't cry, I'll cry for you." Alma said.

Toni could not explain what had happened. But she was left with two thoughts when she could dry the last tear. One, Alma did love her and always would. And two, just a thought that when she could not see what was in front of her, submit to the invisible pilot, Jesus, to lead her. She did not understand the last thought, but found comfort in it anyhow.

The bags had begun coming off of the belt by the time Toni had composed herself. She and Alma picked up her bag and walked to the car rental counter. The process to rent the car was easier than Toni had thought. The credit card had certainly made the process an easy one. Toni and Alma agreed that Alma would park her car and they would use the rental so that she could go see Henry before going to her mother's house.

Toni called her uncle's house from a pay phone. Henry answered and sounded like he was not in the best of spirits.

"How you doing?" Toni asked, trying to fight back the tears she felt.

"I'm okay. A little nervous, but I'm okay. Where are you?" Henry asked.

"I'm at the airport, just got in. I rented a car so I wouldn't have to tie up Alma's time. I'm on my way there to see you."

"I sure need to see you, too. I just want to talk to somebody who love me."

"I'll always love you, Henry, don't you ever doubt that. See you in a little while, okay."

Toni told Alma that she would follow her home and they would go to Clifford's house and spend some time with Henry.

"How is Henry doing Toni?" Alma asked.

"I don't think he's doing too good, Alma."

"I went over there week before last and sat with Henry for a while. Some other girl was there too, but I just sat there and spent time with him. Some other female don't make me no never mind, this is family. Girlfriend tried to out sit me but it must have finally dawned on her from me and Henry's conversation that it was family and she seemed to loosen up a little bit."

"Some of these heifers can pick the worse time in the world to play games. That's why so many of them get their behinds kicked."

Toni was almost in shock when she saw Henry. He had lost a tremendous amount of weight; the situation had taken a toll on him. Henry's pants were nearly falling off of him, his skin looked ashen and his eyes looked like small saucers of sorrow. The tears welled up inside of her as she and Alma circled Henry and hugged him. The tears welled in Henry's eyes, too. But he would not allow one to fall or roll down his face.

Toni's confidence was shaken by what she was seeing. Alma went out to the backyard and turned her back to the house. Toni knew that she was crying and her heart went out to her friend and sister. Her family's problems had become Alma's problem because she loved Toni and her family. It was nearly dark when Alma and Toni left Henry. The ride to Trudy's house was like a period of mourning. Not a word was spoken between Alma and Toni until Toni pulled up in front of Alma's house.

"You wanna go to church with me tomorrow?" Alma asked.

"Yeah, I'll meet you there at eleven."

Toni pulled away with a sadness enveloping her like a blanket. She could not shake the feeling and the flashbacks of how thin and gaunt Henry was made her even sadder. Jeremiah was the first to see her pull up. He was not his happy self. It looked like everybody was suffering somewhat from what was about to happen.

Clifford was sitting at the kitchen table with Joyce playing a card game when she walked in the house.

"Hey, what's going on up in here?" Toni said.

"Hey, babe, how was your flight?" Clifford asked.

"It was okay. I sat down and went to sleep until we were almost ready to land."

"That's how I like to fly." Joyce laughed. "I get on and don't know anything until the plane lands."

"Listen at you. You've only flown twice." Toni remarked.

"Well, for right now, that's enough." Joyce responded.

Toni was holding Jeremiah in her arms. He had laid his head on her shoulder and wrapped his arms around her.

"Jerry, ain't you getting little too big for Toni to tote you?" Clifford asked.

Quietly and with the sweetest and most innocent voice, Jeremiah replied, "No sir, not ever."

No one challenged him and he kept his arms around Toni with his head on her shoulder.

"Where's mama?" Toni asked.

"Upstairs in the bathroom. She took a laxative. Trying to clean herself out." Joyce responded.

"I went by the house and spent some time with Henry right after I got in."

"Yeah, he said that he was waiting for you and Miss Magnolia to come by. So I just stayed right here and played card with cheating Joyce." Clifford responded as he winked.

"Ooh, Uncle Clifford, who reneged about ten times?" Joyce asked, staring at Clifford who refused to acknowledge the stares.

Trudy came downstairs and asked how her daughter was doing. There was no hugs or kisses. There had never been any before, so it puzzled even Toni why now she had anticipated one.

"Jeremiah been looking for you to come in that door since last night." Trudy said.

"Didn't I tell you that I'd be here today, Saturday, not Friday, Jerry?"

"Uh, huh."

"Then why were you looking for me last night?"

"I don't know, something said you was coming Friday."

Toni sensed that Jeremiah had been fretful and wondered whether anyone had been talking about the trial or what had happened the night that Isiah had been shot and Jeremiah had heard it. But there was no doubt that he was sad, like he had been and still was grieving. Toni thought about what she could do to cheer him up.

"Let's go to Burger King and get a milkshake and something. How's that?" she asked Jeremiah.

"Just me and you?"

"Yeah, just me and you, unless you want Alma and Troy to come along."

"Yeah, let them come with us."

Toni put Jeremiah on the floor and called Alma to see whether she wanted to go. Alma said that she had thought about what to eat and Burger King sounded like a fantastic idea. Toni and Jeremiah drove to Alma's house. The boys sat in the backseat and acted like little boys while Toni and Alma listened to the music and acted like adults.

Jeremiah seemed to be happy after they got to Burger King. He and Troy Pierre played around and cut up like they had not seen each other in months when in fact they went to the same school. They were in different classes because of their last names and went to lunch and recess at different times, passing each other in the hallway.

When they returned to the house, Joyce told Toni that Henry had called saying that it was rather important. Toni did not know what to think when Joyce said that it was important. She picked up the phone and called Henry immediately. Clifford answered

187

the phone and whispered that Henry seemed to be depressed, then told her to hold on while he go get Henry.

"Hey Toni, I just wanted to be with you. I'm feeling kind of in a rut. Can you come and get me?"

"Yeah, I'll be right there."

Toni told Joyce that she was going to pick Henry up because he wanted to get out for a while. Before she could get her jacket on, the phone rang again. It was Alma. She told Alma what Henry wanted and that she was on her way to Clifford's house.

"Shoot, girl, come on by here and pick me up. No need in riding by yourself. I think we're all kind of feeling something."

Toni called Henry backed and asked whether it was okay to bring Alma.

"Oh sure, Miss Magnolia is family. There've been some days that me and Miss Magnolia just rode to the battery and sat there talking and listening to the water slap against the piers. Matter of fact, let's just go down there and walk around, I'll put on a jacket."

"Okay, see you in just a little while then."

Toni picked up Alma and told her what Henry wanted to do. That was fine as far as Alma was concerned.

"Toni, you know how sometimes in your gut you know that something is happening but you don't know what it is. I mean you just feel it, but you don't really know what it is you're feeling?"

"I think I really know what you're talking about, Alma. I've been having some strange feelings in my spirit, Lord knows I can't explain them, nor do I understand them. It's like I know something is coming, but it just hadn't got here yet. Kind of like you're being prepared for something, but you don't know what."

"I talked to Pastor about that a few weeks ago, and he said that God is bringing us to a crossroad. He said, as we get closer to that crossroad there'll be all kinds of things to come before us. Sometimes we don't know and can't even see what's before us because things are happening in the spirit. But Pastor also said that even though we know in our spirit that something is happening we don't always know what it is and that's when we must become submissive and let the will of God take over and guide us where we're supposed to be."

"Kind of like when you can't see what's in front of you or ahead of you let your invisible pilot guide you." Toni responded.

"I think that's what Pastor meant. Right now, I feel like I'm being led somewhere. I don't know where it is, but it's not where I had planned to go, but it seems like it's where I'm supposed to go, but I'm afraid."

"I feel the same way, too, Alma. It's like I've got a choice to make, but I don't exactly know what the choice is that I'm supposed to make. So, I guess that's where my fear comes in. I think I'm afraid of what I just might have to go through to be where I should be. Choices aren't easy to make, Alma."

"Toni, it feels like in the next few days God is gonna show up in our lives in a way that we could never imagine."

"I believe that. I pray that we can live through it and still have our minds intact."

There was silence as the friends drove to pick up Henry. Alma broke the silence just before they reached Clifford's house.

"Toni, what do you think Henry is going through right now?"

"I don't know, Alma. But I don't believe that it's fun. His life will certainly change and I don't know whether that's for the good or bad. I can tell by the way he looks and the way he sounds that he is more than just a little bit worried about this trial. Alma, suppose, just suppose something comes up that sends Henry to prison?"

"Toni, I can't receive that, so I have to rebuke you in love. I just cannot imagine Henry going to prison. I have prayed and asked, I have begged God to have mercy on him for your sake and your family's sake."

"I prayed as well, Alma. But I always prayed for the perfect will of God. Funny thing though, I don't know what the perfect will of God is or means."

There was silence between the two friends. For both of them, no matter how they tried to speak, nothing would come up, or out. So they were both compelled to let the silence take control of the moment.

Henry was happy to be with his sister and Alma, who was just like a sister. As Toni drove Henry sat in the backseat and made fun of Alma and a few of her former suitors. Alma also made fun of him and his former girlfriends. They laughed and slapped their knees as though there was no trial before them. Toni was glad that so little had done so much to put the sparkle back in Henry's eye. As they rode along Alma pointed to a new club that had just opened up.

"Hey, when is the last time we've been out dancing?" Alma asked.

"Hell, I don't know." Henry replied. "What is the latest dance, anyhow?"

"I know y'all ain't asking me." Toni said.

"Pull in, Toni." Alma said.

"Girl, you couldn't be serious. We ain't dressed to go in there." Toni said.

"Shoot, come on, Tee, let your hair down and let's just go slumming." Henry said.

"Well, I guess if you guys are game, so am I."

Toni found a place where she could turn around and they drove back to the club and parked. As they walked to the door they giggled like teenagers.

"Girl, if your Pastor sees us, I'm gonna be the first one to confess that it was your idea, then I'm gonna start crying to show my innocence." Toni remarked.

"Well if Pastor is out here and sees us, I hope he's gracious enough to at least buy us a champale or a beer." Alma replied.

"He ain't gotta buy me nothing just pay for his own." Henry added.

They laughed like a trio of hyenas as they entered the club. As they opened the door, the music seemed to make the walls pulsate. Alma and Henry started snapping their fingers immediately. The club was nearly packed and the dance floor was crowded. It was truly a disco and one song after another played. The waitress asked if they wanted a table or wanted to sit at the bar. Toni took the table. Henry took off his leather jacket and put it on the back of the chair. Before Toni could take off her jacket, a brown skinned female was standing at the table grabbing for Henry's hand to take him to the dance floor.

"Dang, that heifer must have smelled Henry, she was over here so quick." Alma commented.

"Who the hell is she?" Toni asked.

"I don't really know who she is, but I've seen her a couple of time with other people."

Tony sat in her seat and danced with the chair to a few of the songs. Alma had had about as much as she could take and grabbed Henry and hit the dance floor. Toni did not see them for a while but was pleased to see that they were having a good time. When Henry and Alma finally returned to the table they were nearly soaked from perspiring.

"Girl, I almost wore Henry's hind parts out on that floor." Alma laughed.

"Please Miss Magnolia, you jazzed up the mash potatoes and threw in the Temptation walk when you got tired. I wouldn't exactly call that dancing." Henry responded.

Toni was laughing at them so hard that she started coughing.

"Toni Spann, how you doing lady?" the voice asked.

Toni and Alma looked around to see who the voice belonged to. It was Victor Washington, someone that Toni thought had died in Viet Nam.

"Victor?" Toni asked.

"The one and only." He replied. "Girl you sure are looking good. I know some guy has taken you out of circulation."

"You make it sound like I'm money and the Secretary of Treasure has given an order." Toni snidely remarked.

She had always hated those come on lines that tried to solicit information that a simple question would have gotten the answer to. But before she could get her undies in a bunch and put up her icy front Victor was hugging her. He acted like he was so glad to see her. Toni found herself returning the hug and sniffing the cologne he was wearing. It was a scent that she had not smelled before. She even surprised herself in how quickly she had examined Victor's body and muscles before the hug was over. She rather liked everything about him. Victor held onto her hand and acknowledged the other people at the table.

"Hey Henry, what's happening, brother. My man you are all grown up now. Alma, you're even more lovely now than when we were in school, how you been lady?"

"Thank you, Victor. I see that time has also treated you with kid gloves."

The disc jockey played a Marvin Gaye song, Let's Get It On. Victor still had Toni by the hand and she did not seem to care whether he held it all night.

"Miss Spann, that's good music, can we dance to this one." Victor asked.

After a brief pause Toni smiled at Victor and said, "why not?" Victor escorted her onto the dance floor where just about every person in the club now was.

"Victor, I have not danced in so long, I hope I can bring it to my memory again."

"Well, since you're not leading, you shouldn't have to worry about anything. Allow me to lead you, Madam." Victor said as he pretended to curtsey.

Toni smiled and shook her head. As Victor took her into his arms she became nervous. His arm went around her waist so gently and his soft smooth hand held her long lean fingers so gently. Her body was pressed against his hard firm body and his cologne gently stroked her senses.

As Marvin Gaye belted out the song, Toni was tempted to sing along, but held her peace. It was like heaven to Toni as she was being held in the arms of a handsome gentleman. Victor was certainly a catch for any girl. Toni had thought that he was phony when they were in school, but now she saw that his tactics, as she called them then, were the kinds of things that she and other women now looked for.

Victor held her tight, but not too tight. The left side of his face touched the right side of her face.

"What is that perfume you're wearing, Toni?" Victor asked.

"I believe it's Shalimar."

"It sure smells good. I like a woman that smells good."

Toni did not say anything, she did know what to say. For a very quick moment Toni had allowed herself to be held and cradled in the arms of a fleeting knight in polyester. When the song was over she and Victor stood on the floor still embraced and talked.

She told him that she was in town for Henry's trial. After explaining, briefly why Henry was on trial, Victor dropped his head.

"Toni, I'm so sorry. I pray that all goes well for him. I would have done the very same thing under those circumstances. No, I would not have. I would have gone out and looked for the joker and blow his dam head off of his shoulder. I just don't understand why they would want to even pursue Henry for that."

"I don't know either Victor, but the trial starts on Tuesday."

"I'll be leaving on Sunday to go back to school, but I'll keep you in my prayers. When are you leaving town? Where do you live anyway?"

"I live in Connecticut."

They began to walk off of the floor and back to the table. Toni had had an opportunity to really look at Victor and see what, if anything, had changed about him. She found him to be even more handsome than when they were in high school together. He had certainly matured, she thought. She thought that it was admirable that Victor was in college at his age, a man of determination, she concluded. Victor was about twenty-five or twenty-six years old, she thought.

Toni felt warm and tingly as Victor held her hand and walked her back to the table. The side of her hand caressed the side of his thigh. In her mind Toni knew that she had backslid and if she had to spend any more time in South Carolina, she would certainly loose her virginity.

When she returned to the table, two more chairs had been added, one for each of the people who had joined Alma and Henry.

"Oh, Alma, I see you've met my buddy and roommate. Toni Spann this is my Army buddy and college roommate, Tim, Tim meet Toni."

Toni reached over to shake hands with Tim. He too, was a rather handsome guy and seemed to be enjoying his conversation with Alma. Henry was having a conversation a female that neither Toni, nor Alma had seen before. She seemed to be a rather nice young lady and she did not drink alcohol. She was sipping a coke and listening to Henry.

Victor told Toni that he and Tim were in their final year of college at South Carolina State College. They both were still in the Army Reserves because they intended to return to active duty as officers.

Tim and Victor toasted Alma and Wilson in absentia, when Toni told them that they were planning to enlist as officers when they graduated from college. The night took on meaning, it seemed to Toni. She was having a good time and so was Alma and Henry. Henry and Shantae were smiling in each other's face and dancing as though they were the only two people in the building. Alma had just let her hair down and Tim was having a good time indulging her.

Toni and Victor sat laughing and talking alone when the others got up to dance. They exchanged telephone numbers and addresses and promised to keep in touch. Victor shared that he had been married for a couple of years to a woman in the Army but that they had drifted apart and finally divorced when she was stationed in Oklahoma. His ex-wife was married, again, he said. They had not had any children and he did not have any children by anyone else. Toni teased Victor about not knowing whether he had any children. Victor looked her eye and told her that he had had many opportunities to sow his oats but that he thought more of himself than to sleep with women because they were available. He reminded Toni that even while they were in high school that there had not been anyone who could truthfully say that she had had sex with him. Toni smiled at him and nodded her head.

Toni was beginning to have thoughts of really being with Victor. But she knew that she had to complete her education and get into law school. She could also see that Alma was having a great time with Tim. She had not seen Alma this happy in a long time. Tim looked like he too, was sincerely enjoying Alma's company. Toni could not wait to get back to Connecticut and tell Kim about her night out. Henry was certainly having a good time and this made Toni forget about what was ahead of her and Henry.

By the time the trio left the club that night telephone numbers and addresses had been exchanged and promises to stay in touch made. Henry asked Toni to drive Shantae home because she was tired and did not want to wait until her cousins had gotten tired of dancing. Victor and Tim left the club with Toni, Alma and Henry. Victor walked Toni to her car held the car door open as she got inside. He bent down and kissed her on the cheek and promised to call her the next weekend.

Toni drove Shantae home and waited while Henry walked her to the door. Toni and Alma took bets whether Henry would kiss her. Shantae shook his hand and went inside the house.

"Now that's a real nice young lady." Henry said as he got back in the car.

"I've got to agree with you there, Henry. She is very pretty and very nice. I can see the two of you together. She's a real fine Christian girl, Henry. The other girl that flew over to the table before we could sit down good she just a little too fast for me. I watched her after you and Shantae sat there talking. She did not seem too happy." Alma said.

"Bump all of that. We're still going to the Battery and watch the waves." Toni said.

"Hold up one minute sister, darling. I saw you grinning and skinning in homeboy face looking like Bucky Beaver at a tryout for a toothpaste commercial."

The comment caused Alma to laugh uncontrollably.

"Oh, so you think that's funny, Miss Magnolia?" Toni asked.

"Yes mam, I certainly do." Alma replied.

"For a minute there, I could hear Miss Magnolia's conversation." Henry said. "Sounded like she had just met Rhett Butler. Man she was so proper I almost asked her to speak normal, but I wanted to make a good impression, too."

Everybody had had a good time and gotten some exercise that night. They stopped at a drive-in restaurant and got something to eat while they walked on the Battery. It was one in the morning but the trio decided that they owed it to themselves to have a good time and they would stay out all night or at least until they were tired.

The trio walked up and down the sidewalk along the Battery laughing and poking fun at each other. Toni and Alma flanked Henry as they walked arm in arm down the sidewalk in the South Carolina fall air. They decided to sit down on a bench and watched the waves slap against the concrete wall.

Although Henry had lost a lot of weight since Toni had last seen him, she could see a sparkle of true joy in his eyes. She saw the same sparkle in Alma's eyes as well. She believed that if Alma and Henry had looked at her, they too, would see the same sparkle in her eyes that she was seeing in theirs. Toni prayed that Henry would be strengthened, if not by her presence, then by her love as his sister who believed in him.

"Hey, you guys look like you just met Mister and Miss Right." Toni teased.

"Girl, what you say, I was just sitting here looking at that water and seeing me and Tim out there on the dance floor. Honey, this is a night that I will never forget. But I'm gonna let the man call me first." Alma said.

"I'm supposed to meet Shantae tomorrow. I didn't tell her anything about what's hanging over my head. But I like that girl and I'll tell her tomorrow so that she wouldn't have to hear it from somebody else." Henry said.

"I think she'll understand, Henry. Don't fret yourself over it." Alma told him.

"Ain't it blip? I meet a girl that I really like and I got a murder rap hanging over my head. Sometimes life just ain't fair."

There was silence for a few minutes. The trio sat in the fall air with the breeze blowing off of the water. A few people came pass and spoke to them as they sat and watched the water.

"What do you think the future holds for us?" Henry asked.

Toni and Alma looked at each other, not sure which of them Henry had asked the question of.

"Sometimes our present seem so bleak, but I believe that we have to go through the dark before we get to the light." Alma said.

"Yeah, but the dark can be a long time." Henry said. "And how about when things you go through wasn't caused by you? How do you walk through the dark when you didn't cause the darkness?"

"One step at a time, that's how, one step at a time. Let the Lord lead the way and the trip will be shorter." Toni said.

Silence fell upon them, again. Toni put her arm around Henry's shoulder and squeezed him. "I don't know what God's plan is for our lives, but I did read in the Bible one day where God said His plan was to prosper us, to give us a hope and a future. I don't fully understand that, yet, but I believe that prosper don't exactly mean getting rich in terms of money."

"I heard my pastor explaining that phrase about prospering and just like you said, it don't always mean that money or wealth is what they talking about. Prospering he said, can mean that every part of our life is in line with what God would want for us." Alma said.

"I'm gonna tell y'all the truth. I am scared." Henry said. "When Wilson went off to college, I sat up all night wishing that I could just leave here and go with him. I would study as hard as I could and we could graduate together. But I can't leave town."

"Henry, we're gonna get through this together and God ain't gonna let you go to prison. So stop thinking about that. You have to go through this process, but God won't let you down." Toni tried to assure her younger brother.

"Henry, I don't care what other people might think, you my brother and all of us gonna get through this. After the trial we just gonna get on with our lives and put all of this behind us. God got too much for us to do and enjoy. But let's don't forget this night. I sure can see myself waking up with that Tim."

"See there, I knew it, I knew it. Alma was digging that guy." Henry said.

Alma started laughing and hitting Henry on the hand. Henry was pushing her away in a playful manner.

"Get off of me, Miss Magnolia. I knew I was reading you right."

"Oh come on, Henry, the pot can't call the kettle black. You looked pussy whipped and hadn't even got none yet." Alma responded.

The three of them burst into laughter almost immediately at Alma's remark. Henry was laughing so hard that he began coughing and had to stand up.

"You got me good this time, Alma. You should have been minding your business rather than minding mine and Shantae's." Henry laughed.

For several moments the trio sat huddled together on the bench laughing every now and then and watching the moonlight as it sat upon the water. Toni stared out over the moonlit water and imagined herself dancing with Victor. A shimmering white dress with sleeves that hung gingerly below her shoulders. The matching shoes with the straps wrapped around her ankles and her hair bouncing in the breeze. She was truly the Nubian Queen she was born to be. Victor stood facing her dressed in a black tuxedo with a white shirt. The shirt was so white it too, seemed to glow in the moonlight. The music started and his arm slipped around her waist and he took her right hand in his left hand and pulled her body close to his as the music intoxicated them both. As she played out the scene in her mind, she could not think of what song was supposed to be playing.

Toni then thought about Jeremiah and how he would feel if she were not there in the morning. But it was more important to her, right now, to just hang out with Henry and Alma. Henry needed her more than anyone now and she would sit on the bench and watch the water until Henry was ready to leave. It was still disturbing to her that Henry had not returned to the home where he had grown up, the home where his mother and siblings where. Deep in her heart, Toni knew that Henry would never again live under the same roof with Trudy, his mother. A sadness accompanied the heartfelt belief that months earlier would have made the tears pour from Toni's eyes like small streams of rushing water. Somewhere, somehow, she had learned or received the ability to absorb the experience of truth and keep walking.

She looked over at her brother and squeezed him with the one free arm. Without turning to look at his sister Henry received the love that was transferred in that hug.

As they sat staring across the water that fall night on the battery Toni saw a light that seemed to glow in Henry's face; a light that seemed to have its power source from somewhere deep inside of him. The light that shone upon Henry's face did not seem to be in its full power, but appeared as a light or fire so deep on the inside struggling to come forth in its fullness.

For now, she was compelled to just live in the moment and let the waves splashing against the pier belt out their watery ballads with tidal wave intensity. Even though they had taken a detour, Toni felt that this evening had been designed with purpose, or for a purpose. Either way, she determined, this was not the moment to try and figure out the thing.

23

As she pulled into the parking lot near the courthouse, Toni realized that she had driven without thinking and almost numb as she turned off the engine of the car. Trudy was in the car with her, and Clifford was driving Henry there. The ride had been one of absolute silence. Trudy would also be called to testify at the trial.

Toni did not want to get out of the car, but knew that she had to go through what was ahead of her and Henry. It was not enough for her, or Henry, to come to the courthouse, the so-called place of justice, and not go through the process. Toni fiddled with her purse as though it would delay what was about to happen. Trudy spoke.

"Huh? You said something, mama?"

"No, not really. I said to myself that them people drove down here."

"What people?" she said looking around.

Toni looked up and around, she saw several people getting out of a green car. At about the same time, Trudy started to wind down the car window. Quickly Toni reached over and pulled her mother's arm back.

"No! Let them go in and we'll go in after them."

Trudy looked a bit startled. Toni had snatched her arm back roughly. She had recognized Isiah's people immediately. She did not want to be walking with those people at the same time. She could also see that Trudy was not pleased by what she had done. But she did not care what her mother's feelings were, right now. Henry was her only concern.

"I was just gonna say good morning to them. My God, the time of day is due to a dog." Trudy said.

"Why don't you just watch them dogs rather than give them the time of day. Those people are more wicked mama than anybody or anything other than the devil, and I ain't too sure that they ain't the devil."

As Toni watched the five people near their car she noticed that Isiah's mother was doing something strange. The old woman turned toward the courthouse and made some motions. Toni could also see that her lips were moving. The brother took out what looked like a handkerchief and waved it. The actions of the family were strange and Toni sensed that they were up to something that was evil. Immediately, her prayer language burst forth. She had not had any warning, nor had she purposed to speak in tongues. She watched Isiah's people continue in their activities and she continued to pray in tongues. She was almost frozen in her posture of watch and pray.

Trudy was in shock to hear what was coming out of her eldest daughter's mouth. Even more surprising was the fact that Isiah's people were doing whatever in the parking lot and had not paid any attention to who else might be around. When the group was finished they began walking out of the parking lot to the courthouse. Toni continued in prayer for a few minutes longer.

"You see how bold the devil is, mama?"

Trudy was speechless. She could only nod her head.

"Mama, those people were not out there acting on the word of Jesus Christ. They're trying some devilishness, again. But I tell you now, as the Lord above is my only witness, whatever they try to do, God's anger is going to rise up and somebody gonna die. Somebody gonna die."

"God just don't go around killing people, Toni. God is merciful, He forgive people for their sins." Trudy said.

"Yeah, God is all that, mama. But God is the one that taught David how to fight. I still say, somebody gonna die."

Trudy did not say another word. She looked at her daughter almost in awe. It was as though she could not take her eyes off of Toni. Toni had been angry with Trudy anyway, because she had a picture of Isiah in the casket on the top of her chest of drawers. Toni's reaction to the picture had been so violent that she and Trudy had had one of the biggest arguments that a mother and daughter could have. Toni had spoken to Trudy as though she was not her mother but another woman, a strange woman.

Trudy had tried to justify the picture by saying that she kept it for memory's sake. Toni told her that that was a memory she should try harder to forget if not for her sake, then for the sake of her children. But Trudy was hell bent on having the picture and not allowing anyone, including Toni, to run her life. The argument had escalated to the point of Trudy telling Toni to take her bags and get out of her house. Toni did just that, but not without having a final word. She told Trudy that her father, had died and left the home not just for Trudy but for his children, but that a dead devil would be responsible for her losing it. Toni went to a hotel and used her credit card, again. She had been very glad that the girl at the credit union had given it to her.

Although she and Trudy had perhaps reached the end of their road as mother and daughter, Toni determined that she would always be as respectful as she possibly could. She would try to give the respect a daughter should give to a mother. She went to the house and picked Trudy up for the trial and would take her home everyday until it was over. She had come to the conclusion that there was nothing that she could do to influence her mother's opinions or truly effect in her the change she would be comfortable with.

Trudy finally opened the car door and started getting out. Toni opened her door and locked the car. Toni walked beside her mother as though nothing had ever happened between them. As they walked up to the courthouse building, Toni's eyes were drawn to the top of the building. There was a black bird sitting on the peak of the roof. She knew that it was a buzzard, but she had never seen a buzzard that large or sitting that high. Matter of fact, she had never seen a buzzard in the city. All of the buzzards that she had seen had been along the side of the road picking at the dead carcasses of animals that had been struck and killed on the road.

Toni's eyes left the roof and fell upon the sidewalk where she saw the shadow of the buzzard. Again, she looked up at the roof and back to the sidewalk. The shadow was still there. Toni stopped briefly and noticed that the sun was in a rising position up and behind the buzzard. The shadow that was cast seemed to be larger than it should be. Although the buzzard was bigger than any she had ever seen, it did not seem large enough she thought, to have cast a shadow as large as what she was seeing. Toni's only comment, "Jesus, that's a big buzzard."

"What? You see a buzzard? Where at?" Trudy asked.

"Look up on the top of the courthouse."

Toni and Trudy had stopped. Toni pointed up at the courthouse but the bird was no longer there.

"I don't see no buzzard."

"Neither do I now. But there was a buzzard up there just a second ago."

"Old folks used to say that when a buzzard come to where living folks is they come to claim somebody before they die."

"Well, I wonder who that buzzard come to claim. I know it ain't claiming nobody in this family cause I've put us all in the hands of Jesus. Now if that buzzard can take one of us out of the hand of Jesus, that buzzard'll get saved and start speaking in tongues."

Trudy laughed a little.

"Huh, can you imagine that, a buzzard speaking in tongues. I guess strangers things have happened."

When they entered the courthouse and looked at the numbers to see where they were supposed to be the attorney called out to them. Clifford and Henry were standing with him. Henry looked so vulnerable, that it made Toni quake on the inside. She spoke to everyone and took Henry by the arm and led him down the hall and around the corner away from others.

"Henry, are you okay?"

"Toni, I don't know. I feel like, like something just ain't right."

"What can I do Henry? What can I do?"

"I don't think there's anything anybody can do, Toni. I think this thing just have to play itself out. That's how I've been feeling. Don't worry about me, I'll be alright."

Toni pulled Henry to her and began to pray. The prayer was so fervent that it caused Henry's body to shake. Toni and Henry walked back to where they had left the attorney, Clifford and Trudy. Trudy watched as her daughter and son approached them. The look in her eyes said so much but the desire in her eyes was not enough to cause her body or mouth to respond.

Henry took a handkerchief from his breast pocket and wiped his face. He gently folded the blue handkerchief and placed it back in his pocket. He walked over to Trudy and hugged her.

"I'll be alright mama. It don't matter what happens, I'll be okay."

Trudy could not speak, her arms could barely rise up to pat her son's back or shoulder. Clifford stood to the side and watched. The look in his eyes was one of sorrow as well. Toni could not shake the quivering feeling that seemed to sit in the pit of her stomach.

Lloyd and Margaret walked in. The attorney had told Toni the day before that Lloyd would be called to testify.

"How you holding up, man?" Lloyd asked.

"I'm okay." Henry responded as they shook hands and hugged.

The attorney told them that it was time to go into the courtroom. Toni walked beside Henry holding his hand. As they entered the courtroom, Toni could see Isiah's people on the right side of the courtroom. They sat almost like statues, stiff and rigid. They watched the family and stared at Henry.

Toni could see Isiah's brother touch the mother and make a motion. The old woman stared at Henry as though she was trying to pierce him with her eyes. Toni reasoned that he was pointing out Henry because they had not seen him that night at the house.

Without notice or thinking Toni began speaking in tongues quietly. As she came pass the row of seats occupied by Isiah's people the volume of her prayer seemed to go up instantly. She glanced over to her right side to see that Isiah's people were blinking and trying to wipe their eyes.

The attorney and Henry walked through the small swinging gate that separated the area where attorneys sat from the other people.

Toni and her family sat just behind the attorney and Henry. Toni felt the hair rise up on her right side. It felt as though there was something trying to cover that side of her body. She began to pray so hard in her mind that she was unable to hear or see what was going on around her. Toni's mind was centered on Henry and Henry's mental state. When everyone stood up, Toni realized that she should follow suit and stood up, too.

The jurors had already filed in and taken their seats. Toni could not believe that she had missed that. As she studied the faces of the people on the jury she noticed at least five familiar faces. She began to feel a little better because at least one of the jurors had been a very good friend of her father, Mr. Lindsey Buchanan. They had been in the same Masonic Lodge. She knew that he would not vote against Henry, his old friend's son.

Then there was a former schoolmate, Yvonne Bowman, who had been in the English Club with Toni. She and Toni were not best friends, but they had been more than friendly and respectful with each other in school. One of Trudy's old church members was also on the jury, Mrs. Sally Ruth Gordon. She and Trudy used to be in the prayer band together, as well as the Missionaries.

Toni's confidence level was rising now. She knew in her heart that these people would surely understand what Henry had done and they would not hold it against him. Toni looked at the jury, again, and thought that Yvonne was staring at her. But Yvonne was staring at Margaret and Lloyd. Toni remembered now that Yvonne had been Lloyd's girlfriend when they were in school together. Matter of fact she and Lloyd had been engaged while he was in Viet Nam. Toni did not know what had happened to that relationship. But there she sat, staring, no glaring, at Margaret and Lloyd. Yvonne's glare seemed to be dripping with venom. If her eyes had been daggers, Margaret and Lloyd would have been cut to death and left to bleed all over the courtroom. That bothered Toni. She wondered whether Yvonne was capable of making the right decision in this case. Already she could see a problem. But Toni was not too shaken by Yvonne's glare because there were two other people that knew her parents, they were parents as well.

Toni recognized another young man on the jury. He was a young white male whose name Toni could not remember, but his face was so very familiar. As she racked her brain to figure out from where she had known him the Solicitor began presenting his case.

Toni was shocked by what she heard. The Solicitor made it sound like Henry had gone after Isiah, tracked him down like a dog and killed him. The Solicitor treated the fact that Isiah had shot Trudy as though it was just a slap on the behind and that Henry had acted out revenge.

David Kingsley, Henry's attorney, got up and set the record straight. He did not miss a beat, Toni reasoned. Now, she thought, the people had the right side of the story. Henry sat next to Mr. Kingsley and never looked back. As the Solicitor called forth members of Isiah's family to testify of how nice a guy he was, Toni watched them as they lied about how Isiah had told them that Henry had threatened Isiah. Toni thought that the lies would make her throw up. The lies were so ridiculous that the Judge looked at them with raised eyebrows.

Mr. Kingsley made mince meat of Isiah's people's testimony. The next day Toni and Lloyd were called to the witness stand. Mr. Kingsley even let Henry testify. The Solicitor could not shake any of the testimonies. He tried to hammer home a point about the number of times that Isiah had been shot, but Toni did not believe that he had made any points with that argument. The Judge sent everybody to lunch. When they returned the closing arguments were made and the jury was sent out to decide the case.

It was nearly two thirty when the jury was sent out to decide the case. Henry was nervous and it showed. Isiah's people had sat and watched for two days now. They did not know how long the jury would be out. Isiah's people sat on the bench outside of the courtroom watching and talking amongst themselves. Toni took Henry outside and they sat on a ledge across from the side of the courthouse. Henry told Toni to come and walk with him; he just needed to stretch his legs. They circled the corner and walked back into the courthouse. Trudy and Clifford were sitting on the other side of the hall, away from where Isiah's people were sitting.

Henry sat down on the bench beside Clifford with his head bowed down. He fiddled with his thumbs. They tried to make small talk to take their minds off of what the jury was doing.

"How is Wilson doing down there in Louisiana? Old college boy now." Clifford asked.

"He's doing great. Studying and trying to decide which fraternity he's going to pledge." Toni answered.

"Yeah, homeboy was determined to get him a college degree. He wants to be an officer in the military. I'm hoping he'll change his mind about the Army and go Navy or Marine." Clifford said.

"How old was you Uncle Clifford when you retired?" Toni asked.

"I had just turned thirty nine. I had twenty-two years in then, it was time to go and do something else. But Wilson will be an officer, not an enlisted man like I was."

"I really think he wants to be in the Marine Corps, Uncle Clifford. You should have heard him talking about the uniforms." Margaret said.

"Hey, I'll be jumping up and down like a grasshopper when they swear him in."

Lloyd sat smiling, but he kept his eyes on Henry. Henry sat next to Clifford looking straight ahead at the wall. Toni doubted that Henry had heard much of what was being said. His eyes seemed to be looking into another world oblivious of everything and everyone around him. Lloyd reached over and patted him on the shoulder and told him to look up to the hill.

As they continued to make small talk, Toni could see Isiah's mother pacing back and forth in front of the courtroom door. Every so often she would stop and look into the door of the courtroom. Toni watched and began praying in her heart. She believed that Isiah's people were up to no good and she would meet their evil with the word of God. She remembered what she had had to endure as a result of their wickedness. But she was not afraid of what they could do anymore. She knew that God would also send help to fight against whatever they might send to her and her family.

"It's four thirty now, maybe the judge will send the jury home and start again tomorrow." Trudy said.

"No, I don't think so. This is going to be over today." Henry said.

The attorney returned and sat on the bench next to Trudy. Henry's statement seemed to be the end of a tiring experience. He sounded like he wanted it to be over whatever the jury decided. A hush fell over the entire courthouse. Nothing could be heard, no voices, no machinery, not even the sound of cars outside. Just deep and thick quiet. No one moved a muscle or blinked an eye.

The old heavy-set black man walked out of the courtroom door and motioned for everyone to come back in.

"Come on, look like the jury got a verdict." Mr. Kingsley said.

Toni held Henry's hand as they walked down the hall toward the courtroom. As they walked in, Isiah's people had already taken their seats and were sitting on the edge them.

Toni felt the anger begin to rise up on the inside. Again she began to pray in her heart. Henry and Mr. Kingsley walked through the little swinging gate and the rest of the family sat on the bench right behind them.

Toni sat straight in her chair, still praying. As her eyes swept over the courtroom she again noticed that Yvonne Bowman was glaring at Lloyd and Margaret. Mr. Lindsey Buchanan sat with his head down. Finally the judge came in. Everyone stood and sat down again after the judge had taken his seat.

The anticipation was great. Toni's heart raced as she tried to read the verdict through the judge's eyes as he read the note from the jury. Trudy's leg shook like she had a spasm in it. Lloyd's hand was folded as though he was praying.

Clifford sat stiff with his eyes fixed on the judge. Everyone seemed to be on pins and needles as they waited for the jury's verdict. Henry turned around and looked back at his family just as the judge had asked him to stand. The jury foreman read the verdict; Henry was guilty of Manslaughter. The only response that was heard came from Isiah's mother who said, "justice done."

Toni's head was spinning like a top, she could not think or see clearly. Henry's knees buckled when he heard the decision. Mr. Kingsley reached over to steady Henry and help him sit down. Henry's head was bowed down, Lloyd cried openly and kept saying, "they're wrong, they're wrong, Lord knows they're wrong."

The judge sentenced Henry immediately to six years in the penitentiary. Toni was so overcome by the decision that she could hardly breath. The deputies came over and put handcuffs on Henry and led him out of the courtroom.

Toni could barely talk, but she managed to tell Trudy that she would go get the car and pick her up in front of the courthouse. As she got up and began walking out of the courtroom she passed Isiah's people. Her eyes did not lower or veer to either side of the courtroom. But, her eyes were fixed upon them, no fear or intimidation.

"All your money couldn't keep him from paying for what he done." Isiah's sister said to Toni.

"And all of your roots and voodoo won't keep God from rendering justice upon you. This ain't over, yet, cause God hasn't spoken. I guarantee that you'll hear Him when He does." Toni responded.

As she walked out of the door she caught a glimpse of her godmother but was moving too quickly to stop and talk. Toni was hurt and felt like God had betrayed and abandoned her. Cold tears flowed down her face. Her heart was absolutely broken, how could God deceive her like this, she thought. There was nothing and no one that could bring comfort or even understanding to her about what had just happened. She had prayed for hours asking God to set her brother free. She had not even depended on the lawyer, her hope and trust had been placed in God and God alone. In the end, she reasoned, the devil had gotten another victory.

She had gotten turned around and walked out of a door that had led her to a street that she was not familiar with. Confused and lost, Toni circled the courthouse trying to get back to the front so that she could find her way to the parking lot from a familiar place. As she came around the corner to walk toward the front of the courthouse she saw the buzzard sitting on the top of the roof. The buzzard began flapping its wings. The wings began moving up and down, up and down, faster and faster. As the buzzard flapped its wings it stirred up a breeze. Several people were standing out in front of the courthouse and there were others coming out of the door. The wind grew stronger and the shadow of the buzzard covered the courthouse and the street in front of it.

Everyone standing in front of and on the steps of the courthouse was covered by the buzzard's shadow. It was nearly dark, but the buzzard cast a shadow like it was noonday.

Toni was in shock. She was frozen in fear as she watched the buzzard. She watched the buzzard and the huge shadow that it had cast over the courthouse and street. The darkness over the courthouse and street caused those standing near and under it to look up in amazement. The wind stirred up by the buzzard's wings was so strong that it blew hats off of heads and caused dresses to be blown over the heads of women. It was like a total eclipse taking place above and around the courthouse.

Someone in the crowd was screaming. The screams were so intense that it caused Toni to snap out of her anger invoked trance and began walking toward the front sidewalk of the courthouse. She did not know what to think but continued to walk toward the front of the courthouse. She now saw that it was Isiah's mother screaming. The old woman tried to run back into the courthouse but the door had been locked from the inside. Toni heard the old woman screaming and babbling something but no one was able to understand or make sense of what she was saying.

Toni stood on the sidewalk in front of the courthouse looking at the people caught in the wind being stirred up by the buzzard and caught in the shadow of darkness that it had cast. She stood down on the sidewalk and looked up at those standing on the steps, including Isiah's people. Isiah's mother looked like she was trying to find a hiding place. Toni thought that old woman had lost her mind. Trudy and Clifford were standing to the left of the courthouse door looking at what was happening.

The buzzard then flew off of the roof and for a brief moment hovered above the street flapping its wings then it took off. The wind that had been stirred up suddenly died down. The darkness that had blanketed the courthouse and the street in front of it was now replaced with the evening light. Isiah's mother and family looked like they had just seen a ghost. Everyone appeared to be in some form of shock and disbelief and trying to figure out what they had just witnessed.

Toni looked up the steps at Isiah's people. She then walked past the building and turned the corner to go to the parking lot where she had parked the car. The walk to the parking lot seemed like a walk in the wilderness, dark with no direction. Confusion occupied her head and pain and disappointment filled her heart. When she reached the second corner from the courthouse she stopped. A car was approaching the corner. As the car came to a stop, she saw Henry in the backseat with his hands behind his back. He shuffled his body to the door and pressed his face against the glass in the backdoor. Toni's eyes met Henry's and she could see the tears rolling down his face. He told her through the glass "I love you."

She could not move. As the car turned the corner she was left with the picture of her helpless and crying brother permanently etched in her mind and memory. She too, felt helpless. She had been unable to secure her brother's freedom and spare him from prison. He looked like an abandoned man. She felt like an abandoned woman. God Almighty had abandoned them. God had kept her afloat, helped her to stay in her right mind and to survive all that she had endured since before Henry killed Isiah. Then when she had come before the enemy seeking justice God had dropped her and left her on the floor for the enemy to have its way with her, it seemed. There was no place for her to go now. Who could she trust? She could not see a glimmer of hope, or peace, no comfort, just the question "why God have you forsaken me?"

24

    The room was dark, except for a sliver of light shining through the edge of the window where the drapes did not extend across the wall. Toni lay in the bed and stared up at the ceiling. She had spent the night reliving a period in her life that nearly caused her to turn her back on God and end her life.
    She thought about the weeks and months that she went through a darkness that seemed to blanket her soul and cripple her spirit. She stopped going to church and lost interest almost in living. For more than six months she could not pick up the Bible that lay on the table in her sunroom.
    Kim had tried to comfort her but it was useless. But Kim remained a friend and continued to pray for her. Alma went to see Henry every other week. Even though Toni's depression had taken her into valleys so deep that she thought that she would never come up out of, she did have the wherewithal to get Henry's prison sentence reduced to fourteen months. She had gotten him transferred to a minimal security facility that seemed more like a halfway house. Henry was able to go home on weekends and to spend holidays with his family. Toni made sure that Henry had sheets for his bed that she had purchased, and not prison sheets. When he said that he could have his own television, she purchased one and sent it to him. Henry had spent his time going to an educational program to learn electronics. He wrote to Toni every week and became the one person to encourage her in his letters.
    Henry had attended a church service while in prison that prompted him to ask the preacher for two copies of the tape. The sermon had been about Joseph, one of the sons of Jacob. The sermon had so affected Henry that he sent one copy to Toni. The tape had laid on the shelf for two or three weeks before she played it. One night as she sat looking around the apartment her eyes fell upon the tape. After listening to the preacher she found herself crying and repenting. God welcomed her home, it seemed, with open arms. After being baptized, again, Toni began the slow walk back to redemption. It was years later that she realized that redemption had been immediate.
    She had learned to walk by herself, knowing that she was never alone. Her belief in God grew into a relationship. She had learned to trust even when she had not understood. She had prayed and believed in the impossible when others had said that she was crazy and her beliefs did not have any logic. Her prayers had brought Aaron Jr., home, safe and sound. He had called her from California where he had been stationed onboard a Navy ship. He had said that something in him had been so strong that he could not go another day without calling her.
    Now, twenty-five years later, she was sure who had killed Isiah and in her mind something had to be done. Toni was in tug of war with her emotions. She had come to bury her mother and something from the past that she thought had died a long time ago was brought back to life. She couldn't tell Aaron Jr., because he had not been there when it all had begun and did not know how he would react. Worse yet, she did not know how Henry would react if he knew that Lloyd had been the one who had shot Isiah.
    Toni sat up in the bed and wondered where Jeremiah was. She had to talk to him, kind of beat about the bush, to see whether he had remembered anything about that night. She took a shower and pulled out one of her sweat suits. She reached for the

telephone and called Joyce to see whether she had spoken to Jeremiah since yesterday. Her plan was to talk to Jeremiah first, then to Henry.

Helen had seen the person who shot Isiah. The killer was carrying Jeremiah. Henry was not carrying Jeremiah it was Lloyd. As Toni tried to put her plans together, there was a little tug in her spirit. She was determined to confront Lloyd before leaving South Carolina. She did not know what she would do if Lloyd denied her allegation and got angry with her. Lloyd and Henry had remained friends, even after Margaret had divorced him and remarried.

Henry was now married and had put that time in his life behind him. There had been a time when Henry had struggled with moving forward but he had bounced back and continued to progress. Was it wise, she thought, to open that wound now? She didn't have an answer but decided that she would do something about it. She wasn't sure what she should do, but determined that she had to do something.

Toni called Lloyd's house and talked with Margaret and her children. Margaret and Lloyd had had a son and a daughter together and they had stayed with their father during the funeral. Now they were all together at his house, just like a family. Jeremiah was also staying there. Jeremiah had moved to Maryland when he began college and stayed after graduating and had gotten a job. Toni spoke with Jeremiah and got him to say that he would meet her for breakfast. She put on her sneakers and socks and grabbed her purse and drove to Lloyd's house to pick him up.

Jeremiah and Lloyd were in the front yard when Toni pulled up in front of his house. Lloyd had built a beautiful house and his flower gardens were so beautiful. Jeremiah beckoned for Toni to get out of the car and join them in the yard. Reluctantly, she turned the car's engine off and walked into the yard.

"How you doing, sis?" Lloyd asked.

"Fine, how you doing this morning?"

"Girl, I'm in seventh heaven. My kids are in there acting like they did when they were just about nine and ten years old and spent the summers with me."

Toni began to feel just a little guilty about what she was about to do. Lloyd had been a good father to his children. Margaret had said that she didn't have to ask Lloyd to pay child support. What the court had put in the divorce decree was much less than what Lloyd had sent. Each summer just after school closed L.J. and Tara would board the train in Baltimore with anticipation to spend the entire summer with their father. Margaret's summers had been free because it was Lloyd's turn to spend time with his children.

"Hey Toni, come around here to the backyard and see this little garden retreat Lloyd built." Jeremiah said.

The trio began walking along the stone walkway to the side of the house. The hedges had been carefully trimmed and even in shape and size. When they got to the backyard, Toni was pleasantly surprise to see how the plants and trees had been organized around a patio. The scene looked like it had been a picture torn right out of a magazine. That, Toni thought, was the scene she had had in her mind so often, but this scene had more details than she had imagined.

It became harder for Toni to do what she had come there to do. But determination was still breathing down her back. She had to confront what she knew was the truth about who had killed Isiah. After a while of sitting in the backyard garden and enjoying the little slice of heaven, as Toni had named it, she and Jeremiah left.

"Wanna go to Burger King like we used to do?" she asked.

"That'll work." Jeremiah responded.

The little boy that she and Lloyd was always carrying around in their arms was now a grown man standing six feet tall with broad shoulders. People used to say that Jeremiah was the one with the Toni face but with a mustache and a small beard. Jeremiah and Toni could pass for boy/girl twins. Jeremiah was now in his thirties and no longer an insecure baby boy. Toni could still see remnants of the seven year boy in the thirty something man, but it was cute she thought.

As they sat at the table with their food. Toni looked at Jeremiah and decided that it was just as good a time now as any other to ask her questions.

"Jerry, I want you to think back for a moment for me."

"How far back do you want me to remember?"

"The night that Isiah died. I remember something you had said that night when you and Lloyd walked in the house just before the cops came."

"What did I say, Toni?"

"You said that the bullets came whizzing pass your head and that your ears were ringing."

Jerry stared at Toni for a long time. She almost regretted that she had asked him about that night.

"Toni, why are you going back there?"

"There is something I need to straighten out in my mind about that."

"What are you thinking Toni?"

"I first need to know what you actually saw that night before I can form a solid opinion."

"Have you spoken to anybody else about this?"

"No, Jerry, I haven't. I wanted to talk to you first."

"Toni, it was years later that I started putting things together and I realized that Lloyd was the one who shot Isiah that night. I saw a man killed that night and didn't realize what I had seen. I am sorry to say this, because no one has the right to take the life of another. But, I was glad that somebody had killed that man. I don't hate Lloyd and never will. I have never said anything all of these years and if you had not brought this subject up, Toni, I never would have."

"Jerry, how long have you known this?"

"Completely, since I was about twelve or thirteen years old. I would have flashbacks about what happened. Finally, it just dawned on me that Lloyd, I think, had got Isiah as he was running from the old house trying to get over to the next street where he had left his car."

"What do you mean, you think? Weren't you there?"

"Like I said before, I was glad that somebody had put a stop to that fool. I believe that Isiah wanted to kill mama and Henry. He got what he deserved, may God forgive me for saying this, but I don't care who killed him, he's dead."

"What about Henry? Do you believe that he should have spent that time in the penitentiary for killing Isiah?"

"Now Toni that's a question that I battled with for a while. But you had bought Henry's time down and he wasn't in the regular penitentiary, so it wasn't so bad. Besides, Henry said that he would do it again, if he had to. So that settled that issue."

"So you never told Henry what you knew?"

"No, Toni, I did not. I wanted to and a couple of times I almost did, but something inside of me would not let me tell him. I had a peace about that Toni and I still do. You're the one that taught me how to trust God for guidance and I believed in my heart of heart that it wasn't meant for me to tell Henry."

Something inside of Toni was telling her that she still had to pursue this matter a little further. Still she did not know what she would do if Lloyd were to admit that he had been the one to pull the trigger that night. But she would go to Lloyd she thought. She would confront him and maybe he would tell Henry the truth and she and Jeremiah would not have to say anything to him.

"What are you going to do Toni?"

"I don't know, Jerry. But I believe that I have to say something about it."

"Well, I just want to say this, please go to the Lord for guidance about this. I love Lloyd just as much as I love Henry, Wilson and Aaron Junior. They are my brothers. Even when Lloyd and Margaret divorced and she married somebody else and divorced him, I never stopped loving Lloyd and we stayed in contact. He would come to Maryland and stay with me. When I came here, I stayed with him. I can talk openly to him and he's just like you, the first thing he would ask me is what did the Lord say about it? Toni, please be careful."

Her baby brother was now admonishing her. On the one hand, Toni admired and respected her brother for his maturity and how he had admonished her in love. On the other hand, she was determined to push ahead with asking Lloyd about his part in the death of Isiah. Toni and Jeremiah sat quietly for a few minutes eating their meals. Their silence was interrupted by Jeremiah's intense stare. Jeremiah's stare was so intense that it sent a chill through Toni. Toni looked back at Jeremiah and for a brief second she did not see him, but a faint look of a familiar face.

Toni did not blink, or look away, but the faint and familiar face faded right before her eyes. Toni drew back but kept her eyes on Jeremiah.

"Jerry, are you okay?"

"Yeah. You okay?"

"Uh, huh."

Toni sat in almost paralyzed silence. There was no doubt in her mind about what she had seen. The face she had seen, although a faint or fading one, it was familiar to her. When she could think again, she began racking her brain and trying to mentally flesh out the face she had seen. No matter how hard she tried as they sat in the restaurant, she could not put a name to the face.

"You know what Toni?"

"Uh, uh. What?"

"I think Lloyd and Margaret might be getting back together after all these years."

"You really think so?"

"Yeah, I really think so. I don't know why they ever divorced. I asked Margaret but all that she would say is that they just drifted apart and she needed to be on her own."

"Well, she certainly has been on her own for a while now. Her children are grown and supporting themselves."

"Yeah. You know L.J. is in the Reserves now, too."

"I didn't know that. He looks up to his Uncle Wilson. Did Wilson say whether he was going to retire soon?"

"Please, you know Wilson think that the Marine Corps will go out of existence if he retires."

Brother and sister started laughing at the remark. Wilson was truly a military man.

"I remember when he went off to college all he wanted to do was get one of those tailored uniforms and have them salute him."

"Yeah, I remember that, too. He couldn't stay anywhere but over at the Officer's Club. The finest hotel in town was not as good as a room at the Officer's Quarters. He tried to get me to stay over there too. I told him get on away from me because I was gonna stay at Joyce, Lloyd, or Aaron Junior's house. Then I decided to stay at Lloyd's house cause Margaret was staying at Joyce's house. Then here come Margaret with her thick hips over to Lloyd's house pretending she checking on her kids. Hell, her kids don't even live with her in Maryland. But Lloyd was glad she was there. So I just went to my room and looked at television until she got through cooking."

"Did Wilson say whether he was coming over today?"

"Ring a pot top or two and he'll hear it and be wherever the pots are steaming in two minutes flat."

"Boy, you are hard on Wilson."

"Wilson hard on himself. That's my big bubba. He ain't stop eating yet. I don't know how Miss Magnolia can keep grocery with him around."

"Well, he buys the grocery and if Alma don't feel like cooking all she's got to do is take him to the chow hall."

By the time Jeremiah and Toni left the restaurant they were laughing like they had been tickled with feathers. Toni was laughing but she was determined to confront Lloyd. She had been laughing but underneath Toni was almost spitting fire.

Jeremiah knew and had known for years that Henry had not been the one to kill Isiah, but he had not said anything. She had suffered depression so badly that she had believed that light would never be a part of her life again. She had scrimped and saved to pay off the lawyer and to get Henry transferred to a minimum-security facility.

As Toni drove she was tempted to scream at Jeremiah but decided that she would hold her peace and let Jeremiah believe that she had accepted all that he had said. But she was seething in anger because Jeremiah had accepted the fact that his brother had spent time in prison for a crime that had been committed by someone else. She was even angrier because he had known for a long time that Henry had not been the one that had shot Isiah, yet he decided that he would not say anything.

A breeze seemed to pass over Toni and left a peace within her about the situation. The anger that had risen so quickly was now gone. Her mind started to focus on leaving South Carolina and going back to Connecticut. If Margaret and Lloyd got back together, that was fine with her. She had divorced the second husband, and there was not even the remotest possibility that she would reconcile with him.

Jeremiah seemed to be happy in his life and he was a God fearing man, attending church on a regular basis. Her siblings were all in good health and together. Toni decided that she could not ask for better than that. She was about to close the door on the past when the haunting truth of Lloyd having been the one who had killed Isiah had surfaced.

Again, she was determined to confront Lloyd. It didn't matter to her now whether he denied his part, or admitted it. She seemed compelled to confront him.

Jeremiah wanted to go to Joyce's house and hang out for a while. So Toni dropped him off there without getting out of the car. She told Jeremiah that she was going over to Lloyd's house to spend some time with Margaret. As she drove, Toni was not sure how she was going to open the subject with Lloyd, but she knew that this day she definitely would do so.

Toni pulled up in front of Lloyd's house and turned off the engine of the car. Slowly she reached for her purse and again tried, unconsciously, to delay the inevitable. She got out of the car and locked the door. Slowly she walked to the front of the house and up the little stone walkway leading to the steps of the front porch. Lloyd and Henry had joined together and helped each other build beautiful homes. She admired the beauty of the house's exterior and how Lloyd had made the yard so beautiful with flowers and trees that accented the outside of the house. This was her idea of a home and it should have a family inside.

As she placed her foot on the second step to go up Lloyd opened the door.

"Hey sis, you back?"

"Yeah. Lloyd, look I've got to talk to you. I have got to ask you something, please tell me the truth."

Lloyd looked at Toni with a bit of sadness in his eyes. The look in Lloyd's eyes seemed to be a look of relief rather than one of shock or disbelief.

"Sis, I've grown beyond lies. I'll tell the truth even if it means I'll die in the next minute."

"Where's Margaret and the kids?"

"Oh they took the car and went to visit Uncle Clifford and his wife."

"That's good because I don't want them to hear what I've got to say."

Toni and Lloyd walked into the house. Lloyd asked whether she wanted anything to drink.

"I need to go to the bathroom. That's from drinking all that watered down coffee. I haven't had a good cup of coffee since I've been here, Lloyd."

"You want me to put on a few cups?"

"Lloyd that would be great."

"I know you like that coffee strong enough to paint a barn."

She went to the bathroom and returned to the kitchen.

"Dag, Lloyd, this kitchen is beautiful. You did some beautiful work in this house. I'm surprised one of them old girls hadn't forced her way up in here and camped."

"Hell no, not here. Them old girls know that I don't fool around like that. Margaret and the kids come here too often for me to have somebody else's spirit all up in here. Me and Henry just decided that we were going to do the best we could with these houses we bought. He and Shantae got that big house over there that he and I worked on. Shantae ain't going nowhere either. We just finished with his daughter, Lil Toni's room. Remember those curtains and comforter you sent her?"

"Yeah, you know that's my baby."

"Well we had to paint girlfriend's room to match what you sent her. Everything have to be perfect for that niece of mine. Oh girl, she had to supervise me and Henry, too, like we didn't know what we were doing. But we got one over on her, though. We built a little window seat for her. That girl was so happy that she didn't want to come out of her room. Shantae had to tell her that if she wanted to eat she had to eat with the rest of them at the kitchen table."

"I've got to go over there before I leave here. I remember the night Henry met Shantae."

"Yeah, he told me about that. She was in college and he was getting ready to go to trial. But she overlooked all of that. Ain't that like God? Here you about to face one the hardest thing of your life and into your life walk the person of your dreams. But God is so merciful that He would keep and hold for you what He has assigned to you."

"God has truly held us throughout the years, Lloyd. We have faced some things that would have killed other people."

"Uh,uh, we have come through a lot of things, Toni. God brought us through a lot of things. Now He is putting me and my family back together."

"Praise God, Lloyd. I bless you and Margaret."

Toni's heart and words were sincere. She believed that whatever was happening or going to happen in Lloyd and Margaret's life was ordained and she would not speak against it. In her heart, Toni loved Lloyd as a brother. But she had come to do something that day and she would finish it.

Toni smiled to herself as she sat on the stool at the kitchen counter. Lloyd still acted as though he was a member of the family. Then it struck Toni, he was a member of the family. They didn't have to have the same mother or father. Her oldest niece and nephew were his children, and Jeremiah loved him so much. Hell, she thought this is her brother.

"Lloyd, did you shoot Isiah that night?"

"I thought that I did. It was my intent to do so. But I am not sure."

Toni was not only surprised by what had come out of her mouth, but by how Lloyd had responded.

"What do you mean that you're not sure?"

Lloyd put up one finger and reached for the telephone. As he dialed the number Toni's mind raced. She didn't know what she had opened up and now wished that she had resisted the urge to confront Lloyd.

"Henry, hey buddy, what you doing? Toni is here and I want you to come over ASAP. See you in a few."

"You mean Henry know that you might have been the one that shot Isiah?"

"Yeah."

"How long have y'all been hiding this, Lloyd?"

"We didn't want anybody to know what we had planned that night, Toni."

Toni's head started spinning. The air seemed light and she began to see little colored speckles of light all around the kitchen. Quickly she stood up and walked to the back door.

"Lloyd, can we sit out there in that little garden patio?"

"Yeah, if you want to."

"I like that little spot you've made out there. I just want to sit out there and have my coffee. It just seems like a little bit of heaven right here in South Carolina."

"It certainly is my little piece of heaven. I like that spot, too. I'm glad that you like it."

Toni poured more coffee in her cup and added the cream. She walked out of the door and stepped onto the little porch just before the garden.

"Please help me Lloyd, to understand what happened that night."

"Isiah called and threatened Henry. Henry and I took that threat serious. I was already hurting inside because mama was in the hospital. I thought about your daddy, Mr. Aaron. Toni, your daddy helped me and my mama and brother and sister to stay alive after my daddy got killed at the mill. Mr. Aaron would see me out there playing or something and he would always give me a dollar or two and tell me buy something for myself. The other kids would have money and he made sure that I had some money, too. Mr. Aaron took me to the store one time and bought me two pairs of shoes. He bought me a pair of sneakers and pair of Stacy Adams."

"I never knew that Lloyd."

"I know you didn't Toni. But those Stacy Adams meant so much to me. All of the other boys were wearing pressed Khaki pants and Stacy Adams. Mr. Aaron bought them for me."

"That's just like daddy."

"You don't know all of the good things that Mr. Aaron did for people, Toni. I used get letters from your daddy when I was in Viet Nam. My God, my God, he was always encouraging me. He wrote me a letter one time and called me son. He also said that he loved me."

The tears began to flow from Lloyd's eyes as he told Toni about her daddy.

"I never saw a letter from you."

"Mr. Aaron would always use Uncle Sammy's address and that's where I would send my letters to him."

"Oh."

"Your mama knew I was writing to Mr. Aaron."

"Oh, I didn't know that."

"Before my mama died, she told me never to forget the bridge that brought me across. She was so grateful for all the fish, greens and potatoes that Mr. Aaron used to give us from the store. Mr. Aaron never denied us credit for anything, even for some cookies or candies. I bought lunch at school, Toni, because Mr. Aaron gave me the money. I loved your daddy."

Toni was crying by now. In death her father was so well loved and remembered by a man who was not his son. Henry could be heard coming around to the back of the house.

"I thought y'all was back here so I didn't bother to ring the doorbell."

Henry kissed his sister on the cheek and shook hands with Lloyd.

"What's happening brother?" Henry asked.

"I was just talking to Toni about the night Isiah died."

Henry looked at Toni. He appeared to be shocked that anyone knew the truth about Isiah's death.

"How did you find out Toni?" Henry asked.

"God has a way of exposing everything that happens in the dark, Henry. I spent every dollar that I had or made to make sure that you didn't spend the rest of your life behind bars. Then I find out that you and Lloyd had planned this man's death. Now Isiah didn't have no right coming to the house that night to try and kill you. I still stand by my word, if there had to be a funeral, then let his family be the mourners. But I can't get over what actually happened. Now Lloyd tells me that he is not sure he shot Isiah. Please tell me for my own mental health, what happened?"

Henry and Lloyd looked at each other. Henry sat down and pulled the chair where he could sit to Toni's side facing her.

Lloyd had his hands folded together like he was praying. Then he stretched his folded hands across the table and looked at Toni.

"Sis, there were two pistols that night. I was packing and so was Henry. I had prayed that Isiah would not carry out his threats, but Henry and I had already decided that we would not be caught off guard if he did. Isiah was evil to the core. I did not know how one person could be so evil, but he was the devil's child. When Isiah showed up that night, we both were shocked. I didn't even know at first that Isiah had even grabbed Henry. When I saw what was going on I wanted to get Jerry out of the way so that he would not get hurt or see anything. The bottom line is there was another guy that came up while Henry and Isiah was struggling."

"What other guy came up? I only saw Henry out there when those shots were fired." Toni responded.

"Toni, I'm telling you that there was another guy out there that night." Henry said.

"Henry, what guy? What did he look like?" Toni asked.

209

"He was a tall kind of light skinned guy. He had real light brown eyes." Lloyd said.

"Did you see the same guy, too, Henry?"

"I looked right in this guys eyes, Toni. He said, 'let him go, this one is mine.' I told Lloyd, I didn't even turn Isiah loose, this guy just snatched him. Everything was happening so fast."

"This is unbelievable, but I truly believe y'all. That guy y'all saw is somebody that you, Lloyd, should have remembered." Toni said.

"What you talking about, sis?" Lloyd asked with wide eyes.

"Lloyd, do you remember our cousin, Joseph? He was the one that got killed in that car wreck with Mr. Lindsay Buchanan son."

"Oh, Lord, have mercy! Sure you're right. That was him; that was Joseph. I remember him now. I remember the guy looked familiar, but I could not remember from where I had seen him." Lloyd said.

"Lord have mercy, Jesus," Henry said, as he began shaking his head. "I remember now. I had forgotten about Joseph. I was a little boy when he died but I do remember what he looked like, with those freckles across his nose. What in the hell happened that night?"

Toni was now wondering why they had to meet this day and discuss an incident that happened twenty-five years ago. Lloyd sat straight up in the chair looking toward the sky in unbelief.

"I don't know what the Lord is doing right now," Lloyd said, "but I have repented at least a million times for what we did, or planned to do. Henry and I tried to piece this thing together years ago and we are no wiser today than we were then."

"What did you and Henry try to piece together?" Toni asked.

"I had Jerry in my arms and I was going to put him down and go around the back to get Isiah. When I got to the back I saw this real tall guy, just like Henry said. The guy had stepped between Henry and Isiah. Before I could put Jerry down I saw Isiah trying to run away. I thought that he had gotten away from both Henry and the tall guy. I didn't know who the tall guy was at first. I thought that it was a guy visiting one of the neighbors and had come out to help us. I knew nobody could see me where I was holding Jerry, so I pulled out my pistol and aimed so I could bring Isiah down. Then all of a sudden it looked like there was I don't know how many other people that just seemed to come out of nowhere and surround Isiah like they were protecting him. I fired a shot or two and the tall guy was standing between me and Isiah."

"Say what?" Toni almost shouted. "Where did the other people come from and where did they go?"

"See, that's the question that I kept asking myself all of these years. I concluded that these were not people, but spirits in the dark. I believe that they were spirits that Isiah called to defend him, but they disappeared as quickly as they had appeared when the tall guy, I mean Joseph, stepped between us." Lloyd said.

"Well let me tell y'all this. That same night when I went out there after I heard the shots. I saw Henry standing there and I had to reach up to pull his arm down with the gun in it. I also saw the face of Joseph over Henry's face. But I couldn't believe what I was seeing. I guess I was in denial. But what I had seen I couldn't deny."

"How in the world could all of us see Joseph in the same night?" Henry said.

"That's not all, I saw his face again today." Toni said.

"What?" Henry and Lloyd said at the same time.

"I sure did. I was talking to Jeremiah at the Burger King and I asked him to tell me what he had seen that night. I thought that I was taxing his memory, but he remembered Lloyd having a gun and firing at Isiah."

"Oh my God, I didn't think that he saw the pistol." Lloyd said.

"It was years later that he started to put things together, he said, but he believes that you and not Henry shot Isiah."

"He has never ever mentioned that." Lloyd said.

"And he never will, Lloyd." Toni said.

"I was in shock when you came out of the house and grabbed my arm. I saw the same thing that Lloyd had seen and didn't know whether I had just entered the twilight zone or what. I just wanted to get away from that place and never go back. I had gotten the best of Isiah and I was definitely gonna shoot him before he got away. I was not gonna fight him twice or even have him out there trying to find me. I was just determined that he was gonna die that night. Then Joseph grabbed my hand just as I squeezed off the shots at Isiah. That's when he spoke to me. But while I'm staring at him I could see these other people behind him. I got to sweating, cause now I thought I have to help this brother fight this crowd. But the brother turned around and the other people weren't there anymore. I almost freaked out. I never saw Isiah fall or anything."

"We switched the pistols before the police came to the house. I knew that Henry had seen something but we didn't have time to really talk to each other about it. Henry and I was talking about that night when you and Alma came to the house the day before you went back to Connecticut, that's what we were talking about. We didn't know which pistol, if either had killed Isiah. I was determined to kill Isiah because he had hurt Mr. Aaron's wife. I did what I did because I loved Mr. Aaron and Margaret. Henry had already said that he would take the rap, we just had to take Isiah out."

"I believe that Joseph and mama had a bond so strong that even from the grave he felt that he had to protect her and us. I can't explain it but that's what I believe." Toni replied.

The trio sat at the table in disbelief. For the first time they had discussed the events of that fateful night twenty-five years ago. The look on their faces was one of bewilderment. They could not explain and did not understand what they had seen individually or collectively. The anger that Toni had had earlier had disappeared and she was left with more questions than answers.

"Y'all would not believe the stuff that happened in that house after that." Toni said finally.

"Oh yeah, I can believe almost anything about that night, or what happened after that." Henry said.

"Mama invited Isiah's people to the house that Monday after he died. I'm telling y'all, those people did something before they came to that house, but it did a number on me and mama. I could feel something so evil going on in the house that night. It tried to kill mama and was holding me down so tight that I felt like I was paralyzed. That's the night that I started speaking in tongues. That's what saved us. Mama threw up some black stuff that looked like flies or bees and a black frog or something."

"Jesus Christ! That was an evil man, Toni. I could not let this man live on the face of the earth after he shot mama. I'll do it again. I don't give a shit whether it was my pistol or Lloyd's pistol that killed Isiah, I did the time for it. I know it cost you a lot to pay the lawyer and all that, and from the bottom of my heart, I appreciate that, Toni. How many sisters would have done what you did? Not many. You damn near gave up your life for us, something a mother should do. You worked and paid every penny that my lawyer charged, I'll always love you for that and I will bath and diaper you, if I had to. But I had to make sure that Isiah died that night. That night when Isiah showed up at the house all that came to my mind is that he had to be dead before the sun rose again. He just couldn't live another day on this earth. I love Lloyd for standing with me. He understood what I had to do. I have asked for God's forgiveness and I did that for years. Then one day it was like the Lord spoke to my spirit and told me that He had forgiven me the first time that I had asked for it. That's when I decided that I was going to live in today and not look back."

"I know what you mean, Henry. You know what I went through after that. I lost my family and even my will to live. I came that close to committing suicide. Henry told me what the Lord had said to him and that thing hit my spirit and caused me to want to live again. I thought about that thing, God had forgiven me the first time that I had asked. I kicked the devil out and laid before the Lord in praise. But I did see Joseph again."

"When?" Toni asked.

"It was the day that we moved mama from the house into that duplex cross the highway. Me and Henry was moving the refrigerator out on the doily to the truck. I was in the front of the refrigerator and Henry was in the back. So I was the first one to go out of the door. I was positioning the refrigerator so the doily could get onto the plank that we had put under the door. I looked up and I saw Joseph standing at the top of the stairs smiling and nodding his head like he approved of what we were doing."

"Yeah, I remember that day, too, boy. Lloyd started speaking in tongues and turned gray. He was too black to turn white but he came dam close." Henry said.

They all started laughing. Toni got so tickled that she could not stop laughing. Lloyd was so full of laughter that he had to get up and walk around the yard to try and get it all out of his system. The discussion had been so serious that they had needed the laughter to lighten the tension of the moment. As they were trying to recover from the laughter, Jeremiah came out of the backdoor.

"What y'all laughing so much about? I bet Henry telling those lies, again." Jeremiah said.

"No, I was telling Toni how Lloyd changed colors when he saw that ghost at mama house that day we moved y'all to the duplex."

"What ghost?" Jeremiah asked. He didn't seem to find any humor in what had been said, but stared at Henry and Lloyd as he waited for an answer.

"You look like you just seen a ghost yourself, Jerry." Lloyd said.

"Tell me about this ghost you saw at mama's house." Jeremiah asked.

"Well, I am not sure that you can call him a ghost. What we saw was our cousin, Joseph, who died before you were even born." Henry said.

"What did he look like?" Jeremiah asked.

"He was very tall, about six three, six four, bright skin with real light brown eyes and freckles across his nose." Toni replied.

Jeremiah looked like he had been hit in the stomach with a sledgehammer.

"No, he ain't no ghost, I always thought that he was an angel." Jeremiah replied.

"You've seen him too?" Henry asked.

"Yeah, I've seen him a lot of times. The last time I saw him was the night before mama died. He seemed to be happy. But I saw him for the first time the night that Isiah died." Jeremiah said.

Henry and Lloyd looked at each other and seemed to stop breathing.

"What did you see that night Isiah died, Jerry?" Lloyd asked.

Before answering, Jeremiah looked around at everybody in the backyard.

"I saw this really tall man step between Henry and Isiah, then he stepped between Lloyd and Isiah. He put his hand over my face and smiled at me. That's when I saw that he wasn't a grown man. He didn't look much older than Henry was at that time."

"Everyone of us saw Joseph that night. Why didn't you say something before, Jerry?" Lloyd asked.

"First I was just glad, God forgive me but it's the truth, that Isiah was dead. After I finally had put it all together, like I told Toni this morning, I didn't want a wedge between us as a family. But there is something to this, all of us seeing the same person at the same time." Jeremiah said.

"Don't forget what happened at the courthouse that day the judge sentenced Henry. Toni you saw it better than anybody because you were walking toward the courthouse from the street." Lloyd said excitedly.

"Yeah, I remembered that day. But I also watched Isiah's people in the parking lot doing some devilish mess before they went into the courthouse. Those people tried to wipe us off the face of the earth. Everything that happens in the dark comes to the light. Remember how Isiah's mama started screaming when that buzzard started flapping its wings? She knew she had tried to hurt us." Toni said.

"Yeah, but this Joseph, what was he doing? I thought that when people died they were gone. If you see anything that look like them it's a familiar spirit. And we know that's from the devil." Jeremiah said.

"Boy you sure getting plenty word at that church in Baltimore. But I believe, I want to believe, that the Lord sent Joseph as an angel." Lloyd said.

"That's what I think I am going to believe," Henry said, "that God loved us enough to bring an angel from our family to take care of us and fight the evil spirits that those people sent."

Margaret returned and yelled from the kitchen to her siblings and ex-husband.

"You guys want me to bring some sodas out there?"

"Yeah, that would be nice." Lloyd yelled back.

A few minutes later Margaret was coming through the door with a two-liter bottle of soda and some paper cups. As she placed the bottle and cups on the table she looked around at everyone. Her right hand was clenched like a fist. When she had gotten everyone's attention she put her hand on the table and released what she had been holding.

"Please tell me why y'all left these on the counter in there?"

There on the table were five bullet slugs, all intact. Henry and Lloyd immediately recognized that they were the slugs from the pistols that they had fired twenty-five years before. They stared at the slugs for what seemed an eternity, then at each other.

What's Next?

But My Heart Won't Lie, So Why Are We Here?

      Eve learns that the head and eyes often work together to aid us in self-deception. But her story reveals that the heart desires the best for us and will not allow us to become satisfied with what is good. The story reveals that the heart will not compromise because it searches those places where the eyes cannot see and the head cannot conceive.

      Trust is taken to a level not seen before. After being taken to that new level, Eve waited as she was being prepared to receive the truth. The heart is always speaking, Eve shows how listening can save our lives.

In Loving Memory Of...

      Just when you thought that you were too old, that all of your dreams had died on the vine, living was just an interruption of life, and youthful desires were only for the young and busy, meet Sandy and her over forty beau, Clarence Alexander Collins.

      You will never look at government employees and lawyers the same, again.

      Obey the rules of the heart.